FANS

Für Waltraud, Ulrich und Ilsa

FANS

THE MIRROR OF CONSUMPTION

Cornel Sandvoss

polity

First published in 2005 by Polity Press

Polity Press
65 Bridge Street
Cambridge CB2 1UR, UK.

Polity Press
350 Main Street
Malden, MA 02148, USA

ISBN 0 7456 2972 5
ISBN 0 7456 2973 3 (pb)

A catalogue record for this book is available from the British Library.

Typeset in 10.5pt on 12pt Palatino
by BookEns Ltd, Royston, Herts.
Printed and bound in Great Britain by MPG Books,
Bodmin, Cornwall.

The publisher has used its best endeavours to ensure that the URLs for external websites referred to in this book are correct and active at the time of going to press. However, the publisher has no responsibility for the websites and can make no guarantee that a site will remain live or that the content is or will remain appropriate.

For further information on Polity, visit our website: www.polity.co.uk

CONTENTS

ACKNOWLEDGEMENTS

I would like to thank the Arts and Humanities Research Board for its support of this project. I am also indebted to the School of Media and Cultural Production, De Montfort University. Finally, I am grateful to a number of colleagues who have provided support, suggestions or feedback at various stages of the writing of this work. These include Tim O'Sullivan, Brian Longhurst, John B. Thompson, Roger Silverstone and Matt Hills. In particular I would like to thank Henry Jenkins for his detailed comments and critical engagement with the final drafts of this book.

I

INTRODUCTION:
REPRESENTING FANDOM

In his hit single 'Stan' American rap star Marshall Mathers, better known as Eminem, describes the obsession of the fictitious fan Stan with his favourite star, none other than Eminem himself. In the song Stan describes his passion for Eminem, the way he identifies with his songs, how his girlfriend is increasingly jealous of his interest in Eminem, proclaiming that he 'will be the biggest fan you'll ever lose'. Yet, as Stan's letters to Eminem remain unanswered, he realizes the one-sided nature of his admiration. In his growing frustration he kills himself and his pregnant wife. Tellingly, despite such a drastic plot, 'Stan' still ranks among the more subtle representations of fandom in that Eminem himself performs the role of the obsessed fan. Yet, in its description of the fan as an obsessed and dangerous fanatic, it echoes a familiar theme.

Tony Scott's *The Fan* (1996) tells the story of baseball fan Gil Renard, played by Robert de Niro, who murders a player of his favourite ball club in order to 'help' the confidence of the team's new star centre fielder Bobby Rayburn. Disappointed by Rayburn's lack of gratitude for his murderous actions, Renard kidnaps Rayburn's son and eventually, like Stan, kills himself.[1] In a similar fashion news media have cultivated a notion of fans as psychologically defunct stalkers and killers. From Mark David Chapman's killing of John Lennon, John Hinckley's failed assassination of Ronald Reagan (attributed to Hinckley's attraction to Jodie Foster), Günther Parche's knife attack on tennis star Monica Seles (described as being motivated by his admiration for

Seles's rival, Steffi Graf) to the death of thirty-five Italian soccer fans following crowd disturbances at a European Cup Final in Brussels in 1985 and the events at Columbine High, where the killers' extensive collection of Marilyn Manson records quickly seemed the only 'reasonable' explanation of their crimes, news organizations and reporters have portrayed such events as partly or wholly motivated by fandom.

One may speculate about the reasons for this negative depiction of fandom. They no doubt contain an element of celebration of the media's own power and influence, an always popular theme among journalists and other media producers. At the same time it fulfils an ideological function in that it displaces fears over media effects on to the imagined 'Other' of psychologically and socially inept fans. Jenson (1992) has argued that beneath this representation of fandom as a social and psychological pathology allowing for such displacement runs an underlying, if nevertheless superficial, critique of modern life and mass culture. With regard to popular representations in the mass media, one may equally argue the opposite: that a critique of the fundamental and complex forces of modern life has been precluded by using fandom as a convenient scapegoat for profoundly disturbing occurrences from Heysel to Columbine. Fandom, as a form of agency, here lends itself perfectly to explanations of such disasters in the mass media, which in their relentless attempt to 'personalize' news and events have always privileged the human actor over structural forces in the analysis of contemporary life.[2]

The balance between structure and agency is also crucial to the academic analysis of fandom. Jenson (1992) notes equal tendencies to pathologize fans in early mass communication scholarship and in 'official' high culture. In contrast to popular representations of fandom, the portrayal of fandom in early academic approaches to the interaction between audiences and popular media, from Horton and Wohl (1956) to Schickel (1986), is rooted in an almost exclusive emphasis on structure. In both approaches fandom is interpreted as a consequence of mass culture needing to compensate for a lack of intimacy, community and identity. If in mass-mediated representation the fan is predominantly the perpetrator, then here he or she is first and foremost the passive victim.

This depiction of fandom as a consequence of psychological or cultural dysfunction constitutes the background against which fans first attracted attention from media and cultural studies scholars in the 1980s. From Fiske (1989a, 1989b, 1992) to Jenkins (1991, 1992) increasingly ethnographic and auto-ethnographic studies revealed a more complex relationship between fans as agents and the structural confines of popular culture in which they operate, a relationship which cannot be reduced to one being simply a consequence of the other. Early fan scholars actively sought this contrast to existing representations of fandom in the media and academia (cf. Jenkins, in Hills and Jenkins 2001). Their endeavour was not only the analytic representation and theorization of fandom, but also a form of political representation: a statement against the double standards of cultural judgement and the bourgeois fear of popular culture; a statement in favour of fan sensibilities which gave a voice to otherwise marginalized social groups.

More than a decade later, the need for such a partisan representation of fandom has disappeared on both sides of the equation: with the proliferation of multi-channel television and the arrival of new information technologies such as the internet, fandom seems to have become a common and ordinary aspect of everyday life in the industrialized world that is actively fostered and utilized in industry marketing strategies (Jones 2003). As Tulloch and Jenkins (1995: 4) report, at one stage 53 per cent of all Americans considered themselves *Star Trek* fans. At the same time, fan studies taking a political stance in representing fandom have themselves become part of the dominant paradigm of audience theory (Abercrombie and Longhurst 1998).

Yet fandom still mirrors conditions of popular culture, consumption and their academic analysis. It has become impossible to discuss popular consumption without reference to fandom and fan theory, just as it has become next to impossible to find realms of public life which are unaffected by fandom – from the intermingling of show business, sports and politics to the everyday life talk about one's favourite music, television show or film. The above-mentioned examples of the representation of fandom in news and entertainment media illustrate how the state of being a fan is part of our schemes of perception: in recent years not only acts of violence committed by fans against their object of fandom – such as sport fans attacking an unsuccessful team or the more drastic case of Mark David Chapman – but any sort of violence committed by individuals who also happen to be fans has been explained in terms of their fandom. Our fan consumption thus becomes a generally understood language through which one's identity is communicated and assessed: the repeated references to the extensive Marilyn Manson collection of the two Columbine killers thus also reflected the attempts of journalists and broadcasters to say something about who they were. In its proliferation, its growing importance in the construction of identity and its social and cultural classification, fandom has something to say about the very substance, premisses and consequences of contemporary life.

Yet the question remains how to conceptualize the role of fandom in modern culture. Given the ethnographic tradition of fan studies often conducted among small groups of fans within a particular cultural and textual context, the problem of theorizing fandom is particularly pressing. Ethnography, as Morley (1991) has argued, must always be placed within wider frames of analysis (see also Marcus and Fisher 1986). Thus the challenges to the scholar of fandom are similar to those faced by the cartographer. The success of either depends on questions of scale versus detail. This is well captured in the following tale reported by Borges and adapted by Baudrillard (1983). In a powerful ancient empire cartographers set out to compile a map that fully represented the empire's wealth and glory. After years of work they finally completed a map so detailed that it covered all of the empire's territory, yet so large that, once unfolded, the empire was covered in its entirety. To Baudrillard the tale illustrates the demise of referentiality, in that eventually the map engenders the territory which is left to rot away under the map. Yet, even if we do not share Baudrillard's concerns with simulation and hyperreality, the fable illustrate the difficulties of processes of abstraction and the compromises that need to be made in drawing a map of fandom. To meaningfully theorize fandom as a practice across various genres – and only if there is a contextual and behavioural kernel in fandom that is evident across different fan cultures does the general term 'fandom' have analytic value – we need to reduce individual fan cultures in scale and move from 'rich descriptions' (Geertz 1975) to the common themes, motivations and implications of the interaction between fans and their objects of fandom. At the same time, it is important to remain true to such detail. I will thus zoom in and out of specific fan cultures, moving towards a theory of fandom that draws on cultural and social theory and existing conceptualizations of fandom, while contrasting these theoretical approaches to fandom with the ethnographic detail of fan studies, often citing the accounts of fans documented in these studies.

A further element of particular relevance to the work of the cartographer is his or her perspective. The work of the social scientist compares to that of the early modern explorer drawing maps from their particular angle of vision. There is no equivalent to satellite and aerial photography when we draw maps of society and culture; we can never step outside the system and look upon it from above. It is therefore all the more important to acknowledge one's own perspective. As Tulloch (2000) points out, the question of whether scholars are fans themselves, or whether they study fandom as something that others do, has profound theoretical and methodological implications (cf. Brooker 2000). Equally, scholars failing to display an adequate level of knowledge about the fan cultures and texts they explore raise suspicion amongst their peers and fans alike.[3] My own position is the following: I have been an avid follower of spectator sports, and particularly football, since my childhood and, more recently since a work-related stay in the United States, baseball. My support for a particular club would qualify me as what we will later, following Abercrombie and Longhurst (1998), describe as a 'cultist', although my transnational mobility has affected my ability to attend *in situ* events such as games and concerts. Either way, my previous qualitative research on sports fandom (Sandvoss 2001, 2003) has inevitably shaped some of the conceptual frameworks with which I approach this book. Since my adolescence I have also been a keen fan of alternative and electronic popular music, particularly bands such as *Kraftwerk*, and have attended many concerts and festivals, while keeping up to date through various niche media. By contrast, my interest in particular television shows, popular books or the work of given directors has taken place only on a committed, yet unorganized level. In a nutshell, then, I, like most of us, have experienced different degrees of fandom within different genres of popular culture. However, as part of the endeavour here to explore conceptualizations of fandom across different genres and sub-cultural contexts, I, as much as the reader, will inevitably be an insider to some of the fan cultures discussed here, but an outsider to others. This is the particular perspective from which this book is written, and which has shaped its argument and structure.

Preceding any analysis, one further issue needs to be addressed. Before we can draw a map, it is essential to define its boundaries and thus the subject we mean to represent. Before we can analyse the premises and consequences of being a fan, it is necessary to define what we mean by 'fan' and 'fandom'. It should be noted that what has formed as a field of academic study of 'fandom' does not necessarily include all fans and their activities, but rather focuses on specific social and cultural interactions, institutions and communities that have formed through the close interaction of committed groups of fans in a subcultural context. In a broader understanding of 'fandom', as on a most basic level the state of being a fan, this focus on communities and tightly networked fans fails to conceptualize important aspects of the relationship between the modern self, identity and popular culture which forms my particular concern here. Some of the different, on occasion conflicting, conclusions I draw in comparison to earlier studies of fandom thus follow from a different and broader scope of analysis. Rather than challenging such studies on their own terms, I have thus, one may argue, changed the subject of study. While this is partly true, this tactical shift in the boundaries of the maps I seek to draw is, I think, a necessary one. However much ethnographic work on fans and audiences has emphasized the specifics of the cases studied, it inevitably carries implicit claims about the relationship between audiences and popular culture which sit uneasily with the absence of a large number of viewers, listeners and readers who in many definitions, not least in their self-description, are understood as fans. In other words, a map that colours in only small sections of the territory may be accurate as far as these sections are concerned, yet of lesser value in navigating through the territory at large. This question of the boundaries of the object of study of course remains a question of judgement and definition, and I will seek to clarify the criteria for my judgement below.

Far from these theoretical considerations of what we can describe as fandom, who or what a fan is seems, as Hills (2002) observes, to be common knowledge. Even if specific assumptions regarding what and who a fan is may vary, it seems safe to assume that we can associate fandom with a particular form of emotional intensity or 'affect' (Grossberg 1992). Notably, however, the self-classification of fans does not necessarily relate to the intensity of their emotions. Sometimes audience groups that from the outside appear as casual viewers identify themselves as fans (Sandvoss 2003). On other occasions emotionally involved viewers and readers shun the label 'fan' as potentially derogatory, at least as far as their own media consumption is concerned. Moreover, emotional intensity is a category which cannot be measured quantitatively. For the purpose of empirical investigation and academic analysis, we therefore need to turn to observable aspects as defining marks of fandom. I thus want to suggest a definition of fandom focusing on fan practices. This admittedly devolves the problem to the question of which fan practices are most indicative of fans' emotional investment and affect. John Fiske, whose work has shaped much of the framework of the first wave of fan studies, offers the following description of fan practices:

Fandom ... selects from the repertoire of mass-produced and mass-distributed entertainment certain performers, narratives or genres and takes them into the culture of a self-selected fraction of people. They are then reworked into an intensely pleasurable, intensely signifying popular culture that is both similar to, yet significantly different from, the culture of more 'normal' popular audiences. ... [Fandom] is...associated with the cultural tastes of subordinated formations of the people, particularly those disempowered by any combination of gender, age, class and race. (Fiske 1992: 30)

The problem with this *de facto* definition of fandom is that Fiske blurs the boundaries between the description and the interpretation of fan practices, and hence presents us with a normative definition. Yet a normative definition ties the phenomenon to be studied to an already formulated hypothesis: if we define fandom as a cultural practice limited to those disempowered, and if we ascribe to it, as Fiske does elsewhere (1989a), a subversive ideological function, we limit our analysis to those fans who *are* disempowered and who *do* utilize fandom as a form of resistance, thus confirming the initial hypothesis. In fact, fans' practices, as well as the socio-demographic background of fans, are broader than Fiske suggests. Extensive quantitative (Wann et al. 1999; Schurr et al. 1988; UFA 1998; Wann et al. 2001) as well as qualitative (Erickson 1996; Sandvoss 2003) research on sports fandom illustrates its popularity beyond groups disadvantaged on accounts of class, gender or ethnicity. Fiske (1992) acknowledges this in the case of sport, but fails to address similar tendencies across other fields of popular culture. Some genres of popular music, for example, attract predominantly white, male fans (Christenson and Peterson 1988), not all of whom fall into lower-class brackets. Similarly, particular shows, such as the BBC radio soap *The Archers*, have attracted a substantial middle-class following (Thomas 2002).

Instead, we need a definition of fan practices that precedes normative evaluation. The clearest indicator of a particular emotional investment in a given popular text lies in its regular, repeated consumption, regardless of who its reader is and regardless of the possible implications of this affection. Many of those who label themselves as fans, when asked what defines their fandom, point to their patterns of consumption. Consider the following definitions of being a fan by three fans of different popular texts:

I spend a lot of time going to football and talking about football, thinking about football. (Samuel, Chelsea FC fan, interviewed April 1999)

Ever since I saw the video I was a fan. In the beginning not a real fanatic, that came later when they got more popular. I started buying magazines, buttons, posters, just about anything that was to buy. (Sally, *Backstreet Boys* fan, interviewed February 2002)

In the beginning I used to watch *Star Wars* over and over again, until one day I was walking through town with my friends and I saw the *Star Wars* novel in a shop and could not resist buying it, I bought that book and read it non-stop for two days until I finished it – and then I went out to buy three more! I have been buying more and more books every week, there are only a few now that I haven't got. (Mike, *Star Wars* fan, interviewed April 2002)

In one form or another the emotional commitment of these fans is reflected in the regularity with which they visit and revisit their object of fandom (see also Brooker 2002). Similarly, Harrington and Bielby (1995) have noted that the vast majority of soap opera fans they studied watched their favourite show five times a week. Hence, drawing on this lowest common denominator, I *define fandom as the regular, emotionally involved consumption of a given popular narrative or text* in the form of books, television shows, films or music, as well as popular texts in a broader sense such as sports teams and popular icons and stars ranging from athletes and musicians to actors.

In this multiplicity of possible objects of fandom spanning the spectrum of popular culture lies a further important aspect. Few studies of fans have sought to explore the parallels between fans of different texts or genres, with some studies even making explicit claims about the assumed uniqueness of the particular fan culture they investigate (such as Rodman 1996). Moreover, most of the work on fandom has focused on readers and fans of forms of popular fiction, with studies of fans of individual performers or popular icons playing a subsidiary role in discourses on fandom. In epistemological terms, the distinction between popular texts and icons Hills (1999) draws is problematic, because at the point of consumption fictional narratives and 'real life' icons are equally encountered as texts which are read and appropriated by their (fan) audience. Whether we find our object of fandom in Britney Spears, *Buffy the Vampire Slayer* or the Boston Red Sox, these are all read and negotiated as (mediated) texts by their fans. The way in which fans relate to such texts and the performances that follow from this relationship vary between different fan cultures, and indeed from fan to fan. Yet, they are all forms of consumption in which we build and maintain an affective relationship with mediated texts and thus share fundamental psychological, social and cultural premises and consequences.

From this definition of fandom as a form of sustained, affective consumption follows the relationship between fandom and 'subculture', a concept which has been popular in the study of specific social groups from mid-twentieth-century sociology (Becker 1963; Cohen 1972; P. Willis 1977) to media and cultural studies (Hebdidge 1977; Gelder and Thornton 1997; Redhead 1997; Redhead et al. 1997). Most – maybe all – of those who participate in subcultures which evolve around a given media text or genre conform to the patterns of regular and emotionally committed consumption by which I define fandom here. In this sense I am repeatedly drawing on studies of subculture, regardless of whether members of subcultural groups describe themselves as 'fans', a term often avoided by audiences trying to portray themselves in opposition to mainstream media (Thornton 1995). Yet, not all fans belong to what has been described as a subculture. Moreover, the academic analysis of subcultures inevitably carries a different theoretical focus on questions of collective rather than individual identity, of group interaction, style and community. While all these are important elements in the study of fandom they are not germane here and will be discussed in further depth only to the extent that they relate to the formation and implications of fandom. The same applies to the growing number of studies of fans which do not examine fandom as such, but related phenomena, such as the proliferation of online communities in relation to fandom (Baym 1998, 2000; Ganz-Blättler 1999; Cumberland 2000; Cohan 2001; Hanmer 2003).

With these boundaries of the map of fandom I aim to draw in mind, I now want to turn to the analysis of parallels and differences in fan practices across different genres, as well as their social, cultural and economic premises and consequences. This entails a journey through the different inter- and intrapersonal aspects of being a fan. We begin this journey by exploring the social and cultural context of fan consumption. Chapter 2 explores the power relations between fans and media producers, as well as power relations within fandom. Moving the discussion from the notion of power to identity, chapter 3 investigates the content and context of fandom by analysing fan performances, the interdependence of such performances on forms of spectacle, and the role of fandom in the formation of communities, as well as territorially bound and unbound identities. Chapters 2 and 3 thus focus most closely on those aspects of fans' experiences that have hitherto formed the key concerns of the academic exploration of fandom: the role of fandom as a social and cultural institution forming interpretive communities socially contextualizing the power of mass media. If these chapters thereby reflect the analytical emphasis on the interaction between fans, the following chapters focus on an equally significant aspect of the fan experience: the interaction between fans and their object of fandom. Chapter 4 turns to the intrapersonal dimensions of the relationship between fan and object of fandom by assessing the validity of different psycho-analytic approaches to pleasure, desires and self-identity in fandom. Moving beyond classical psychoanalysis, chapter 5 draws on social, cultural and medium theory to develop a model of fandom as a form of self-reflection, in which the object of fandom functions as an extension of the self. Conversely, chapter 6 explores the changing role of mediated texts in the relationship between fan and object of fandom and, on the basis of a critical reflection on the notion of polysemy, assesses how fan texts can function as a mirror to the self. What at first sight may then seem to be an investigation of different fans and fan cultures – with the first chapters focusing on fan communities and the later chapters on individual fans – is in fact an exploration of the various social, cultural, psychological, technological and textual dimensions of fandom, with different studies and thematic emphases highlighting varying aspects of the fan experience. The way in which these different aspects of fan consumption, practices and performances combine will vary from fan group to fan group and from fan to fan. For some fans, as we will see, the communal context of their fandom, or even their own textual productivity, form the true core of their fandom, while for others, their fandom is driven more by an idiosyncratic bond with their object of fandom. If, as I suggest here, fandom functions as a mirror, we must not forget that what we see will ultimately depend upon on our angle of vision.

2

THE DOMINANT DISCOURSE OF RESISTANCE: FANDOM AND POWER

I want to begin my analysis of fandom with the debates which conceive of fandom as a form of cultural institution and interpretive community: the questions of power and resistance which, as is illustrated in Fiske's aforementioned definition of fandom, have shaped the scope and theoretical orientation of a substantial share of fan studies since the late 1980s, a focus that reflects the wider tradition in Media and Cultural Studies of evaluting the premises and consequences of media consumption in terms of power.

Popular culture and empowerment

John Fiske's work on popular culture and fandom (1989a, 1989b, 1992) provides a useful starting point. While Fiske is not the first scholar to confront questions of power and popular culture empirically and theoretically, and his conclusions are not generally endorsed in the various approaches to fandom that have emerged since, he has formulated an overall paradigm of power and resistance in the analysis of fandom that has continued to shape much of the field. Fiske's (1989b) concept of popular culture hinges on the notion of the polysemic popular text – in other words, the ability of popular texts to incorporate a variety of different meanings, which allow fans to construct alternative readings and interpretations of such texts, thus distinguishing them from 'normal' audiences. Fiske (1989a) compares the popular polysemic text and its negotiation by audiences to the use of jeans in everyday American culture. Fiske argues that, while being a true mass commodity, jeans do not only allow for a variety of different uses by different social groups in different situations, but that they are also an illustration of how the meaning of mass-produced, standardized commodities is created in the course of their consumption. It is only in everyday life, when jeans are worn, washed out or cut, that their true meaning unfolds. The same, according to Fiske, holds true for our consumption of mediated texts. Popular texts, especially those for which we hold a particular affection, are the textual equivalent of jeans: their meaning is created in everyday life. It is through the processes of appropriation in everyday life that these mediated texts become objects of fandom, as we make the mass-produced product our own, creating its particular emotional significance. The emphasis on continuous consumption in Fiske's approach corresponds to my definition of fandom here, as well as to the particular attention to everyday life in media consumption in the discipline as a whole (cf. Morley and Silverstone 1990; Scannell 1996). It thus highlights an important aspect of fan consumption, in light of which we need to assess the way in which fans construct their identities and how power is distributed in fandom.

With regard to the latter, Fiske (1989b) argues that popular culture and the pleasure that fans and viewers derive from it, exist in opposition to official, bourgeois 'high culture'. The consumption of popular culture in fandom thus forms part of the struggle of disempowered groups against the hegemonic culture of the powerful:

> Everyday life is constituted by the practices of popular culture, and is characterized by the creativity of the weak in using the resources provided by a disempowering system while refusing finally to submit to that power. The culture of everyday life is best described through metaphors of struggle or antagonism: strategies opposed by tactics, the bourgeoisie by the proletariat; hegemony met by resistance, ideology countered or evaded; top-down power opposed by bottom-up power, of social discipline faced with disorder. (Fiske 1989b: 47)

Consequently, fandom constitutes a form of cultural subversion that reflects the different spheres of operation between strategies and tactics. While the textile industry continues to develop new marketing strategies to sell us their particular jeans, we are left to wear them or cut them up as we see tactically fit. Popular texts and icons such as Madonna may be commodities and means of capital accumulation to the media industry, yet they are appropriated by fans as meaningful resources in their everyday lives.[1] Fiske illustrates how the Madonna fandom of teenage girls, whom he describes as one of the most disempowered groups in society, is turned into an important symbolic resource that enables the girls to evade patriarchal conceptualizations of gender. To Fiske, the polysemic nature of Madonna as a popular text, offers as much as it problematizes traditional representations of gender and sexuality. When 14-year-old Madonna fan Lucy describes Madonna as 'tarty and seductive ... but it looks alright when she does it', she seeks to establish 'a satisfactory sexual identity within an oppressing ideology' for herself as much as Madonna (Fiske 1989a: 98–9). Through their Madonna fandom, teenage girls thus articulate and display their struggles by adopting Madonna's looks, listening to her music, or participating in look-alike contests such as MTV's *Make My Video*. With regard to the latter, Fiske (1989b: 149) argues that the 'pleasure lay both in the girl's ability to project herself into the Madonna image and in the productivity that transformed this from its normal form of an interior fantasy into material, and potentially public, text'.

To Fiske (1989b: 47) fandom is thus subversive by design, as the pleasures of fandom are rooted in its subversiveness, in 'the pleasures of producing one's own meanings of social experience and the pleasure of avoiding the social discipline of the power bloc'. In this respect Fiske's conceptualization of fandom is firmly rooted in de Certeau's (1984) understanding of everyday life in industrial capitalism as a site of struggle in which those disempowered do not create their own products and symbols but subvert the meaning of those imposed on them. Fans 'make do' with mass-produced popular culture through their own distinct and oppositional readings, through what Fiske (1989b), in reference to Eco (1986), calls 'semiotic guerrilla warfare'. In its subversion of symbols and its intense involvement with popular culture, fandom thus becomes a carnivalesque space, which, as Bakhtin (1968) argues in his canonical analysis of carnival, allows for a temporary subversion of the existing social order.

Yet, Fiske's use of military analogies constructs a polarity between empowered and disempowered that raises the question of whether the pleasures of fandom are indeed *necessarily* constructed in opposition to the dominant power system, and, secondly, whether such pleasures work to erode or sustain power relations in society. Fiske's difficulty in answering either question lies in the amorphous nature of what he calls the 'power bloc'. The 'colonizing army' (Fiske 1989b: 104) may be much more difficult to identify than Fiske implies.

While Fiske pays close attention to those on the receiving end of cultural hegemony, his understanding of the origins of hegemonic power seems too singular to account for complex power relations. Despite deriving his understanding of official, bourgeois culture from the work of Pierre Bourdieu, to whom I turn in more detail below, Fiske lacks Bourdieu's detailed attention to the interplay of society, culture and economy. Given his usage of Marxist terminology with regard to class, it is surprising that Fiske locates the centre of cultural power and discrimination in bourgeois official culture while paying little attention to those who control the means of cultural production, which by the end of the twentieth century lie well beyond the reach of the bourgeoisie as a class entity. Transnational corporations such as Bertelsmann or News Corporation and their subsidiaries are producers and distributors of fan texts ranging from *Run DMC* (BMG) to the *X-Files* (Fox), which clearly pursue different goals from bourgeois 'high culture'. Moreover, as the recurring spats between musicians and their record labels, such as in the high-profile case of George Michael, or between athletes and their clubs illustrate, even within the realm of the production of popular culture we find conflicts of interest between financiers, producers and performers. Hence it is increasingly difficult to identify 'dominant' and 'oppositional' readings. As Livingstone's (1998) analysis of audience readings of the popular British soap opera *Coronation Street* demonstrates, within the convention of a particular genre such as soap operas, dominant or preferred readings are often in opposition to otherwise hegemonic cultural values. A 'cynical' reading of a love triangle constitutes a dominant reading within the genre conventions of soap opera, but an oppositional reading in light of the dominant ideology of romantic love in the Western capitalist societies and vice versa.[2] Similarly, the endorsement of the aesthetics of *Dallas* by Dutch viewers that Ang (1985) observes, may be the preferred reading within the context of the programme and its industrial origin, yet an oppositional reading in the context of official Dutch culture of the 1980s. By contrast,

Tulloch illustrates how British and Australian fans of *Dr Who* endorsed a bourgeois cultural consensus in opposition to American cultural production, juxtaposing the BBC programme to American science fiction productions:

> *Dr Who* is 'inventive' and 'ingenious' in its scripts, while *Buck Rogers* and *Battlestar Galactica* are 'plastic' and 'glossy' in their action. *Dr Who* is 'flexible' and 'liberal' in its politics, whereas *Star Trek* is inflexibly 'moralistic' in presenting the 'American ideal'. (Tulloch and Jenkins 1995: 167)

In other cases, such as Barker's study of *Judge Dredd* fans (Barker 1993; see also Barker 1998), the fan text accommodates a range of ideological positions from the political left and right, leaving fans uncertain as to the author's intentions. These cases do not preclude the possibility of Fiske's notion of subversive pleasures in fandom. The articulation, for instance, of racist or sexist beliefs by Teddies (Hebdige 1979) or football fans (Sandvoss 2003) may reflect a pleasurable opposition to official bourgeois culture. Yet, it points to the need to explore under which circumstances, and against whom, fandom constitutes a form of resistance. Or, to return to Fiske's analogy, the question of who cares about the way we consume media text as fans, is the same as who cares about the holes we cut into our jeans.

Fandom and gender

On this level the jeans analogy already gives the game away: it is ultimately of little significance to the culture industry what we do with texts and commodities after the point of purchase. The way we wear our jeans or engage with the symbolic resources of popular culture does, however, have a profound impact on our social and cultural environment and interpersonal relations. The implications of forms of power and empowerment in fandom are therefore primarily located in the micro field of media consumption, the private and the domestic sphere. Within this sphere, which naturally tends to be homogeneous in terms of class, gender constitutes the most significant marker of asymmetrical power relations. Morley (1986) has demonstrated how long-standing gender inequalities in modern nuclear households shape mass media consumption. To assess notions of power and resistance in fandom further, I now turn, therefore, to the role of gender in fan consumption.

Curiously, fandom has been identified as both a distinctly masculine and a distinctly feminine space. Popular fan texts such as 'pop music, romance novels, comics, Hollywood mass appeal stars' (Fiske 1992: 30) have traditionally attracted a strong female following, and as Harris (1998a: 7) notes, 'most research on fans foregrounds female participation'. In particular, fan activities and discourses revolving around popular televisual texts are often driven by female fans. As Jenkins observes, '*Star Trek* fan writing is a predominantly female response to mass media texts, with the majority of fanzines edited and written by women for a largely female readership' (Tulloch and Jenkins 1995: 197).

At the same time, many other areas of fandom appear to constitute explicitly masculine domains. The overwhelming majority of respondents in Barker's research on fans of the superhero comic *Judge Dredd* (Barker 1993; Barker and Brooks 1998) are male. Similarly males have accounted for a share of between 90 per cent (J. A. Brown 1997: 16) and 100 per cent (Tankel and Murphy 1998) in other studies of comic fandom. Both qualitative (Erickson 1996; A. King 1998; Sandvoss 2003) and quantitative (Gantz and Wenner 1991; UFA 1998; Sportfive 2002) studies confirm the overwhelmingly male fan base of spectator sports. However, as I have argued elsewhere (Sandvoss, forthcoming), the growing number of female fans in football fandom suggests that such areas of male fandom are reflective of the socio-historic gendering of leisure in industrial societies (cf. Hargreaves 1986; Holt 1989; Brailsford 1991), in which female leisure had long been confined to the home and restricted with regard to any temporal and monetary expenses. Hence, it is also subject to contemporary social, economic and technological transformations which have broadened the accessibility of fan texts. The increased availability of sport on television, and therefore its greater accessibility in the domestic realm, has thus substantially transformed gender relations in sport fan cultures.

Fandom, then, cannot be described as a form of consumption that lends itself to either gender position. Instead, the different socio-historic development of male and female fan cultures, the variations in chosen fan texts, and the usage of different media are indicators of the different power positions articulated in fandom.

A number of studies illustrate how within particular socio-historic positions female fandom has fostered subversive pleasures and constituted a form of resistance. Dell (1998) identifies such a moment of subversion in female wrestling fandom in the United States in the 1940s and 1950s. With the end of World War II, the comparative autonomy and equality that women had enjoyed as part of the war effort, particularly through their work in the arms industry, were successively eroded by a counter-movement seeking to return women to their 'natural' roles as housewives (Spigel 1992). According to Dell, female viewers in this situation found refuge in a particular genre of entertainment that defied all patriarchal expectations of femininity in its emphasis on spectacular bodies, physical confrontation and assertive sexuality: professional wrestling. Following its decline in the 1930s, wrestling was revived by the influx of committed female fans to its auditoriums, as well as on television. In its emphasis on physical pleasures arising out of the excessive emphasis on the (male) body, wrestling thus constituted a form of social, carnivalesque transgression. Analysing the representation of female wrestling fans in the popular press, Dell also draws on de Certeau's distinction between strategy and tactic: newspapers, from a position of power and in their strategic effort to sustain patriarchal order, derided the pleasures of female fans. Yet, female wrestling fans evaded the constraints of such representation:

> Women successfully insisted on watching televized wrestling two or three times a week and then openly admired the parade of male bodies that filled the screen, transgressing the roles set out for them as wives and mothers, while disgruntled husbands and sons looked on. In doing so, they created a temporary space within the home, employing tactics that allowed them to supplant the normative domestic, demure, caregiving role expected of them with an assertive, self-gratifying, sexualized role. (Dell 1998: 105)

In this instance of fans reading objects of fandom in marked opposition to their dominant mode of address, Fiske's formula of fandom as pleasurable resistance appears most accurate. Female fandom drawing on apparently masculine genres of popular culture such as wrestling, soccer or action and horror films can thus be identified as a subversion of existing gender roles and their accompanying power relations. However, as the negative coverage of female wrestling fans illustrates, such forms of fandom attract substantial resistance themselves. As Cherry (2002) points out in her study of female horror fans, these fans then require a particular commitment in the face of dominant opposition.

Moreover, as noted above, few popular texts are as clear-cut in

their implied meaning and readership. In particular, the representation of gender roles in popular texts is often ideologically complex.
Fiske's (1989b) own example of Madonna fans is problematic.
Because the popular texts surrounding Madonna are highly
polysemic, they can not only accommodate group-specific readings, but they themselves cannot be located easily on either side of
the polarity between 'power bloc' and the disempowered. As
Kellner (1995: 292) argues, 'Madonna is a site of a genuine
contradiction', in that she 'sanctions revolt and individual
construction of image and identity, yet the form in which she
carries out her revolt is that of the models of the fashion and
consumer industries.' Thus, while teenage girls resist a reading of
Madonna as 'boy toy' and symbol of female submissiveness,
Schulze et al. (1993) identify a group of readers who oppose such
readings of Madonna as emancipatory pop icon precisely because
it, in turn, legitimizes existing power positions of the culture
industry and simplifies complex social issues. In her study of *X-Files*
fandom, Clerc (1996: 42) illustrates how the assumed differences in
reading according to gender position – 'men are usually more
interested in the "factual", women in the "emotional"' – are
inverted in the show's representation of the lead characters, Scully,
the woman, as scientifically trained sceptic, and Mulder, the man,
as emotional and intuitive, and thus transgress gender roles in the
texts and audience alike. The difficulty in determining dominant
and oppositional readings in all these cases follows from the
ambiguous nature of the power bloc. Fiske identifies the 'power
bloc' as dominant, bourgeois cultural values (against which
Madonna or other objects of fandom open a space of resistance);
yet the media industry, which has substantial powers of
representation and agenda setting itself, the strongest and most
inherent of these being commercialism, constitutes another power
bloc whose discourses do not necessarily correspond with Fiske's
assumed cultural hegemony of the bourgeoisie.

Such distinctions between different fields of power are even
more intricate in those genres that have been aimed particularly at
female audiences, such as soap operas, television drama and
romance novels. In their regular patterns of reading which Radway
(1987) describes, the female readers who frequent a bookstore in an
unspecified Midwestern town to purchase and discuss romance
novels clearly qualify as fans. Against a background of dominant
gender identities, Radway (1987) sketches the complex interplay
between these readers' expectations, authors, some of whom have
previously been devoted romance readers themselves, the publish-

ing industry and the role of gatekeepers, such as the bookshop assistant Dot, who helps and guides women seeking her advice towards particular books that they will enjoy. The particular motive for reading romance novels that emerges in interviews with these female fans is that they offer a form of 'relaxation', a term preferred by most participants to that of escape, and an activity and space far from the domestic pressures that otherwise structure the everyday life of these female fans, many of whom are married with children. In helping fans to establish an autonomous temporal space in everyday life, as well as a textual space which fosters fantasies that address their ideas and desires of ideal romance, this fandom is a source of pleasure as well as emancipation and empowerment. However, the position of their fandom with regard to hegemonic gender relations is complex, and does not constitute a form of direct resistance. As Radway observes:

> 'good' romance continues to maintain that a woman acknowledge and realize her feeling only within traditional, monogamous marriage. When another text portrays a heroine who is neither harmed nor disturbed by her ability to have sex with several men, I suspect it is classified as 'bad' because it makes explicit the threatening implications of an unleashed feminine sexuality capable of satisfying itself outside the structures of patriarchal domination. (Radway 1987: 74)

Yet, while Radway is under no illusion about the potential conformity of romance to dominant ideological positions of patriarchy, the cultural consequences of female fandom remain ideologically ambiguous. While she notes that 'the happy ending [in romance novels] restores the status quo in gender relations when the hero enfolds the heroine protectively in his arms' (Radway 1987: 81), fans interpret this moment as 'an occasion for the vicarious enjoyment of a woman's ultimate triumph' in maintaining her integrity and achieving a formal commitment from the hero and thus a sign 'of a woman's attainment of legitimacy and personhood in a culture that locates both for her in the roles of lover, wife, and mother' (Radway 1987: 84). The break with existing power structures and patterns of hegemony is thus at best partial, especially since, as Heinrich Triepel (1938/1974) reminds us, hegemony is always located on a continuum between influence and direct rule, and is thus based on a hegemonic compromise, which allows for diversion and self-rule by those in the weaker power position without challenging the broader framework set by the hegemon.

In Radway's study we thus find a more nuanced account of the relationship between fan audiences, media industries and hegemonic culture, in which the last is not *a priori* questioned through the interaction of the first two. McKinley's study (1997) of female fans of the 1990s Fox hit series *Beverly Hills, 90210*, by contrast, poses another challenge to Fiske's understanding of fandom as a form of resistance in which popular culture is identified as a reiteration of hegemonic culture. McKinley describes how the show is consumed in regular, often communal, pleasurable and playful ways by its female fans of different age-groups. Yet, while McKinley acknowledges that the series constitutes a polysemic text which attracts a variety of different readings and interpretations, she is particularly concerned with how it simultaneously 'inoculates' viewers against truly opposi-tional readings. In discussions following their viewing of single episodes, female fans draw on the visual representation in, for example, the depiction of female beauty and the show's narrative portrayal of characters in their understanding of themselves as well as their social realities. 'In memorising and reproducing *90210* narratives', as McKinley (1997: 136) argues, 'viewers organized and prioritized life options that, I would suggest, worked hegemonically to win pleasurable consent to a world of limited potential for females.' Focusing on particular narrative strands, such as one involving college professor Lucinda, who after divorcing her husband has an affair with the male lead character Brandon and attempts to seduce his friend Dylan, McKinley reports how the ideologically dominant reading of the show prevailed among its fans. Lucinda, who, by comparison with the show's other characters, is an older woman, who is sexually assertive, professionally successful and non-monoga-mous, opens up different ideological positions in the reading of the text, only for these to be rejected even more forcefully. When Kelly, the young heroine and Dylan's girlfriend, confronts Lucinda over her attempt to seduce Dylan in class, the audience is invited to, and does indeed, side with Kelly. In the words of one of McKinley's (1997: 208) interviewees: 'Go, Kelly!' In this partisan identification, 'the text firmly closes down Lucinda as a viable identity possibility' (McKinley 1997: 208). Identification is therefore a key factor in fans' relationship to the text and its empowering or disempowering potential. The female fans of *90210* create an imagined community with the show's lead characters, thus locating fans' identification within a framework of hegemonic gender positions:

This process constituted a 'misrecognition' of themselves in the idealized capitalist and patriarchal subject that irresistibly hailed them. The centre of ownership of the programme concealed ways in which their talk pleasurably blended fictional and self-narratives that privilege certain meanings and silenced others. (McKinley 1997: 236)

While McKinley acknowledges that some, if few, fans adopt oppositional readings, in admiring Lucinda's independence, for example, the true hegemonic power of the show lies in its ability to set the agenda. Even when Lucinda's character was read more positively, this evaluation was tied 'not to her academic achievements or independent lifestyle, but rather to the ways in which she relates to men' (McKinley 1997: 237). McKinley's study thus highlights the problems in Fiske's conceptualization of the power bloc. First, the power relation between fan and text that McKinley observes seems considerably more asymmetric than Fiske suggests. Polysemic texts and readings function as implicit reaffirmation — and integration through identification by the viewer — of a patriarchal hegemonic compromise. There is a further, if implicit, challenge to Fiske's conceptualization of fandom in McKinley's work. While Fiske remains ambiguous as to the basis of the power bloc in either hegemonic cultural values or the media industry — if the two can indeed be separated analytically — McKinley's study illustrates that spaces of negotiation and consequently empowerment and resistance in fandom arise only if there is a disunity between traditional hegemonic cultural values and the ideological canon of media producers (as in the case of Madonna). If, however, the two coincide, as in the case of gender representations in *90210*, fans rarely challenge dominant meanings.

On the one hand, then, we need to examine the distribution and constitution of power in culture and society in more detail than Fiske's notion of the power bloc suggests. Yet, whereas Fiske underestimates the complexity of the power bloc, McKinley underestimates the complexity of fan practices. From the lack of oppositional readings displayed by *90210* fans in McKinley's study, we cannot construe a general inability of fans to challenge dominant meanings. Instead, these are dependent on the interplay of fans' readings and fan texts, which, through textual productivity, can ultimately be removed from media producers' control.

Fan fiction and slash writing

In this context Jenkins's (1992) study of the fans of the CBS drama *Beauty and the Beast*, cancelled after three seasons in 1990, is particularly illustrative. While Jenkins acknowledges that popular texts can be read from different perspectives of genre expectations, he confirms that most members of the Boston group of fans of the show whom he studied approached the programme as a popular romance. As in Radway's (1987) study, the reading of the female protagonist (Catherine) by female fans evoked notions of 'ideal romance' which overcomes gender difference and discrimination: 'the fans' Catherine' – much like the show's female fans, who all worked outside the home – 'must reconcile her desires for professional autonomy and romantic affection' (Jenkins 1992: 138). The emphasis on the developing romance between the lead characters Catherine (the beauty) and Vincent (the beast) thus functioned as the leitmotif of fans' reading of the show, as it 'posed an ideological solution, a reconciliation of differences, the possibility of trust and intimacy between two people who are so different and yet so alike' (Jenkins 1992: 142). However, in the comparative narrative closure of the television programme, the fandom of these female viewers of *Beauty and the Beast* was dependent on the continuation of narrative strands that would allow for romantic consummation. Yet with the departure of lead female character Linda Hamilton and the network's concerns over a predominantly female audience, the third season of the series adopted a more action-oriented style which accommodated less and less the romantic reading preferred by the fans in Jenkins's (1992) study. When the relationship between the lead characters finally progressed to a physical level, the show fell dramatically short of the romantic expectations of its female fans. Worse, the possibility of romantic fulfilment is eradicated shortly afterwards, when Catherine is killed and Vincent's rage becomes exemplary of the shift towards violent story-lines. Feeling disappointed and betrayed, many female fans rejected the third series as fan text. Whereas fans had initiated a large-scale letter-writing campaign to save the show only months earlier, cancellation of the show after the third series was now seen as a blessing by many fans whose fandom had become irreconcilable with the text it was built upon. The female fans of *Beauty and the Beast* were thus ultimately denied the symbolic resources in popular culture that cater to their pleasures and needs. Jenkins nevertheless does not break with an understanding of fandom as a tactic of resistance. Instead, he observes how, following the cancellation of the show, fans took on the task of developing the narrative in writing their own stories about Catherine and Vincent, stories which finally fulfilled their generic expectations. The *Beauty and the Beast* fans thus negotiate popular culture not only within the constraints they were set by the text, but are willing and able to create their own symbolic resources when their mass-produced object of fandom fails them. To Jenkins a key dimension in tactical resistance of fans lies in fans' creativity and the production of their own fan texts.

These forms of fan productivity beyond the actual consumption and reading of fan texts, ranging from group interaction in the form of conventions, online discussion groups, or regular fan meetings, to the writing or creating of artwork, can be observed across different fields of fandom such as sport, music, film or television. Fanzines, for example, have formed an important source of subcultural knowledge in areas as diverse as football (Haynes 1995; Jary et al. 1991), rave (Thornton 1995) or Goth cultures (Hodkinson 2002).

With regard to gender, the genre of fan activity that has been most closely associated with female fandom is the writing of fan fiction drawing on television shows, including its best known genre 'slash'. The etymological and historical root of slash fiction lies in early *Star Trek* fandom. In the early to mid-1970s erotic stories focusing on the relationship between the two lead characters of the show emerged in various places and became known as Kirk/Spock or K/S (Jones 2002; Green et al. 1998). Initially available in the form of hand-copied or printed magazines at fan conventions or through mailing lists, fan fiction has proliferated with the spread of internet access, and has diversified in terms of its distribution, focus and content. However, boundaries between slash and other areas of fan fiction remain sharply demarcated and debated by fans and scholars alike. Some, such as Jones (2002), focusing on a range of different shows, including programmes such as the *X-Files* or *Xena: Warrior Princess*, have argued that slash has moved from a near exclusive focus on homoerotic relationships between male protagonists to serve a wide spectrum of scenarios of sexual same- and cross-gender interaction. Yet, Brooker (2002: 144) observes that while he himself questioned whether slash connotes same-sex pairs exclusively, his argument 'cut no ice with the writers ... who are clearly happy with the not quite logical convention as it currently stands'.

On the surface, slash writing confirms Fiske's definition of fandom as a discriminative, productive form of resistance of subordinated groups. Female viewers take on the symbolic resources of popular culture – exemplified through the potentially patriarchal focus on two leading male protagonists – and reformulate them according to their own needs and desires. In contrast to the female viewers of *Beverly Hills, 90210* or Radway's romance readers, they overcome the structural constraints of the culture industry and, quite literally, rewrite popular culture. This textual activity thus coincides with the degree of self-reflexivity that Giddens (1991) identifies as a key aspect of the formation of self in modernity. As Cicioni, for example, concludes:

> slash fans are ... much more than passive consumers. [They] participate in a valuable learning and liberating process: they recognize and verbalize their own – at times problematic and contradictory – needs and desires and begin to analyse the relationship between their sexuality and their subjectivity. (Cicioni 1998: 175)

Despite claims that the thematic diversity of slash stories renders questions of power and resistance obsolete (Jones 2002), the question of how the alternative spaces of articulation in slash fandom described by Cicioni relate to existing power structures remains controversial.

The different positions with regard to this question are well illustrated in Jenkins's (1991, 1992) and Camille Bacon-Smith's (1992) studies of *Star Trek*-related slash writing. While the particular emphasis in academic studies on *Star Trek*-based fan fiction (see also Tulloch and Jenkins 1995; Penley 1991; 1997), resulting from the origin of slash in *Star Trek* fandom, has been criticized by a number of slash authors (Green et al. 1998), and both Jenkins and Bacon-Smith also document slash writing surrounding other shows such as *The Professionals* or *Blake's 7*, these studies are nevertheless well suited to juxtapose different positions and theoretical orientations. Bacon-Smith and Jenkins both describe the textuality and social context of slash writing in rich detail, giving extensive space to the reproduction and narrative summary of fan fiction, as well as to the debates and discussions among fans. While I cannot replicate such detail here, the following extract from Lesley Fish and Joanne Agostino's 'Poses' quoted by Jenkins (1992: 199) gives a flavour of the stylistic and narrative orientation of slash.

Kirk squirmed in the command chair, feeling sweat soaked into the shirt between the shoulder blades. His senses seemed to have expanded; he could feel Spock sitting only ten feet away, watching, waiting, saying nothing, but acutely aware of it. It was as if an invisible electrical current connected them, keeping them painfully conscious of each other. He couldn't keep the Vulcan out of his thoughts, couldn't ignore him or stop musing about him or concentrate on anything else.

Slash writing has thus enabled female fans to break into the male domain of science fiction fandom and establish their own distinct space of reception, productivity and discussion. Bacon-Smith (1992) further categorizes slash as part of a number of genres of *Star Trek*-centred fan fiction arising out of the broader divisions between stories dedicated to 'us' (women) and 'them' (men), including so-called Mary Sue stories which focus on a young heroine, non-sexual relationship stories, slash stories with a mixture of sex and romance, matriarchal stories in which an alter-ego heroine has a sexual relationship with the male protagonist (so-called 'lay-Spock' or 'lay-Kirk' stories) and 'hurt-comfort stories' in which characters undergo particular forms of suffering and are subsequently comforted. Jenkins (1992), by contrast, focuses on the 'formulaic structure' of slash writing, which moves from the actual relationship between the characters in the conventional television programme, through an often dystopian problematization of their relationship within the confines of the initial text, to a cathartic phase of confession and resolution which culminates in the achievement of a 'masculine utopia' (Jenkins 1992: 215) through the establishment of sexual intimacy. The conventional popular text is in both cases fundamentally revised and rewritten.

Beyond this textual output, slash writing is accompanied by the establishment of tight social networks of fans. Bacon-Smith, for example, explains in great detail the processes of initiation through which she gained access to what she calls the fan 'circle' she studies. Her membership to and understanding of the group, however, deepens only over time, and it is not until she starts writing and circulating slash stories herself that she learns about the identity of many slash writers who use synonyms, as well as the particular fantasies and problems of individual group members. The group's evasion of the public gaze, according to Bacon-Smith, reflects the risks which are not only countered but on occasion also created through slash fandom, as is illustrated in the case of women working in commercial publishing who were ordered by employers not to participate in writing fan fiction.[3] In the resulting secrecy such groups are reminiscent of Fiske's notion of fans' 'guerrilla' tactics, as they resort to camouflage to avoid the danger of detection, following which they would be confronted with the conventional might of the dominant system. Yet, Bacon-Smith's account — which, drawing on the notion of 'play', avoids such martial comparisons — offers the opportunity to take the logic of the resistance analogy beyond the level developed by Fiske. The female fans in Bacon-Smith's study are not motivated predominantly by an aspiration for a utopian future. Rather, much as in the case of actual guerrilla fighters, their activity is a response to their everyday life struggles and deprivations and the lack of opportunity to counter these within the dominant power system. As Bacon-Smith (1992: 294) concludes: 'the search for expression feeds the struggle for social organization and vice-versa, but always both are founded not upon an ideal of how things might be if they were different, but how women feel right now, and how they can sanely hold on to what they are.' This assessment of the relationship of fan subcultures to dominant forms of power which are therefore maintained rather than subverted through fandom is rejected by Jenkins. To Jenkins, Bacon-Smith, in her focus on pain and risk, portrays the female fans in her study as victims of their social and cultural situation, and thereby fandom as an expression of social or emotional poverty, coming, according to Jenkins, 'close to restoring the pathological stereotype of fans' (Tulloch and Jenkins 1995: 203). In response, Jenkins focuses on two stories written by the fan writer Jane Land as an illustration of how fans have sought to rewrite the series' secondary female character, Christine Chapel, and her evolving relationship with fellow Enterprise crew member Spock. To Jenkins, Land's fan stories depict a careful negotiation of gender roles and relationships, balancing male biological needs (as symbolized by Spock's 'mating urge') and female autonomy, as well as respective social structures which grant females professional and private fulfilment. With reference to the polysemic nature of the original televisual texts of *Star Trek*, Jenkins concludes:

> The generic multiplicity and ideological contradictions of *Star Trek* invite fans to construct their own utopias from the material it provides ... By rethinking the utopian vision of *Star Trek*, [Land] finds a way to rescue the female characters from the stereotypical on-screen behaviour while explaining, within the fiction, rather than

in terms of the programme's production and reception context, those forces which do not allow *Star Trek's* women to achieve as much as their potential suggests. (Tulloch and Jenkins 1995: 212)

These contradictory conclusions drawn by Jenkins and Bacon-Smith warrant further explanation. In the first instance, Jenkins's and Bacon-Smith's different assessments of the utopian and progressive potential of fandom follow from different empirical and ultimately ideological positions, reflecting different generations of feminism. Jenkins (Tulloch and Jenkins 1995) rejects what he describes as the victimization perspective in Bacon-Smith's work in its contrasting account of feminist empowerment. From these differences also follows the different weight placed on particular aspects of fan fiction: while Jenkins seems particularly interested in its communal, interpersonal aspects, Bacon-Smith focuses on the impact of fan fiction within individual fans' everyday life. Yet, beyond a focus on different aspects of fan practices, they also explore different fans, particularly if we take into account the wide selection of fan groups of different socio-demographic backgrounds in Jenkins's later work (Tulloch and Jenkins 1995). The significance of these variations is highlighted in Jenkins's conclusion to *Textual Poachers*:

> I am not claiming that there is anything particularly empowering about the texts fans embrace. I am, however, claiming that there is something empowering about what fans do with those texts in the process of assimilating them to the particulars of their lives. Fandom celebrates not exceptional texts but rather exceptional readings. (Jenkins 1992: 284)

If, then, fandom is based primarily on forms of exceptional reading rather than a shared symbolic basis, levels of resistance displayed in fandom are likely to vary between different fan groups. While Jenkins and Bacon-Smith thus seem to study the same fan culture of slash writing in the first instance and *Star Trek* fandom in the broader sense, they – at least in parts – follow a different empirical focus. On those occasions where Jenkins's findings on *Star Trek* fans differ most substantially from Bacon-Smith's conclusions, the background of the fans – students at the Massachusetts Institute of Technology where Jenkins teaches, and members of the Boston branch of the Gaylaxians, an urban group that is also actively involved in the gay rights movement – shows a marked contrast in age and class as compared to the Pennsylvania based women in

Bacon-Smith's study. It is easy to see how the fandom of students at one of America's elite universities or a group of urban civil rights campaigners differs in its utopian promise from the fandom of middle-aged suburban service workers and housewives, confronted with a range of discriminative gender expectations. An important line of distinction in fandom thus emerges along demographic lines and with respect to different social, cultural and economic positions. However, class position alone is an insufficient category to account for the different meanings constructed by different fans in slash writing and beyond. The *90210* fans, including students at another of America's leading universities, Princeton, whom McKinley (1997) interviews, for example, do not display similar forms of ideological resistance or utopian vision. Yet, neither do they engage in extensive textual production or subcultural exchange comparable to Jenkins's *Star Trek* fans. In these varying patterns of fan productivity, then, lies a second axis of distinction, which I want to explore further, before turning to fans' socio-demographic variations and their consequences.

Fan productivity

While slash writing has long constituted a key concern in the analysis of fan cultures and thus continues to constitute a well-documented and illustrative example of fans turning producers, it remains only one of many different fan practices (cf. Jenkins 1992). Equally, the interest in slash appears to vary significantly between different fan cultures. Brooker, in his study of *Star Wars* fans (2002: 132), for instance, struggles to record fan interest in slash corresponding to what he describes as 'the enthusiasm with which media scholars approach and report on slash': 'I ended up ... with only three mentions of slash, two of which I had prompted myself.' Yet, as much as the boundaries of slash are contested, the distinction between slash and other forms of fan fiction has relatively little impact on their respective social and cultural significance. As Brooker argues:

> My core argument here is that *Star Wars* slash fiction plays exactly the same game with primary texts, on a formal level, as does genfic, its heterosexual counterpart. Stories that do nothing more than fill in the gaps in Luke and Biggs' platonic relationship or expand on Han's evolving romance with Leia are no less radical than slash in

terms of their relationship with the primary texts. Slash relies on the films as much as genfic does; genfic departs from the films as much as slash does. (Brooker 2002: 133)

In turn, fan fiction itself accounts for only a part of the wide variety of fan performance and productivity. Fiske's work (1992) again provides a useful starting point, as he distinguishes between three different forms of fan productivity: semiotic, enunciative and textual. Semiotic productivity refers to the creation of meaning in the process of reading, and therefore takes place on an intrapersonal level. Enunciative productivity, by contrast, describes the forms of social interaction that are cultivated through fan consumption. A key dimension of such productivity is the regular verbal exchange between fans (cf. M. E. Brown 1994; Baym 2000) in form of fan talk and gossip, which, according to Fiske (1992: 38), accounts for 'much of the pleasure of fandom'. Enunciative productivity also includes pleasurable forms of non-verbal communication, such as replicating a star's appearance or wearing shirts or buttons to display affection for one's favourite sports team or television programme. Textual productivity, finally, refers to materials and texts created by fans which are manifest concretely, in that they are either written, edited or recorded, such as fanzines, fan fiction, self-produced videotapes or 'filk songs' (see Jenkins 1992).

While, according to Fiske, these forms of productivity constitute the ground on which mass culture is turned into popular culture through the pleasurable and subversive creation of meaning, McKinley's (1997) analysis of *90210* fans illustrates that neither semiotic nor enunciative productivity is a guarantor of a critical negotiation of the ideological framing of fan texts. Textually productive fans, however – such as those studied by Bacon-Smith (1992), Jenkins (1992) or Cicioni (1998) – reformulate the fan text in ways that necessarily move it out of its industrial framing and thus invite emancipation from, and resistance to, such frames. Consequently, fandom *can* be subversive, especially when based on textual productivity; yet there is no automatism which positions the tactics of reading in necessary opposition to the strategies of (mass) production.

Moreover, while all fans are semiotically, and most fans are enunciatively productive, only a minority of fans participate in textual production. This challenge to an understanding of fandom as a form of pleasurable subversion, in Fiske's work (1989b, 1992) in particular, has been addressed in two ways: the first has upheld the normative basis of Fiske's definition of fandom and instead redefined the empirical object. In particular, ethnographies of tight-knit, textually productive fan communities have relied on a narrow definition of fandom, studying only those actively participating in fan communities through conventions and meetings and textual production. In their discussion of science fiction audiences, Tulloch and Jenkins (1995: 23), for example, distinguish between 'fans, active participants within fandom as a social, cultural and interpretative institution, and followers, audience members who regularly watch and enjoy media science fiction programmes but who claim no larger social identity on the basis of this consumption'. The problem is that Tulloch and Jenkins's second assumption, since it lies outside the scope of their study, is never explored, Tulloch's (2000) later reflection on his own initial status as a 'follower' aside. Yet many viewers and readers who do not actively participate in fan communities and their textual productivity[4] nevertheless derive a distinct sense of self and social identity from their fan consumption (cf. Sandvoss 2003). Alternatively, in maintaining an inclusive, non-normative defini-tion of fandom, we need to develop a taxonomy of fans which accounts for the varying degrees of productivity and social organization in fandom.

The particular challenge, then, is to explain the ambiguous relationship between the consumption patterns of fans and non-fans. Fans who are semiotically and enunciatively productive and those who are textually productive engage in what at first sight appear to be fundamentally different activities. Semiotically and enunciatively active fans negotiate and appropriate their object of fandom, whereas textually productive fans create (new) objects of fandom. To return to Fiske's analogy, it is the difference between wearing jeans to make them fit, and tailoring your own trousers. This seemingly irreconcilable division has led many scholars to limit their theoretical ambitions to the group of textually productive fans. There are, nevertheless, lines of continuity. Abercrombie and Longhurst (1998) recognize these various forms of fan productivity in locating fandom in the transitional space between consumption and production, and develop a continuum leading from ordinary consumers on one end to petty producers on the other. In between these polarities we find three different groups of fans: fans, cultists and enthusiasts. Two aspects are important here. First, the notion of a continuum implies a difference of degree, rather than kind, between different audience groups. Fans are therefore conceptualized as part of our understanding of everyday life consumption in consumer capitalism, not in opposition to it. Secondly, while their categorization of different fan groups recognizes differences in productivity, it equally accounts for further differentiating factors without resorting to problematic claims regarding the individual importance of fandom in creating a sense of self or identity, as Tulloch and Jenkins (1995) do. Abercrombie and Longhurst distinguish fans along three axes: media use (the distribution and availability of media used), connectivity (the degree to which fans are part of fan networks or communities) and focus (the specificity of the object of fandom). The first group, 'fans', intensely follow a particular cultural text or icon almost exclusively through the mass media. They are part of an atomized audience and are not linked with each other on an organizational level. Cultists' media usage is more specialized, as is their object of fandom. Additionally, they tend to develop through albeit largely unorganized ties with others who share their fandom. In the case of enthusiasts, finally, it is not so much the original mass-mediated object of fandom (such as, for instance, a particular pop star, television programme or football team) as their own activity and textual productivity that constitute the core of their fandom. Enthusiasts consume highly specialized texts produced by fellow enthusiasts, such as fanzines, which are exchanged through organizational structures such as fan conventions, fan clubs or online communities. All three factors are thus interdependent, and in turn relate to different degrees of productivity.

This taxonomy lends itself well to the study of fandom across various genres. Elsewhere I have illustrated how the wide range of different fan practices within football fandom can be usefully conceptualized drawing on such a model (Sandvoss 2001). The case of football fandom, however, points to the problems arising out of Abercrombie and Longhurst's chosen terminology. Few football fans, or for that matter fans of most other genres, would describe themselves as cultists, while all participants in my study described themselves as fans. The use of the term 'fan' to describe only a small section of consumers whom we have identified as fans, as much as the religious connotations that terms such as 'cultist' carry, is misleading. As Hills (2002: p. ix) remarks, 'it seems unhelpful to produce a taxonomy in which the definition of 'fan' is at odds with the use of this term in almost all other literature in the field.'

This, however, is primarily a problem of terminology, not substance. Abercrombie and Longhurst's model illustrates a range of important issues in relation to fandom and power. In quantitative terms, it is important to note that the continuum between fans, cultists and enthusiasts is a pyramid instead of a linear continuation. Box office takings, audience ratings and market research on music or football fandom all illustrate that fans who regularly follow a particular fan text in its mass-mediated form outnumber those attending live events or conventions, or even become producers in their own right.[5] 'Fans' thus account for by far the largest segment of the fan continuum, with a substantially smaller number of cultists and even fewer enthusiasts.

Furthermore, such a taxonomy of fandom enables us to read the different conclusions concerning the potential for empowerment and emancipation in fandom in light of the different groups of fans studied: the *Star Trek* and slash fans in Bacon-Smith's (1992) and Jenkins's (1992) work clearly form a group of enthusiasts, while McKinley (1997) and Fiske (1989b) are also concerned with fans and cultists. Despite all parallels among fan groups, this also highlights an important difference in the focus of fandom. While for fans and cultists their object of fandom lies in a given mediated text, enthusiasts find their object of fandom in their own textual productivity. Yet, enthusiasts, despite the radical shifts in the object of fandom through textual productivity, share the same motivations and needs articulated by cultists and fans. All three groups seek textual forms that allow for the creation of a particular sense of meaning that is evaluated with regard to its ability to correspond to fans' wishes, desires and sense of self. In other words, fandom and the power relations within fandom, are based upon the capacity of popular texts, whether produced by the media industry or by fans, to carry meaning that articulates fans' identity and their objective and subjective position within society. In this sense I now want to turn to the social, cultural and economic framing of fandom articulated in fans' identity, as well as their external classification.

Fandom, taste and distinction

The problem in evaluating notions of popular culture and fandom as forms of pleasurable deviation or subversion is thus the following: fans' semiotic, enunciative and textual productivity may allow for oppositional appropriations, but who or what these fan readings are oppositional to is dependent on factors outside the interaction between fan and fan text. The opposition of, for example, fans of classical music against what they would see as 'dumbed down' mainstream pop clearly differs in its aims and motivations from the oppositional readings of teenage Madonna fans. We therefore need to turn to the context of the interaction between fans and their objects of fandom. If there were a simple division between those empowered and those disempowered in modern societies, as Fiske implies, this would be a relatively easy task. However, when Fiske argues (1992: 30) that fandom is 'associated with the cultural tastes of subordinated formations of the people, particularly those disempowered by any combination of gender, age, class and race', he fails to account for the power relations between these fields. Drawing on Bourdieu (1984), Fiske recognizes the multi-polarity of power, but he does not address its consequences in his understanding of fandom. Here, Fiske's analogy of fandom as semiotic guerrilla warfare does not stand up to critical scrutiny: guerrilla tactics require a clear division – and inequality – of power. Instead, the power relations in many fan cultures, particularly those marked by a pronounced opposition to official culture, are more complex. In England the lawlessness and violence of football fans, for example, constituted an open confrontation with the existing political power bloc of what was from 1979 onwards a neo-liberal government. On the other hand, their opposition was also directed, and probably most felt, by other disempowered groups: older spectators, women, and particularly non-white fans and players (cf. Williams and Taylor 1994). The distribution of power in fandom is more adequately reflected in a different historical analogy. With the diffusion of power following the demise of the Soviet Union and, consequently, the bipolar world, guerrilla fighting as a dominant form of military confrontation during the Cold War has given way to new forms of civil war and factional fighting, which result from the complex relationships *between* disempowered groups as much as their opposition to any definable power bloc. In order to understand the complex power relations and hierarchies in fandom reflected in the analogy of factional fighting, a number of studies have returned to Bourdieu's analysis of consumption on which Fiske (1989b, 1992) draws so partially.

Bourdieu's sociology of consumption (1984) has formed a popular theoretical framework of fan studies for two reasons. First, it accounts for the multiple factors through which identity and class position are defined in modern societies. In addition to a Marxist definition of class in terms of economic capital, and hence means of production, Bourdieu identifies further important resources that shape class positions, such as social capital, education capital and cultural capital. While all these different forms of capital are interrelated, they are not identical. The owner of a small construction business may, for example, be considerably wealthier than a higher education teacher or freelance artist, yet will possess lower cultural capital – that is, forms of knowledge and cultural expertise. Bourdieu thus develops a multi-dimensional model of class accounting for the diverse power relations between various class positions.

These class positions – and herein lies the further importance of Bourdieu's work for the study of fans and audiences – are articulated through consumption preferences that also constitute the very basis of fandom: the principle of taste as the privileging of defined, distinct objects of consumption. Taste, according to Bourdieu (1984), is based on the 'habitus', which in turn reflects any combination of social, cultural and economic capital. Thus 'the habitus', in Bourdieu's words (1984: 101), 'enables an intelligible and necessary relation to be established between practices and a situation, the meaning of which is produced by the habitus through categories of perception and appreciation that are themselves produced by an observable social condition'. For Bourdieu, taste thus functions as a premiss and consequence of class positions, rather than as a form of empowerment. Taste, through the habitus, functions as 'structuring' as well as 'structured structure' (Bourdieu 1984: 170). It is, put simply, a forced choice. This is not to argue that the habitus is necessarily experienced as restrictive by consumers or fans themselves. Indeed, it seems plausible to suggest that the emotional intensity and public display of consumption in fandom constitutes a celebration of one's habitus. The habitus articulated in fandom thus fulfils a double function that is of crucial importance to our sense of self in a media-saturated world. It functions as a simultaneous form of communication and identity building: as communication, in that our consumption choices articulate our complex class position, and as identity building, in that this communication is as much directed inwards as outwards, forming a sense of who we are and believe ourselves to be. Taste thus 'functions as a sort of social orientation, a "sense of one's place"' (Bourdieu 1984: 466). This role of the habitus in fandom has been conceptualized in three different ways: first, by exploring the extent to which fans' habitus reaffirms existing cultural social hierarchies; secondly, by examining the opposition between fans' habitus and existing cultural hierarchies; and thirdly, beyond the scope of existing cultural hierarchies, by focusing on the role of fans' habitus in the creation of new hierarchies within a subcultural context.

There is substantial evidence in support of an understanding of fan tastes as yet another segment of the process of distinction through consumption, in line with an orthodox reading of Bourdieu's analysis in studies which have correlated the choice of the object of fandom to fans' class position. In her study of the grass-roots fan group Viewers for Quality Television, which campaigns for the continuation of shows with low ratings but considerable fan following (such as *Cagney & Lacey*, *Alien Nation* or the above-discussed *Beauty and the Beast*), Harris (1998b) describes the participation of fans in the group and their respective 'fan tastes' in such terms (see also Brower 1992). The role of fandom within existing cultural hierarchies, according to Harris (1998b: 51), is therefore 'to protect and enlarge the social space bound by our cultural capital'. Similarly, Thomas (2002), in her study of fans of the British detective drama *Inspector Morse* and the BBC radio soap opera *The Archers*, demonstrates how the choice of these programmes as object of fandom is motivated by particular combinations of the social, cultural and economic capital of fans. The majority of respondents in her research on *The Archers* are lower middle class. Similarly, Thomas illustrates how her own 'taste' for *Inspector Morse* is structured through her habitus and class and background:

> On one level I found the images of middle-class life – tea on the lawn, sherry parties, Morse's own taste for classical music and good country pubs – reassuring. In the same way, the leisurely tea at five and supper at seven which I consumed in my Oxford college seemed a more adequate protection from the collapse of civilized life than the hastily put together bacon and egg 'teas' – an amalgamation of both meals – that we had at home. These images, and the class trajectory of Morse himself, mirroring my own, make me feel that what sometimes seemed like a fragile veneer of middle-classness was not just a figment of my own imagination, but an external reality. (Thomas 2002: 2)

While Thomas is hesitant to describe her own fandom as a simple articulation of class position or 'as an aspiration of middle-classness' and instead elects to summarize it as 'a search for a cultural home' (Thomas 2002: 2), she thereby illustrates the dual, inward- and outward-looking framing of the habitus. However, while both Harris and Thomas establish a link between class position and choice of object of consumption in fandom, other socio-demographic factors – and none more than gender – emerge as equally if not more important lines of distinction. Members of the Viewers for Quality Television Group are 'primarily female' (Harris 1998b), while 78 per cent of respondents in Thomas's survey (2002) on *The Archers* are female, and almost 100 per cent are white. While class is an important factor in fan consumption and distinction, it is only one of a number of important socio-demographic variables. Similar observations apply to sports fandom (Sandvoss 2003) and music fandom (Christenson and Peterson 1988), in which gender emerges as an important axis of distinction alongside, and at the expense of, class (Erickson 1996). Even those studies attesting to a relationship between class and fan tastes thus point to the need to broaden our understanding of the structuring influences on the habitus in contemporary popular culture beyond class.

The discrepancies between Bourdieu's emphasis on class and the emergence of different lines of distinction in fandom echo two prominent criticisms that have frequently been directed at Bourdieu's work: first, his too narrow and deterministic under-standing of class as a structure of entrapment (Gans 1966; Honneth 1986; DiMaggio 1979), and secondly, his misunderstanding of objects of consumption as assuming fixed meanings (Grossberg 1985; Frow 1987; Fenster 1991), as a consequence of which he comes to underestimate the individual freedom that consumers and audiences exercise through consumption choices. Both points are inextricably linked with the proliferating role of (electronic) mass media in the consumption and distribution of popular culture. On the surface, the universal accessibility of popular culture has led to a proliferation of fan consumption across different classes and the disappearance of an official culture that is driven by bourgeois cultural interests, which, as Frow has noted, also remains insufficiently explored in its power relations by Bourdieu. Mass media, according to American critics such as Lewis (1987), thus create a classless space of consumption (cf. Peterson and Kern 1996). However, as we have already seen, it seems at best premature to claim the disappearance of class as a factor of distinction in popular culture.

Fiske (1992: 43), pointing to the specific practices of fan consumption based on an extensive knowledge of both text and context of the object fandom, distinguishes between the 'dominant habitus' of official culture, which is used as an agent of discrimination, and the 'popular habitus', which by contrast functions as an agent of participation and a form of empowering knowledge, which allows fans 'to see through the production processes normally hidden by the text'. Yet, Fiske remains vague when it comes to how and against whom the popular habitus empowers the fan. His example of a fan being inspired by a fellow black athlete's success hardly suggests an anti-hegemonic disposition of the popular habitus. In order to answer either of these two questions, we need to look in more detail at fans' practices of distinction.

While it has become increasingly difficult to link specific fan texts, particularly those distributed through mass media of virtually universal reach, such as television, to specific positions in a multi-dimensional class model, this does not mean that they cease to function as signifiers of class, age or gender positions from the subjective position of the fan. Thomas's (2002) study of *Inspector Morse* illustrates this point well. While she observes how her own and her respondents' socio-economic positions are mirrored in their readings of the show, she equally acknowledges that 'the programmes contain the whole hierarchy of taste analysed by Bourdieu: put simply, there is perhaps something for everyone, from the most ascetic intellectual to the radical feminist, taking in the Radio 2 listener en route' (Thomas 2002: 94). Rather than ceasing to signify cultural hierarchies, objects of fandom popular across socio-demographic divisions represent a multitude of such positions subjectively.

On a side-note, it is worth mentioning that the same process applies not only to objects of fandom, but also in reverse to textual discrimination through rejection of particular popular texts in an effort of 'negative distinction' by those viewers who have been labelled 'anti-fans' (Theodoropoulou 1999; Gray 2003). Jancovich (2001), for example, observes how the popular critique of *Playboy* magazine, particularly through the notion of 'middlebrow', reinforces cultural hierarchies.

While the ability to appropriate fan texts from a range of class positions raises important questions concerning the nature of the meanings articulated in fandom, to which I will return in chapter 6, its challenge to Bourdieu's understanding of taste as structured and structuring structure maintaining cultural hierarchies is a relative one. It illustrates a shifting emphasis from texts and commodities to consumption practices as agents of distinction. This in turn is already recognized in Bourdieu's attention to *what* is consumed as much as *how* it is consumed. With regard to the example of sport, he argues that:

> Because agents apprehend objects through the schemes of perception and appreciation of their habitus it would be naive to suppose that all practitioners of the same sport (or even any other practice) confer the same meaning on their practice or even, strictly speaking, that they are practising the same practice. (Bourdieu 1984: 211)

Thus variations in fan practices – rather than in objects of fandom – are increasingly indicative of social and cultural differences. The contrast in the following accounts of two football fans – the first from a retired engineer, the second from a middle-aged, female social worker from a working-class background, who at the time of the interview was unemployed – reflects the importance of consumption practices as signifiers of fans' socio-demographic position (quoted in Sandvoss 2003: 23-4):

> It [supporting Bayer] is part of my leisure time. I play chess, I worked for the local energy services and I founded a sports club there. We have played football there for years. I played tennis, passionately. They also have a very good basketball team [Bayer]. My wife and I have season tickets there ... Apart from that, there are other leisure activities, sometimes we go to the theatre ... I would say, football is only one component of all this. (Mr Perschul, Bayer Leverkusen fan)

> I need this [supporting Bayer] as an outlet, when I have accumulated two weeks of frustration. I am much calmer during the football season. I just shout it all out. I shout 'you arsehole', 'you wanker' and when the game is over, I can go home and feel much better. (Chris, Bayer Leverkusen fan)

Through such variations in consumption practices, cultural hierarchies continue in the field of fandom, despite an increasing lack of external signification through particular objects of fandom. However, as specific cultural objects are less and less recognized as universal signifiers of specific socio-demographic positions, as distinctions are more and more based upon practices of consumption, the audience to which such distinction is performed changes. It is mainly fellow fans who will recognize the nuanced differences in consumption choices – between a season-ticket in the supporters' end or elsewhere in the stadium, or between white label bootlegs and compilation albums – and consumption practices, such as appropriate forms of appearance and participation at, for instance, a screening of the *Rocky Horror Picture Show*.

Consequently, within fan cultures new cultural hierarchies are formed.

In this spirit recent studies of fandom drawing on Bourdieu (Thornton 1995; Erickson 1996; J. A. Brown 1997; Dell 1998; Harris 1998b) have not only positioned fandom within the hierarchies of official culture, but highlighted the replication of hierarchies within subcultures. Thornton's (1995) influential study of club culture in the early years of Acid House sets out to illustrate how the seemingly classless spaces in fan subcultures, particularly in youth cultures, are – contrary to Hebdige's (1979) interpretation of the formation of style as *bricolage* – not constructed against, but in line with, power relations in society at large. In her analysis of interactions between various groups, such as occasional clubbers, dedicated record collectors, and semi-professionals such as DJs, Thornton finds a replication of the habitus in subculture that, in contrast to Fiske's popular habitus, continues to carry the discriminative power of the official habitus. On this basis Thornton distinguishes between *being* empowered and *feeling* empowered. While the latter is fostered through the relative insignificance of class in the formation of youth culture, given the 'still considerable discretionary income amongst the bulk of people aged 16 to 24' (Thornton 1995: 103), wider forms of social discrimination continue – for example, through quotas in the admission of black males to rave venues – and new cultural hierarchies are created.

Within these hierarchies bourgeois aesthetic norms are replaced by the subcultural leitmotifs of 'authenticity' and 'hipness'. Being hip, being in the know about clubs, records and fashion, become signifiers of cultural status, and thus function as 'subcultural capital'. Such subcultural capital is constructed in opposition to class, yet maintains other social power relations, as it functions as 'the linchpin of an alternative hierarchy in which the axes of age, gender, sexuality and race are all employed in order to keep the determinations of class, income and occupation at bay' (Thornton 1995: 105). And, like other fan cultures – such as the fans of *Dr Who*, who define themselves against other science fiction programmes such as *Star Trek* or *Blake's 7* (Tulloch and Jenkins, 1995), or the horror fans who construct their own fandom with reference to sub-genres or fanzines they reject (Cherry 2002) – it is constructed against the imagined Other as 'the social logic of subcultural capital reveals itself most clearly by what it dislikes and by what it emphatically isn't' (Thornton 1995: 105): the notion of the 'mainstream' which is primarily defined through different forms of (mass) media. Subcultural capital is obtained through niche media, such as pirate radio stations, bootlegs or relatively low circulation subcultural magazines, while simultaneously being threatened *and* maintained through mass media coverage. As Thornton illustrates in relation to the coverage of rave culture in Britain's largest tabloid paper, the *Sun*, the initial, negative mass media coverage and media panics about rave events, and the related drug culture, served to reinforce the subcultural legitimacy of rave fandom, whereas more appreciative coverage in subsequent years including tips on how raving is 'the perfect way to lose weight' constituted the 'subcultural kiss of death' (Thornton 1995: 135). This opposition between fan culture and mainstream culture not only reflects different forms of media usage and productivity as outlined by Abercrombie and Longhurst (1998), but becomes a source of discrimination itself. The imagined Other of the mainstream in club culture is predominantly projected on to female participants. The handbag, brought along by the unhip female clubber unaware of subcultural fashion conventions, becomes a signifier of female mainstream (Thornton 1995). Instead of empowering female fans, the subcultural logic of hipness and authenticity thus evokes the feminization of mass culture by cultural theorists (cf. Huyssen 1986):

> Among youth cultures there is a double articulation of the low and the feminine: disparaged *other* cultures are characterized as feminine *and* girls' cultures are devalued as imitative and passive. Authentic culture is, by contrast, depicted in gender-free or masculine terms *and* remains the prerogative of boys. (Thornton 1995: 105)

Through subcultural capital, then, discrimination and power relations are maintained and reconstituted in fandom, and Bourdieu's logic of distinction through consumption is extended even to fans seeking to position themselves in opposition to official culture. According to Brown (1997), who analyses the role of cultural capital in comic book fandom, fan culture thus functions as a substitute for cultural status 'denied elsewhere', replicating the official culture in its details: 'the shadow cultural economy of comic fandom observes all of the same markers of aesthetic good taste that official culture does' (J. A. Brown 1997: 28). The structuring and classifying momentum of, and within, fandom also operates, of course, in relation to those who investigate fans academically. Hills (2002) in particular has pointed to the similarities in the construction of fan as well as academic hierarchies.[6] Indeed, on occasion, academic discourses inform such hierarchies within fandom, as is illustrated by the notion of 'cult'. The confusion over what is meant by 'cult' is illustrated by the profound lack of basic agreement on which particular texts can be accurately described as cult (Grant 2000).[7] To further complicate matters, the label 'cult' has been promiscuously attached to texts across different media and genres. Cult films, for example – if we, for the moment, assume that we can describe them as cult films prior to the existence of a common definition – come from a range of established genres, including Western, musicals, or science fiction, film noir, war films, crime films and romantic comedy. In the absence of a generic definition, cult texts are thus defined by their particular modes of reading and their consumption by fans. Mendik and Harper (2000b) thus resort to the audience rather than the films themselves in their definition of cult:

> The cult film draws on a (hard)core of audience interest and involvement which is not just the result of random, directionless entertainment seeking, but rather a combination of intense physical and emotional involvement. . . . The effect it produces is not merely an affectionate attachment to the text, but a ritualistic form of near obsession. (Mendik and Harper 2000b: 7)

This use of the notion of cult is in turn reflective of the habitus of the fan. Mendik and Harper (2000b: 7) evidently engage in a process of distinction when they proclaim that the pleasures experienced by the cult film viewer are superior: 'Such stimulation is more than pleasurable, it's orgasmic!' What can be described as cult, then, cannot defined in textual terms, but must be judged *a posteriori* in relation to consumption practices, which in turn are reflective of the fan's habitus. Herein lies the importance of 'cult' as an element of distinction within fandom. Through these classifications of their object of fandom as superior, cult fans tend to communicate social and cultural capital defined against the mainstream.

Looking beyond its structuring potential at the structured use of the term, it comes as no surprise that the notion of cult has enjoyed popularity with academics and scholars who are under particular pressure to legitimize their own consumption patterns in relation to educational capital. Whether in the case of Hunter's (2000) defence of Paul Verhovens' *Showgirls* (1995) or Osgerby's (2000) study of *Thunderbirds*, the label 'cult' establishes cultural legitimacy with respect to otherwise little regarded texts, ranging from the graphic depiction of violence to kitsch, or even hard-core pornography (Krzywinska 2000). The notion of cult thus replicates cultural hierarchies in the consumption and appropriation of the text. As Jancovich (2002: 312) argues, cult cinema (or 'paracinema') is 'at least as concerned to assert its superiority over those whom it conceives of as the degraded victims of mainstream commercial culture as it is concerned to provide a challenge to the academy and the arts cinema'.

Fandom, in a nutshell, then cannot be defined through inherent principles of resistance. In the media-saturated world the habitus is no longer signified through the external object. Consequently, the centre of gravity of social signification has shifted from objectively identifiable textual structures associated with particular class positions to subjectively constituted readings and appropriations of fan texts which also reflect a multi-polar distribution of power in the complex connectivity between class, gender, age and ethnicity. Thus the object of distinction in fandom is no longer the text, but the meaning that is constituted in the interaction between text and reader. By the same token, the key to understanding the emotional rewards of fandom, as well as its social and cultural consequences, shifts from the macro questions of power, hegemony and subversion to questions of self and identity in fandom.

Summary

In this chapter I have revisited the original theoretical concerns over power and resistance that motivated the first and second waves of fan studies. Critically examining Fiske's notion of fandom as a form of empowerment, I have underlined the need for a detailed analysis of both the 'power bloc' and fan practices. The different articulations of gender in fandom illustrate that neither mass-mediated fan texts nor fans' reading of such texts can easily be identified as hegemonic or subversive. Different fan practices in particular, which Fiske usefully categorizes as semiotic, enunciative, and textual productivity, constitute different degrees of appro-priations of the fan text, which itself cannot be easily classified ideologically. Moreover, textual productivity in particular, as in the case of slash writing and other fan fiction, often breaks with the cultural and ideological frameworks of the fan text and radically reformulates its substance. Equally, the social and cultural background of the fan is essential in eroding or reaffirming existing power relations. Consequently, I have conceptualized fan practices by distinguishing between different fan groups, as well as exploring fans' reading position in light of their habitus as, following Bourdieu, a structured and structuring structure. In combination, these illustrate not only the position of fandom within existing cultural hierarchies that do not allow for simple bipolar oppositions between media and audiences, but also the tendencies to replicate such hierarchies within fan culture. While the question of power is clearly important, given the prominence of fandom as a symbolic resource in everyday life, the diverse emotional qualities of fandom can thus not be subsumed under the heading of 'pleasurable resistance'. Instead, we need to turn to the significance of fandom to the self and its representation to others.

3

A TEXT CALLED HOME: FANDOM BETWEEN PERFORMANCE AND PLACE

The growing body of fan studies drawing on Bourdieu (1984) documents how hegemony and resistance are constituted not only in the relationship between text and reader, between production and consumption, but in the social and cultural fields in which fan consumption is located. The consequential paradigmatic shift from the immediate dialogue between media and its audiences to questions of self and identity, however, does not equal an abandonment of questions of power. Instead, it enables us to move beyond the too narrowly defined questions through which various approaches to popular culture have sought to explore manifestations of power in fandom. As hegemony and resistance are constituted in the context of fandom as much as in the relationship between fan and text, I now turn to the analysis of those cultural fields within which fandom is located: fans' identities, the interaction between fans, their performance of self, and the territorial framing of fan consumption in place and space.

Performing fans

In contrast to semiotic and enunciative productivity, fan performances are always constituted between text and context by turning the object of consumption into an activity with a given micro field of social and cultural relations. Performance implies the existence of an audience for fan consumption and a process of interaction between performer and spectators. Performance, in Abercrombie and Longhurst's words (1998: 40), is thus an 'activity in which the person performing accentuates his or her behaviour under the scrutiny of others'. While consumers of (mediated) performances in the form of books, music, films, television shows or sports events, fans also become performers as others acknowledge their consumption. As Cavicchi (1998: 19) observes in his study of Bruce Springsteen fans: 'the interesting aspect ... is that they have a significant relationship with a performer and also perform themselves in various contexts'.

The notion of performance thus offers an alternative theoretical framework for the micro analysis of fan practices. The benefits and limitations of conceptualizing fandom as a form of performance are usefully illustrated in Lancaster's (2001) study of fan performances surrounding the mid-1990s science fiction series *Babylon 5*. Instead of extensive qualitative work with other fans of the show, Lancaster's account is based on the insider perspective that arises from his own regular participation in the viewing of the programme, web-based discussion groups, role-playing, card games and multi-user domains. These 'imaginary entertainment environments' constitute, according to Lancaster (2001: p. xxviii), 'sites of performance', performances which are as valid and as important as professional performances in theatres or on television. Drawing on his detailed account of rules and play of *Babylon 5*-based card and board games, Lancaster argues that fan performances are based upon a form of 'immersion' in which the fan becomes an active performer within a given text. Immersion is therefore based upon the simulation of narratives in play through fantasy. Contrasting fan performers with conventional viewers or readers, he asserts that the latter groups 'do not participate as performers in that action. In immersive performances, on the other hand, participants perform the actions, and, because of this, the fantasy seems more real. ... Immersion occurs as the fantasy frame expands around all other frames, causing it to seem *as if* it were a real environment' (Lancaster 2001: 83, original emphasis).

While fantasy thus constitutes a necessary premiss of performance, performance as the process of interaction between the fan and the fan text before an audience (as in the case of the *Babylon 5* board game) also constitutes the premiss of fantasy and immersion. When the spaces for such performances are limited or absent, as in the case of the official *Babylon 5* CD ROM, the

performance/fantasy circle is interrupted: 'the high-tech performance of the software designed never delivers what is indicated
through to packaging: immersion. ... Instead, through the
bureaucratic performance of press reviews, advertising, and
packaging, the producers have effectively reconfigured potential
participants' (Lancaster 2001; 116–7). While Lancaster's account
thus reinforces the significance of semiotic autonomy in fandom as
a constitutive element of fan culture, his definition of fan
performances is problematic on a number of counts. For, once it
reintroduces an assumed diametrical opposition between fans and
'normal' consumers and audiences, the criteria for distinguishing
between fans and non-fans do not match a distinction between
consumers and performers: not all fans engage in performances of
game-play, and not all performers in role-play or fantasy games are
fans. More importantly, Lancaster has little to say about what lies
behind fan performances. While he associates fandom with play – a
notion to which we will return later – the wider social and
psychological implications of 'fantasy' or 'play' remain unexplored
(cf. Hills 2002). This is particularly problematic in relation to the
textual and technological framing of fan performances. Despite
Lancaster's acknowledgement that the different texts and games
evolving around *Babylon 5* constitute realms of simulation and
hyperreality, as described in the work of Jean Baudrillard (1983,
1993b), he evades the question of whether fan performances
constitute part of a hyperreal, and hence intrinsically hollow and
superficial, media culture by simply stating that fans 'desire to
recapture an emotional moment through [performances] in an
attempt to relive the immersion experience in viewing the original
text' (Lancaster 2001: 155). Why, and to what effect, fans want to
create this emotional experience remains unanswered.

One approach that offers a broader contextual understanding of
performances, which Lancaster turns to in his discussion of the
show's producer, Joe Straczynski, is the work of Erving Goffman.
Goffman (1959/1990) develops an account of the self as
constituted through processes of performance as communication,
ritual and the adoption of different roles in everyday life. To
Goffman self and identity thus become immediately interconnected
and almost interchangeable categories (Gleason 1983), based upon
the performances of individuals in their routine social interaction.
Whereas in the 1940s and 1950s these roles were often defined
through the context of public space and/or professional work – as
in Goffman's frequently quoted example of the different roles acted
out by a waiter – in an increasingly mass-mediated world the

performances of media consumption, of being a fan, are increasingly important everyday life roles. Fandom thus becomes one of the many facets of the multiple self. Yet, in contrast to other socially prescribed roles, fandom offers a greater degree of autonomy in performance. Consider the following dialogue between two 18-year-old grammar school students and football fans:

MARTIN: [Football] is always the highlight of the weekend and it is a highlight because you are a Bayer fan.

ALEX: Yes, it is, for example, being here at the fan meeting place. However, in my case I have observed, that I, at least in part, really display a very different personality, when I appear in my role as a football fan, as opposed to being a normal student.

MARTIN: You can't deny that you act in a more aggressive way towards, for example, other fan groups and that you kind of give way to your aggressions. That sounds like a cliché, but in these moments, you are really completely different than you would be in school for instance, because when certain people would see us watching football – like our parents – they would really think, 'my god, what is going on? Our children wouldn't be doing this . . .'

C. S.: So you consciously take up another role?

ALEX: Yes.

MARTIN: Yes, I do see this role, whether this is a primary role or secondary role, that is a question of definition. Actually, it would be terrible if it was the primary role.

(Martin and Alex, Bayer Leverkusen fans, interviewed October 1998)

While not all fans may display this level of self-awareness, performances in fandom are organized in relation, either in accordance or deliberate opposition, to persisting social and cultural conditions. While these performances are neither necessarily emancipatory nor oppositional, they nevertheless – closer to Bourdieu's than Fiske's understanding of (popular) consumption – form fans' sense of self. Fan performances in everyday life thus become a source of stability and security, performing one of many areas of social interaction. In light of Linville's (1985) 'self complexity model', fan performance and fandom as social role then appear as a device of spreading social risks. According to Linville, individuals differ in the number and the interconnection of the social roles they perform. The higher the role complexity, the better equipped the self is to deal with the breakdown of one of the many social roles upon which it is based. McAdams summarizes the sense of stability that the self complexity model proposes as follows:

> A threat to one's 'self-as-father' ... may have little negative impact on one's 'self-as-best-friend-to-Jim' if these two different self-aspects are separated from each other by a large number of other, clearly delineated self-aspects that act as buffers to the threat. Through multiplicity and self-understanding, therefore, a person can distribute his or her precious self-esteem eggs into many different self-baskets (or bins), spreading out the risk and minimizing the chances of a big break. (McAdams 1997: 53)

Fandom provides of one of the most stable eggs in the basket, one that through its point of reference in a mediated object of fandom is shielded against the usual risks of interpersonal relationships in marriage, employment and friendship. While it is, of course, still at the mercy of external risks, such as the bankruptcy of football clubs, the decision of a television executive to pull the plug on one's favourite show, or the retirement or death of one's favourite performer, all of these can be countered through fans' textual productivity. Conceptualizing fans as performers, rather than recipients of mediated texts, thus offers an alternative explanation of the intense emotional pleasures and rewards of fandom. As the fabric of our lives is constituted through constant and staged performances (Goffman 1959/1990), the self becomes a performed, and hence symbolic, object. In this sense fandom is not an articulation of inner needs or drives, but is itself constitutive of the self. Being a fan in this sense reflects *and* constructs the self. The concept of self in the analysis of fandom as performance, as well as, incidentally, in Goffman's work, thus coincides with symbolic interactionism and its emphasis on the creation and continuous re-creation of the self in everyday life (see Blumer 1969; Mead 1934). However, it is important to note that performances constitutive of the self in fandom are inherently tied to an external, mediated object. The performances of teenage Madonna fans, football fans or followers of a cult television series are interlinked to the industrial and technological context of the production of their object of fandom.

Fandom and spectacle

In this sense performance and identity in fandom are specific forms that arise in the context of the technological and economic particularities of industrial, modern life. Departing from Goffman's claims of performance as universal human condition, Abercrombie and Longhurst (1998: 74) argue that the everyday life performances of fans and audiences 'are *specific* to contemporary society', as through the intrusion of media into everyday life, 'formerly innocent events become turned into performances with the further result that the people involved in those events come to see themselves as performers' (1998: 72). Their argument is thus based on the media saturation of everyday life which is reflected in performance-based identities in fandom (cf. Nightingale 1994). Performances are thus intrinsically linked with a particular mode of economic and social organization highlighted in the concept of spectacle:

> In arguing for the importance of spectacle, the proposition is that the world, and everything in it, is increasingly treated as something to be attended to (Chaney, 1993). People, objects and events in the world cannot simply be taken for granted but have to be framed, looked at, gazed upon, registered and controlled. In turn this suggests that the world is constituted as event, as a performance; the object, events and people which constitute the world are made to perform for those watching or gazing. (Abercrombie and Longhurst 1998: 78)

It is easy to see how this nexus of spectacle and performance applies to a range of popular media genres and their fans. The rise of reality television and game-docs such as *Big Brother*, while hitherto largely unacknowledged by fan studies, has attracted a considerable share of avid followers in different European countries (Schultz 2000; Hill and Palmer 2002; Mathijs 2002), and is a vivid illustration of the spectacularization of everyday life through mediated representations. Recent research on *Big Brother* has – although on occasions only fleetingly – begun to develop this apparent connection further: Couldry (2002), drawing on Dayan and Katz (1992), attests the constructed liveness and, consequently, 'event' character of the show; Hill (2002) acknowledges the potential connections between her research on *Big Brother* audiences and Abercrombie and Longhurst's (1998) spectacle/performance paradigms, without developing such links in any further depth. More usefully, Scannell (2002: 277) draws on Goffman (1968) to illustrate how the institutionalized context of the staged performance in the media spectacle of *Big Brother* leads to the 'destruction of the civil self of everyday life existence and its replacement by an institutionalized self, the model prisoner, schoolboy, soldier or nun'. While Scannell's argument remains firmly with the contestants of the show, it would be worth investigating to what extent these performances reveal an institutional framing of spectacle which in turn promotes an institutionalized self in audience performance: the model viewer and model fan, who will follow the show through its multi-mediated layers and participate in its interactivity, charged at premium call rate.

Yet, the media spectacle of *Big Brother* also highlights a further aspect of Abercrombie and Longhurst's notion of spectacle: its interrelation to the aestheticization of everyday life through the increasing significance of style and the modelling of everyday life after art, and art after everyday life, and the proliferation of imagery and emphasis on vision. Shows such as *Big Brother* have been pivotal in the process of aestheticization of the everyday through their eradication of boundaries between private and public and between life and its own representation. In their detailed textual and visual analysis of the first German *Big Brother* series, Mikos et al. (2001) illustrate how the programme, through its use of montage, camera angles, soft-focus lenses, and its direction of performance frames, constructs a condensed and intensified, dramatized form of everyday life narratives. 'Reality shows' such as *Big Brother*, alongside other examples of media spectacle such as American basketball star Michael Jordan or the science fiction drama *X-Files* which Kellner (2003) identifies, demonstrate the advancement of spectacle in the medium of television to an extent that its spectacular nature is no longer recognizable: 'There is no longer any medium in the literal sense: it is now intangible, diffuse, distracted, in the real, and it can no longer even be said to be distorted by it', as we witness 'the dissolution of TV into life, the dissolution of life into TV' (Baudrillard 1983: 55). Hence, it becomes increasingly difficult to separate fandom and its related performances from the spectacular nature of mass-mediated texts.

Whether or not they function as a space of articulation for utopian fantasies as described by Lancaster (2001), the everyday life performances of fandom are thus embedded in the (dystopian) macro cosmos of spectacle. Spectacle in turn is inherently linked to capitalist modes of production and ownership. Abercrombie and

Longhurst, for instance, point to Berger's (1972) work, in which he traces the rise of a possessive gaze in the art of early modernity to the mounting importance of property and commodities in capitalist societies. This linkage between capitalism and spectacle is further examined in the work of the French situationalist Guy Debord. To Debord (1995), market economies are the all-encompassing framework of contemporary social life. In turn, the modes of capitalist production in market economies lead to a commodification of the object world or, to be precise, a constant perception of the world as potential or actual commodities. The world is increasingly seen and performed as commodities, forming economies of signs and symbols and, consequently, a society of spectacle. In Debord's words (1995: 24, original emphasis) 'spectacle is *capital* accumulated to the point where it becomes image'. In this understanding of spectacle, fan performances are in fact performances of symbols and images representing texts and commodities tied to the economic and symbolic power of the media industry. Lancaster's (2001) *Babylon 5* fans play officially licensed card and board games; football fans pay premium prices to wear the symbols of the public limited companies they support; and music fans are often willing to invest significant amounts of money and time to attend the spectacle of pop concerts. Yet, Debord's account implies that these performances of spectators can only ever function as hollow ersatz to the lost emotional qualities and rewards of authentic, non-commodified life. Stardom in Debord's eyes (1995: 38) functions as 'the object of an identification with mere appearance which is intended to compensate for the crumbling of directly experienced diversifications of productive activity'. While it is important to note that Debord's work thus requires an implicit point of reference in the same romanticized and fictitious notion of a pre-modern 'golden age' of direct experience that spans from Heidegger to Marxist accounts of postmodernity such as Harvey (1990),[1] a closer analysis of the frequently cited cases of fans becoming professional producers of fan texts, whether as scriptwriters, musicians or athletes, supports Debord's distinction between 'directly experienced productive activity' and spectator productivity. A keen interest in watching professional cycling on television, for instance, does not prepare the respective fan to participate in the Tour de France. On the level of the individual fan, such interests of course often coincide with nevertheless separate forms of amateur activity. A keen cycling fan may him- or herself participate in the sport. As the many examples in chapter 2 illustrate, those with a particular interest in particular genres or television series may themselves take up creative writing. Yet, these forms of what Fiske (1992) describes as textual productivity are of course not forms of spectatorship or consumption. Instead, they are modes of production which, when crossing the divide between amateur and professional activity, often exclude the possibility of fandom as they become integrated into the capitalist logic of exchange. This is well captured in the memories of former Uruguayan international footballer Gustavo Poyet:

> My father was always Peñarol [one of the two most popular teams in Montevideo] ... But as soon as I started playing professional football, I put the Peñarol stuff to one side. I used to be a great Peñarol fan, but once I had to play against Peñarol, I pretty much stopped. I'd gone from being a fan to being a professional. (Quoted in Taylor 1998: 38–9)

As performances of consumption and performances of production thus remain sharply demarcated, they reinforce the tendency of spectacle to replace any direct experience of the world with mediated representation. Thus the 'as if'-performances of media consumers and fans are mirrored by the 'as if'-nature of contemporary spectacle. In other words, we cannot separate fandom from its symbolic basis. Whether we are a fan of a sports team such as the Chicago Bulls, a television show like the *X-Files*, or a pop star like Michael Jackson, our fan performances are inherently tied to the spectacular nature of industrial capitalism. In this respect Debord's understanding of spectacle carries many of the hallmarks of the work of another French theorist whose account is so hastily dismissed by Lancaster (2001): Jean Baudrillard. Baudrillard has characterized constant textual reproduction, copying and pastiche, the proliferation of self-referentiality and the increasing visualization of culture, which in turn are all intrinsic features of a society of spectacle, as 'simulation' and 'hyperreal'. Baudrillard's foremost concern is the disappearance of referentiality in mediated representation. The hyperreal is neither real nor unreal – it seeks to supplant the real: 'the real does not efface itself in favour of the imaginary; it effaces itself in favour of the more real than real: the hyperreal. The truer than true: this is simulation' (Baudrillard 1990: 11). What is notable is the frequency with which Baudrillard and other commentators identify as hyperreal those sites of contemporary consumption that are widely associated with fandom, such as sports stadia (Baudrillard

1993b) or theme parks (Eco 1986; Ritzer 1998). They seem to constitute the space in which the hyperreal nature of media spectacle, on which the performances of fandom rest, manifests itself in territorial place. However, as much as a continuation of a spectacular media universe, these places mark the return of hyperreal spectacles into the 'real world' and a space in which individuals come to negotiate such spectacles. It is here that the notion of fandom as a reflection of a hyperreal culture or a society of spectacle has to stand the empirical test.

The place of fandom

In the following I want to pursue the question of, quite literally, *where* our discussion so far leaves fandom. Territorial place, inhabited and frequented by audiences as part of their fandom, exemplifies the different forces that shape fandom. On the one hand, the physical places of fandom, such as sports stadia, the venues of fan conventions, or a living room decorated with fan memorabilia, constitute sites of appropriation of popular culture as well as sites of interaction between and among fans. On the other hand, such places often amount to the crudest display of commercialism, commodification and a society based on an economy of signs, simulation and spectacle. While the following discussion of places of fandom will not resolve such oppositions, it highlights the cultural implications of fandom as audiences develop a sense of place and home, and, consequently, identities and communities in fan consumption.

Given that fandom at its core remains a form of spectatorship, fan places are places of consumption. Yet, they reflect the diversification of consumption environments in mediated societies. First, electronic mass media have created a non-territorial, virtual space of media consumption. This space, while physically non-existent, is nevertheless socially manifest. It exists through fans' readings and negotiations in the realm of fantasy, as well as in interpersonal communication. These spaces include the imagined realms of mediated narratives, from the planetary universe of *Star Trek* to the suburban neighbourhoods of popular soaps such as *Neighbours* or *Eastenders*. Secondly, fandom is physically located in places of *in situ* consumption, such as sports stadia or theatres. These places, while often ascribed a particular emotional or even mystical significance, are in themselves early forms of mass media.

The sports stadium, for example, introduced mass spectatorship, and hence the separation of spectator and actor, before the rise of electronic mass media. Such places are therefore most frequently found in forms of popular culture pre-dating the television age. These places, however, have themselves become subject to popular representations, to the extent that their contemporary significance derives predominantly from their mass-mediated image, and thus have shifted into the virtual realm. By the same token, the virtual spaces of media consumption are re-manifested in place through the creation of new landscapes of fandom that find their point of reference in a particular fan narrative. Such places include the various theme parks built by Hollywood studios and, more generally, places of the production of cultural texts, ranging from Granada's *Coronation Street* set in Manchester (Couldry 2000) to the streets of Vancouver where much of the *X-Files* was shot (Hills 2002). Finally, alongside these spaces and places, which are all publicly accessible, the most common place of fandom is the private realm of domestic media consumption – our living rooms and homes – in which the virtual worlds of fan texts are consumed and lived.

Despite their profound impact on the three other categories of fan places, the first category of fan place, the virtual worlds of fan narratives, does not include places in any physical sense at all. Consequently, such spaces have invited debates on fandom as site of fantasy and escapism. Robert Aden (1999), drawing on Bourdieu's notion of the habitus and locating it within the physical territorially of our everyday life, argues that the spaces constructed in fan narratives open alternative realms for a new habitus. Examining fan texts such as *Dilbert* comics, the *X-Files*, the American sports magazine *Sports Illustrated*, and the baseball film *Field of Dreams*, Aden argues that the escapist visions fostered through such texts 'can be envisioned as a purposeful play in which we symbolically move from the material world to an imaginative world that is in many ways *a response* to the material' (Aden 1999: 6, original emphasis). In this sense such texts, as Aden acknowledges, are places of textual travels. Fans are in this sense engaged not so much in textual poaching as in textual roaming.

The textual spaces of fan texts are of course public, and the practice of textual roaming within them is shared by many fans. According to Aden (1999: 93), these textual travels, which he describes as symbolic pilgrimages, 'create a sense of community through our interactions – sometimes imagined, sometimes real – with other fans of the story. These communities surround the personal promised land of the individual fan, yet sufficiently share in its characteristics to be a site of sharing.' Thus communities in fandom, in Aden's account, are constituted outside fixed territorial place. A similar observation is made by Cavicchi (1998) in reference to Bruce Springsteen fans:

> The Bruce fan community is not a village, it's not a street, it's not affiliated with an institution or organization, but it brings people together with a remarkably strong commitment and goodwill. Fans create community or 'a sense of belonging together' not with actual shared experience but with the *expectation* of shared experience. It begins the moment a person reaches out to Springsteen as he or she becomes a fan and reaches fruition in the ways in which they reach out to each other for good conversation and debate. In the end this sense of belonging together is part and parcel of fans' social world. It shapes the tenor and quality of fans' interactions not only with each other but also with other non-fans like family members, friends and coworkers. (Cavicchi 1998: 161, original emphasis)

Cavicchi's discussion is also helpful in highlighting the mixture of virtual and physical places and spaces which are utilized by fan communities, including niche media such as fanzines, computer discussion groups, concerts, and social gatherings and fan conventions organized by fans. Both Aden's and Cavicchi's accounts thus correspond with the changing understanding of community in mediated environments that has been encapsulated in Benedict Anderson's (1991) notion of 'imagined communities' – communities which are based on shared symbolic, mediated events as well as the knowledge of such shared activity. In the realm of popular culture, the media at the centre of such ritualized consumption are often less defined within the frames of national broadcasting but range from globally distributed shows such as *Dallas* (Ang 1985) to local sports events or festivals and concerts (Crafts et al. 1993). While they thus bypass the nation-state on both the local and the global level, thereby contributing to the simultaneous processes of globalization and localization (Sandvoss 2003), the process of constituting communities through, in Cavicchi's words, the 'expectation of shared experience' remains the same. That such communities are imagined does not preclude their very real social and cultural impact. As one of the Bruce Springsteen fans in Cavicchi's (1998: 163) study remembers: 'eventually, in '88, [I] found all these people in the Bruce world. ... And this is how my life completely changed, because I would say the majority of the people I now know, am friends with, converse with, talk to constantly, are all Bruce fans.' Alongside social networks based on face-to-face interaction, the steep rise of internet access over the past two decades has provided an alternative space of dialogical communication that mirrors the virtual space of mass media such as radio and television, in which new 'computer mediated fan communities' (Baym 1998: 127) have formed. While the debate as to whether online networks can be accurately described as communities is ongoing (Rheingold 2000; Turkle 1997), there can be little doubt that many fans themselves imagine these networks as a community and equal to other friendship ties. In the words of Hannah, who runs a web page dedicated to British pop singer Melanie C:

> I share my fandom with other fans on the internet and I think this has made me more of a fan because it made me realize I wasn't the only one. I can call a few of these people friends, even though I've never met them in the flesh, but we have this interest in common to talk and send e-mails ... I can safely say I have good contacts in America, Canada, Europe and even Brazil now ... something I would have never imagined before. (Hannah, interview March 2002)

In light of this deterritorialized nature of fan communities and their nevertheless manifest social consequences, it is worth revisiting Meyrowitz's argument concerning the changing nature of place. Meyrowitz (1985) argues that electronic mass mediation has severed the link between communicative situations and places, and hence eroded the boundaries of group territory: 'electronic media may begin to blur previously distinct group identities by allowing people to "escape" informationally from place-defined groups and by permitting outsiders to "invade" many groups' territories without ever entering them' (Meyrowitz 1985: 57). While fan studies have naturally focused on the communities generated in fandom, rather than those communities outside yet affected by fandom, many illustrate the informational escape that Meyrowitz portrays. Remember, for example, the women in Bacon-Smith's (1992) study of *Star Trek* fandom or Radway's (1987) romance readers who create their own fan space in opposition to their established roles within their families. Similarly, the proliferation of soccer on television in Europe, resulting in its increased domestic availability, has allowed female fans to gain access to previously fiercely guarded male group territory inside football stadia (Sandvoss, forthcoming). Being able to bypass traditional masculine domains of football, female football fans now regularly enter such territories not only symbolically but also have become regular visitors to stadia and even members of organized fan clubs. Hodkinson (2002) likewise illustrates how Goth subculture in Britain allows its members to take on new forms of deterritorialized group identity, often initiated through mass media consumption, at the expense of other forms of social and cultural organization. While the singular link between locality and community is thereby eroded, it is worth noting that this does not lead necessarily to an absence of 'a sense of place', as in Meyrowitz's phrase, but rather to 'a new sense of place', as these new group territories, whether virtual or territorial, are experienced as emotionally significant by fans. It is, then, as Massey (1994) notes, important to avoid myths of authenticity of place by acknowledging that the identities of places are never fixed. This said, it is equally important to note that the point of reference for all such new places, and the communities they encapsulate, is a particular object of fandom, which is located in the first category of symbolic space outlined above.

This is further illustrated by the fact that there is no automatic link between the membership of imagined fan communities and actual social ties. As the classification of different fan groups in chapter 2 highlighted, regular interaction and networks commonly feature only among fans engaging in enunciative or textual productivity (cultists and enthusiasts). Yet, even if no such ties to other fans exist, fans construct an imagined, implied community or a bond between themselves and the object of fandom as well as other, imagined fans (see Sandvoss 2003). Crucially, then, the initial point of reference of these fan communities, the binding symbolic frame, lies in the symbolic, virtual spaces that Aden (1999) explores. While the fan communities evolving around such symbolic frames are manifested in all four forms of physical and virtual fan place outlined above, these places are constructed in reference to a specific community. In turn, fan communities evolve around a chosen object of fandom, and while this choice is, as we have seen, pre-structured through the fans' socio-demographic position, it is, in contrast to one's nationality or ethnicity, experienced as voluntary. Fan communities are therefore imagined in terms not only of *structure* but also of *content*, not only in terms of who the other members of such communities are, but also in terms of what such communities stand for. The symbolic and ideological core of communities imagined by fans is therefore structured through fans' appropriation of their object of fandom. Doss's (1999) account of Elvis fan culture underlines this pivotal role of the object of fandom in the organization of such communities:

> Many fans talk about Elvis's charisma ... about how he 'connected' with them individually ... this sense of intimacy and closeness corresponds to the way in which many fans claim Elvis on familial terms — as kin, as blood. ... They talk about how Elvis makes them feel like they were part of *his* family. ... Even those who became fans only after Elvis's death tend to shape their fandom around his broader familial image, seeing others, themselves, and other fans as one big Elvis family and claiming the private Elvis — his tastes, his things, even his ex-wife, Priscilla, and his daughter, Lisa Marie — as stuff of their own personal devotion. (Doss 1999: 12)

As fan communities are thus imagined in content and structure through the symbolic space of fan texts, the physical places in which fandom takes place are under pressure to accommodate the imagined symbolic content of such communities. The physical fan places of the second and third categories hence need to be 'all things to all fans' as fans' respective understandings of the symbolic core of the fan community are dependent upon their appropriation of the object of fandom. Or, in the more prosaic terms of Paul Simon's (1984) homage to Elvis Presley's former estate and now territorial focus of Elvis fandom: 'I have reason to believe, we all will be received, in Graceland.' Just as fan texts across the genres of popular culture are polysemic in their ability to accommodate different, sometimes diametrically oppositional readings, so landscapes of fandom are under pressure to provide a place corresponding to all such divergent readings. Consequently, landscapes of fandom, from sports stadia to large concert halls, out-of-town hotels and conference centres in which fan conventions are held, to the urban dwellings and suburban streets of everyday life fan consumption, often match the criteria of what the geographer Edward Relph (1976: 18) has termed 'placelessness'. Relph describes as placeless those modern spaces in which 'different localities both look and feel alike, and in which distinctive places are experienced only through superficial and stereotyped images'. Alongside other factors, such as a lack of human scale, uniformity and standardization, a key aspect of placelessness lies in what Relph describes as 'other-directedness', places not experienced in and for themselves but in reference to absent codes and symbols. The themes of the theme park, for instance, are not the themes of the actual landscape but, as in the case of Disneyland, the themes of the virtual, symbolic spaces of entertainment media. Such other-directedness is thus an inherent condition of places in fandom, as they are necessarily constructed with reference to the symbolic spaces of fan texts. Even conventional urban spaces are subject to such 'other-directedness' if approached from the angle of the fan. As Hills (2002: 149) notes in his analysis of Vancouver from the perspective of the *X-Files* fan, 'the fantasies which these places materialize are always to some degree dependent upon the generic and other formal qualities of the source text'; and hence, we may add, such places are necessarily experienced as 'other-directed'. The resulting lack of inherent meaning of fan places thus forms the premiss of fans' appropriation of these places in accordance with their reading of the object of fandom. In this sense, the placeless and hyperreal condition of places – their lack of any intrinsic meaning in and for themselves – is the premiss of their utilization as sites of fandom.

By the same token, placelessness, like hyperreality, remains virtually impossible. Places are, as Bale (1998: 68) argues, 'peopled spaces'; the physical spaces of our world are turned into places through human interaction (cf. Augé 1995). However much sites of fandom may lack authentic 'directedness' and are constructed and made sense of with reference to textual absences, such as Graceland in the case of the dead Elvis and his songs – however much they may be turned into spectacle and places of consumption and commodification through official and unofficial merchandizing and souvenir shops – however much they may be standardized to appeal to the largest possible number of people, they are turned into peopled places by the fans who occupy and transform them into places of particular emotional significance. Doss (1999: 89), for example, observes the ordinariness of Elvis's Graceland estate: 'the house itself isn't that remarkable: a pseudo-Georgian structure of about 40,500 square feet and a teeny guitar shaped pool.' Yet, southern kitsch or not,

> fans repeatedly talk about Graceland in terms of its emotional intensity ... Graceland is the most visible public place where they can comfortably and collectively express their private feelings for Elvis ... there is an immense emotive power in the transformative bond of communitas that going to Graceland generates amongst Elvis fans. The fans who gather there during Elvis Week bond as a 'community of admirers' and a 'community of sorrow' brought together under their love for Elvis and a profound grief that he is gone. (Doss 1999: 90)

Doss's description of Graceland corresponds with Tomlinson's (1999: 112) broader analysis of 'non-places': 'the point is that non-places can be seen as particular, distinct instances of "deterritorialized" locales, embodying distant relations, but this does not necessarily render them socially and culturally sterile'. Public places of fandom thus fulfil a dual function. First, they provide a physical locality of face-to-face interaction among fans. They therefore become the focal point of fan communities in their face-to-face as much as their imagined form. As Rodman, to stay with the example of Graceland, notes:

> one of Graceland's more important functions is that it serves as a 'real world' site where the type of temporary community that arises at fan conventions can take on a more stable and permanent existence. The specific fans who are at Graceland will, of course, change from day to day and even from hour to hour ... but some critical mass of Elvis fans can almost always be found there: a fan presence that provides enough continuity to foster a lasting, a tangible sense of an Elvis-centred community. (Rodman 1996: 124)

While Rodman's otherwise insightful analysis is based on the problematic assumption that Elvis fandom is unique in its form and content, a constant presence of fans can in fact be found in many fan cultures: during the months of the baseball season, ballparks host games most days of the week; sports stadia and television or film studios now often host museums and attract groups of visitors on a daily basis; bus tours and individual visitors gather in public spaces of fandom such Hollywood Boulevard's Walk of Fame every day of the year.

In addition to the importance of communities which are manifested there, such places offer something beyond the promises and even realization of face-to-face interaction with other fans. To return to Tomlinson's discussion of place (1999: 149, original emphasis), 'there is the simple but important fact that we are all, as human beings, *embodied and physically located*'. With this comes the recognition that our sensory apparatus works at its fullest within physically manifest settings. In this sense, objects of fandom as the textual spaces of the symbolic pilgrimages that Aden (1999) describes cannot re-enact the immediacy of the experience of place. In the words of the following Elvis fan (Doss 1999: 88): 'seeing his home, Meditation Gardens, the planes and many of his personal belongings, I realized that he was a real person with a real life'. There are numerous ways to explain the motivations of fans in seeking out physically manifest places of fandom: a search for authenticity, a search for the real. Most importantly, however, it is a search for unmediated experience, of putting oneself, literally, in the place of the fan text and thus creating a relationship between the object of fandom and the self that goes beyond mere consumption and fantasy. As Doss observes (1999: 89) 'resonant with Elvis – his possessions, his body, his spirit – fans go to Graceland to walk in his mansion, gaze at his things ... and be that much closer to the man they adore.' These fans do not visit Graceland to find the real or authentic Elvis, but to experience *their* version of Elvis in unmediated form. The fan sites of fictional fan texts, of course, do not even hold the promise of the real: there is no *Gotham City*, no *Coronation Street*. Yet, as Couldry's study of visitors to the set of *Coronation Street* demonstrates, this does not diminish their emotional importance. In the words of interviewee Susan: 'for us [the Granada Studios Tour] was just a wonderful experience, something we will remember for the rest of our lives' (2000: 78). As in the case of Elvis fandom, here the emotional significance of visiting fan places lies in the ability of fans to put themselves physically into the otherwise textual universe of the programme. As Susan's friend explains, 'we've got a photograph ... on our wall in our room at work, of the two of us outside the Rovers [the show's local pub] and that's us ... we've got lines all around so everyone can see it. We have been there' (Couldry 2000: 80).

Fan places between the holy and the homely

The physical places of fandom clearly have an extraordinary importance for fans. The climactic and in Aden's (1999) words 'cathartic' experience of place has invited religious analogies, in which the travel to and consumption of such places is often described as 'ritual' and 'pilgrimage' (see also Hills 2002), analogies which have found wider currency in fan studies beyond the question of place. Such comparisons seem motivated in particular by similarities in terms of form and language: the intense emotional significance, the regularity of consumption – which in more theological terms we might call 'devotion' – and a sense of emotional stability that mark fandom and religion alike, on the one hand, and the representation of objects of fandom in fan talk and art reminiscent of (Christian) iconography, as in the Jesus-like portrayals of Elvis, on the other. Yet, they nevertheless remain problematic. With regard to the use of religious symbols in forms of representation or even practices, it is important to acknowledge the difference between references *to* religion in fandom and fandom *as* religion. As I have argued in chapter 2, the context of fandom informs the appropriation of the object of fandom and the construction of meaning in the process of fan consumption. It is therefore no surprise that, for example, the deeply Christian Elvis fans in Doss's (1999) study choose depictions of Elvis that bear clear references to portrayals of Jesus. However, far from implying that Elvis fandom has superseded their religion, these 'icons' are signifiers of the importance of Elvis to these fans *as* Christians. As Nightingale (1994: 9) argues, religious analogies to fandom are useful, but ultimately limited, as in the acts of impersonation in fandom, 'identity, not similarity, is desired'; thus, fans aim to take the place of the star in a way that is unlike religious devotion (in which devotees do not seek to supplant God). Equally, the religious symbols and language in fandom are, as Jenkins (1992; cf. Hills and Jenkins 2001) observes, not conditions of fandom as such, but clustered within particular fan cultures; comparisons based on emotional significance and regular engagement are no more or less precise than comparisons with other structures or institutions shaping and affirming identity, such as nation-states or ethnicity. Thus such analogies simply point to the fact that fandom has become an additional realm of identity construction alongside other long-standing factors such as religion, the nation-state, ethnicity or work: 'there are more differences between fandom and religion than there are similarities, and similarities extend to any social organization that serves multiple functions in the lives of its members and becomes a site of meaning and emotion' (Jenkins, in Hills and Jenkins 2001: 30).

The broader difficulties of the fandom-as-religion analogy lie in the fundamentally different point of reference from which they evolve. This problem is evident in Couldry's adaptation of Durkheim's sociology of religion. Couldry (2000) argues that the distinction between the world of the media (and its territorial manifestation in fan places such as Granada's *Coronation Street* set) and the world of ordinary everyday life resembles Durkheim's distinction between the sacred and the profane. Based on this division, a 'symbolic hierarchy of the media frame' is constructed, in which the mediated and the ordinary worlds come in contact only through the controlling framework of pilgrimage and ritual, which allows the ordinary fan access to the sacred places of the media world (Couldry 2000: 44). This adaptation of a framework of social relations constructed in relation to a transcendental point of reference to fans and audiences is epistemologically problematic. Couldry (2000: 15) himself acknowledges that the division between media and ordinary life does not constitute a social fact in the Durkheimian sense, and is 'not beyond contestation'. This, however, points to the wider issue of the validity of religious metaphors in the absence of any (significant) transcendental points of reference in fandom. In contrast to religion, fandom lacks an absolute, other-worldly framework through which social realities are constructed and legitimized. If fandom differs so radically in its premisses from religion, it is difficult to juxtapose their consequences meaningfully. The pilgrimages of fans, for instance, lack the universal cultural acknowledgement of the places of pilgrimage of the monolithic world religions. Rather than a communal search for a future place in another world, they are individual journeys seeking a sense of place in *this* world. This distinctly relative and subjective nature of fandom and its textual and physical spaces is also recognized by Aden (1999). Aden traces what Weber called the 'disenchantment' of the modern world through rational systems of industrial production (cf. Ritzer 1996, 1998) and consumerism, in which any form of generally recognized religious faith system has disappeared (cf. Bell 1979). Fandom, according to Aden, does not function as substitute religion, but fills a void created by the absence of this-worldly and other-worldly utopia:

> For those of us who have subscribed to dominant visions of promised lands, their decreased relevance is no doubt disturbing, but the lack of a *single, universal* alternative promised land presents all of us with the opportunity to develop and appreciate *multiple* versions of promised lands – for each promised land is a vision of how to create a good and just society. (Aden 1999: 41, original emphasis)

The notion of 'promised lands' thus entails a compromise between fandom as a mundane, yet spiritually significant, realm of everyday life and the importance of place within fandom. However, given the fundamentally divergent points of reference of fandom and religion, I want to suggest a different analogy, in which references to religion are omitted in favour of a heightened emphasis on the significance of place in fandom. In less religiously suggestive language, Hodkinson (2002: 195) concludes that those regularly participating in Goth subculture, through, we might add, fan nsumption, 'shared a translocal sense of affiliation and collective stinction, which tended to be prominent in their overall sense of ...entity'. At the same time he reveals how his respondents repeatedly emphasized a strong sense of individuality. This projection of self-identity on to a collective, resulting in a distinct sense of belonging, illustrates the ambiguity of identity construction between self and community in fandom. Yet, such 'individualized collectivity' is not particular to fandom, but resembles the wider patterns of identity construction that have formed the relationship between self and territory in modernity. In this sense, I believe, fandom best compares to the emotional significance of the places we have grown to call 'home', to the form of physical, emotional *and* ideological space that is best described as *Heimat*. Fans themselves often associate fandom with a sense of home. Fans of team sports, such as football, describe their football club and its respective stadium in such terms (Bale 1993, 1998; Sandvoss 2003; Roversi 1994). Similarly, fans in different fields of popular culture often refer to their fandom in terms of 'emotional warmth' or a sense of security and stability, which in turn are associated with *Heimat*.

Understanding fandom as a form of *Heimat* thus accurately combines the significance of symbolical, personal space in fandom with the importance of territorial place within which such fandom is physically manifested. However, these spaces differ from the territorial place conventionally understood as *Heimat*. Rather, as our discussion here has illustrated, they can be physical as well as textual, and hence can be accessed by fans in different mediated and unmediated ways, at different times, and from different localities. The sense of home in fandom is in fact a mobile *Heimat*. Fandom thus emerges as an extension of the profound restructuring of everyday industrial life that Raymond Williams (1974) has characterized as 'mobile privatization', explaining fandom's popularity in an increasingly phantasmagoric, deterritorialized world. Places of media fandom are of such particular importance to fans, then, because they offer the rare opportunity to relocate in place a profound sense of belonging which has otherwise shifted into the textual space of media consumption.

But the notion of fandom as a form of *Heimat* comes with its own implications with regard to the social and cultural consequences of fandom. The idea of *Heimat* is based upon notions of security and emotional warmth, but *Heimat* also always involves an evaluation and categorization of others. As Morley (2000) argues, drawing on Rathzel's (1994) study of immigration in

Germany, *Heimat* implies a sharp division between 'us' and 'them' in the form of a constructed 'Other'. Fandom, as I have argued above, is always based on such acts of textual and social discrimination articulated through taste. In *Heimat* as well as fandom, such divisions and their respective communities are always constructed and imagined. As Rathzel's study demonstrates, the notion of *Heimat* does not relate to any past experiences, but rather marks a search for, in Aden's words, 'promised lands'. However, such promised lands – much like the promised lands of economic prosperity – are fiercely guarded, to the degree that the imagined Other functions only as negative point of collective identification. The conclusions that Morley (2000: 253) draws from Rathzel's research apply equally to fans – whether committed football enthusiasts, resenting the rising numbers of new, socially diverse fan groups, fans of television shows rejecting substantial changes to existing formats, or rave fans distancing themselves from what they perceive as mainstream: 'people who hold a reified, harmonious image of *Heimat*, as something necessarily stable and unchanging, are particularly likely to be hostile to newcomers – who are held to be the cause of all manner of disorienting forms of change'. This is the common, yet, it should be noted, not inevitable consequence of *Heimat*. There are, as Morley (2000) demonstrates, many possibilities for reconciling a sense of *Heimat* with the endorsement of difference. Equally, some fans seek to endorse and celebrate difference and overcome discrimination in their own fan cultures. Nevertheless, *Heimat*, whether territorially or textually, is a projective term, describing an imagined relationship between the self and the external world, in which part of the world is experienced as inherently related to and constituted through the self; it is one's place in the world, in which place and community become an extension of one's self, and the self a reflection of place and community. In the next chapter I thus want to turn to the psychological processes through which this projective relationship between the fan's self and the external object of fandom as a symbolic space is maintained.

Summary

Highlighting the importance of fan productivity, I have explored aspects of fan performances. Such performances, as the reference to

Goffman's work suggests, are constitutive of fans' identity. Yet, fan performances are firmly located and constituted within the social and technological context of industrial, mediated modernity. In the case of fandom, this means that we have to account for the dependence of such performances on increasing media saturation, which results in the spectacularization of contemporary everyday life. The spectacular or hyperreal nature of the symbolic resources of fandom, however, is countered by the inherent territorial manifestation of all media consumption. In fandom, as in other areas of everyday life, place remains a fundamental point of reference. Places of fandom thus take on a dual meaning. On the one hand, they incorporate tendencies to placelessness for their other-directedness with respect to the fan text; on the other, they are transformed into the territorial focus of individual and group identities. Arguing against comparisons which equate the emotional significance of fandom with forms of organized religion, I have suggested that the particular emotional qualities of fandom resemble a sense of *Heimat*, as a claim to the fan's place in physical territory, mediated space, and everyday life culture and social relations.

4

THE INNER FAN: FANDOM AND PSYCHOANALYSIS

For all the attention to the social and cultural context of fan consumption in the approaches to fandom discussed so far, the psychological basis of the pleasures, desires and motivations that form the relationship between given fans and their objects of fascination have remained comparatively unexplored and under-theorized. This is not to say, however, that fan studies have ignored the pleasure of fandom. Fans' emotion, or what Lawrence Grossberg (1992) has described as 'affect', are as crucial to Fiske's understanding of subversive pleasures as to the notion of fandom as textual *Heimat* that I proposed in chapter 3. Yet, in their broadly sociological framework, many studies of fan cultures have, by definition, been limited to *inter*personal explanations of pleasure, desire and motivation. The hesitation of fan studies to adopt psychoanalytic perspectives to explain fans' actions and experience is under-standable. It is not only the risk of 'pathologizing fans' that makes the relationship between psychoanalysis and fan studies uneasy. If the study of fans is primarily the study of a social subject, and hence sociological, psychoanalytic and psychological approaches to fandom present a methodological and empirical minefield. Whereas audience research in its qualitative tradition resorts to all aspects of fandom that are socially and culturally visible — such as fans' chatter, their everyday life performances and their textual productivity, which in turn are recorded through in-depth interviewing or participant observation — psychoanalytic approaches to fandom explore processes and motivations which remain concealed from the researcher as much as the researched. We thus move our focus from 'social facts' to the metaphors and speculation with which psychoanalysts have sought to conceptualize conscious, unconscious and hence extra-verbal foundations of self.

This is an uncomfortable step for the reader and scholar alike, in which we leave relatively charted territory for the bog of fans' motivations, fantasies and desires. But it is also a necessary one, as the emotional core underlying our continuous consumption of the object of fandom cannot be explained in interpersonal terms alone. The premiss of my argument here is that there is something that lets us develop a passion for our favourite sports team, the particular affection in which we hold a comic superhero or our favourite television show, something upon which our fascination with a given pop or film star rests, that goes beyond the interpersonal. To fully understand fandom and the relationship between fan and object of fandom, we thus have to understand the psychological foundations of the self.

Freud, fans and fantasies

Having said this, the question of how self and identity are constituted of course remains among the most complex and widely debated fields of human science (cf. Anderson and Schoening 1996). As amorphous and changing phenomena, 'self' and 'identity' 'defy hard and fast definitions' (Ashmore and Jussim 1997: 5), and thus any analysis of the intrapersonal aspects of fandom lacks a clear framework of reference. Moreover, despite the popularity of psychoanalytic approaches in film studies and amongst a small group of fan scholars, many fans are openly hostile to psycho-analytic explanations of their fan practices. In the words of one slash writer:

> I'm sick and tired of being told why you write slash. I am sick and tired of being told what the deep, dark psychological reasons are. ... I am sick and tired of having other people tell me what I really think and feel — as opposed to what *I* think I think and feel. I'm really tired of being told I'm writing 'from my pain' or my guilt, or my inhibitions, or my lack of self-worth, or my repressed this that or the next thing. ... I am tired of being told I'm writing because I want a man, want to be a man or actually am a man and just didn't know it. ... I'm tired of being told its penis envy or vagina hate. (M. Fae, quoted in Green et al. 1998: 31)

While providing us with important clues, the degree to which fans enjoy and subscribe to particular theoretical approaches to fandom is no sole indicator of their validity – if explaining a joke is never particularly funny, analysing pleasures rarely tends to be particularly pleasurable. More importantly, however, Fae's statement also illustrates that in areas of fandom explicitly involving pleasures, fantasies and desires such as slash – and we will assess below whether there is not at least an implicit direct or indirect element of such pleasures in all forms of fandom – it is near impossible to think about such pleasures outside the basic concerns and language of psychoanalysis. When trying to explain her involvement in slash writing in common-sense terms, Fae inevitably returns to fields of psychoanalytic concern:

> Some of us ... read slash because it turns us on. Some of us read slash because it's sexy, arousing, fine, one-handed reading, as satisfying to the emotions and the intellect as it is to the libido. ... slash is often a masturbatory aid, or a marital aid, or just the inspiration for a rollicking good time. ... It's about emotional orgasms, and physical orgasms, lust and/or love fulfilled. It's about libidinous excitement, descriptions that make us quiver. (M. Fae, quoted in Green et al. 1998: 31)

The references coinciding with psychoanalytic vocabulary in Fae's explanations of her own pleasures are hard to overlook: autoeroticism, drives and libido, as key notions of Freudian psychoanalysis, all feature prominently in her account. From her use of such terms it does not follow that Freudian psychoanalysis necessarily provides the most accurate account of her pleasures and desires. Nevertheless, it indicates the pervasiveness of psychoanalytic discourses as we approach the intrapersonal dimensions of fandom.

Turning to Freud as the founding father of modern psychoanalysis, and to his original writings, may seem a rather outdated starting point for our analysis here, not so much for the fact that his work continues to sit uneasily with attempts of positivist empiricism to appropriate many branches of psychology, but because his work has been appropriated so widely in psychoanalytic and cultural theory throughout the twentieth century from Marcuse to Lacan.[1] These interpretations, rather than Freud's initial work, have formed the conceptual core of psychoanalytic approaches to media consumption. Psychoanalytic theories of cinema spectatorship in particular have tended to draw on Lacan's interpretation of Freud, rather than on Freud himself (Metz 1974; Mulvey 1975; Baudry 1986; Merck 1987). However, beyond these particular interpretations of his work, Freud himself provides us with a useful framework through which to approach pleasures and fantasies in fandom.

In contrast to an understanding of the self as a coherent, rational subject, which implicitly underlies the accounts of fandom discussed so far, Freud's concept of self (1905/1977, 1927/1982, 1923/1984) assumes a partitioning of the self into three, potentially conflicting layers: id, ego and super-ego. These layers are in turn reflective of the polarities between which the self is formed: on the one hand the pressures, conventions and regimentation that arise from the organization of social life – in other words, civilization and culture – and on the other, the inherent inner drives of the self that form its psychological core. The ego is thus constituted within a field of tension between the super-ego, as a realm of internalized culture, and the id, which is structured through our inner drives and desires, which form between its most basic formulations Eros (libido) and Thanatos (death drive). The state of our self is hence always one of repression, in which conscious and unconscious fantasies on the level of the id and the ego articulate what the super-ego does not permit.[2]

The root of such fantasies and the self's search for pleasure lie in early childhood. According to Freud, pleasure is first experienced as a form of wholeness by the unborn child, who is as yet unable to distinguish between him or herself and the surrounding world. In the absence of an ego the child is thus in a state of omnipotence, in which no external subject exists and everything is assumed to be under the child's control. In this state of omnipotence the child engages in a form of pleasurable 'autoeroticism'. External objects such as the mother's breast are experienced as a pleasurable form of nurture, 'and for that reason should be termed sexual' (Freud 1923/1984: 154). Yet the experienced unity between the child and the mother's body upon which these pleasures rest is soon disrupted by the child's realization of its lack of control over external objects. At this point the child's sense of wholeness and the pleasures that arise from it are lost. The self is henceforth a construct of lack, marked by a profound sense of loss of (sexual) pleasure, and the resulting attempts to fill this void through fantasies and action are the basis of what Freud (1923/1984) labels the 'pleasure principle'.

Within the context of modern everyday life the consumption of popular mass media provides a space in which such pleasures, enjoyment and sexual desire can be lived and fostered. There can be little doubt that such pleasures form a key motivation for the continuing relationship between fans and their object of fandom. Whether we write fan fiction, support a sports team, collect newspaper clippings of our favourite film star, watch and debate our favourite television show or listen to our favourite music, we pursue such activities only to the degree that they are, all temporary frustrations aside, an essentially pleasurable experience and site of enjoyment. Freud allows us to conceptualize this search for pleasures and, potentially, even sexual excitement in fandom – as most obvious in areas such as slash writing and fandom evolving around particular celebrities (cf. Vermorel and Vermorel 1985; Rojek 2001) – as a reflection of a universal human condition – a condition which is hence independent of particular socio-cultural circumstances, although these of course determine levels of pleasure fulfilment and repression (cf. Marcuse 1956/1987).

While it is easy to see how fandom relates to the self's search for pleasure and enjoyment, the question that follows is why fandom is better suited to this quest than other forms of cultural practice or social interaction. The answer lies in the relationship between pleasures, drives and fantasies. While the drives are firmly rooted within the realm of the id, fantasies are manifested on both conscious and unconscious levels, and hence are subject to social and cultural contexts. Drawing on Freud, Laplanche and Pontalis thus usefully define fantasy as an

> imaginary scene in which the subject is a protagonist, representing the fulfilment of a wish ... in a manner that is distorted to a greater or lesser extent by defensive processes. Phantasy has a number of different modes: conscious phantasies or daydreams, unconscious phantasies like those uncovered by analysis as the structures underlying manifest content, and primal phantasies. (Laplanche and Pontalis: 1973: 31)

These different conscious, unconscious and primary fantasies have in turn informed different approaches to pleasure, fandom and spectatorship. Primal fantasies as the fundamental unconscious formulations of desire and fear are located deep in the unconscious and pre-verbal. Consequently, primal fantasies have attracted particular attention in approaches to spectatorship foregrounding visual and textual analysis, such as psychoanalytic film theory, which has focused on violent and fantastic genres such as science fiction, horror or splatter films. Creed's (1993) analysis of female protagonists as perpetrators in horror and science fiction cinema indicates the benefits and limitations of such approaches. Creed (1993: 17) emphasizes the relationship between the 'primal scene' portrayed in films such as *The Thing, Invasion of the Body Snatchers,* or *Altered States* and the three primal fantasies Freud (1905/1977) defines as the witnessing of parental coitus, seduction and castration: 'These fantasies are about origins: the primal scene represents to the child its own origins in parents' love-making; the seduction fantasy is about the origin of sexual desire; and the fantasy of castration pictures the origins of sexual difference.' In her detailed analysis of *Alien* (1979) Creed seeks to illustrate such primal fantasies in the visual representations and narrative structures: from the birth-like awakening of the spaceship crew wholly dependent on the 'mother ship' as a representation of incestuous desire to the find of alien eggs as a primal scene in which the subject imagines travelling back inside the womb. Yet, Creed, like other scholars in the field (Lebeau 1995) finds herself arguing for additional primal fantasies, such as of death, as the three stipulated by Freud do not sufficiently account for her reading of *Alien* and other horror films (cf. Hills 2002).

This liberal reinterpretation of primal fantasies is problematic, given that psychoanalytic approaches to popular culture focusing on the unconscious are already a form of metaphorical speculation. Yet, this does not mean that psychoanalysis lacks any empirical basis. While its findings are rarely verifiable through forms of numerical or verbal documentation that is called upon in fields such as cognitive psychology or sociology, its assumptions are nevertheless based on clinical practice and observation. In psychoanalytic film theory, however, the actual, empirical viewer or fan is dismissed as an object of study (cf. Stacey 1994) in favour of visual and textual analysis. This, in purely epistemological terms, is a legitimate strategy as long as such an analysis uncovers visual and narrative elements which correspond with psycho-analytic theory that has been formulated on the basis of clinical, empirical observation, such as Freud's formulation of the three types of primal fantasies. Yet, what the textual analysis of films or any other popular medium does not equip us to do is to reformulate psychoanalytic conceptualizations of the self of the fan/viewer, as it fundamentally lacks the empirical basis for such claims. If psychoanalytic film theory can shift its focus to the text by assuming an implied reader derived from psychoanalytic theory – in other words, by assuming that every viewer's self will under all possible conditions and contexts always share three types of primary fantasies – it cannot then retrospectively reformulate the basic premises upon which its textual analysis rests. The exclusion of actual viewers and fans from the analytic scope of film theory, moreover, carries the risk of a cosy dialogue between producers, whose work reflects their own awareness of psychoanalytic theory, and scholars as academic *Schreibtischtäter* who, from the comfort of their own desks, excitedly recognize precisely these discourses in the final text.

Even if we accept that there are realms within the self which evade empirical verification, the exclusion of spectators and fans as social subjects in such research renders it of little value to the study of fandom. In its focus on singular texts, it cannot account for fandom as a *social process* and continuous form of consumption organized and structured in the everyday life actions of actual – rather than implied – readers. Psychoanalytic theories of spectatorship offer interesting perspectives on how pleasures are constituted in watching Hitchcock's *Rear Window* (Mulvey 1975) or about the visual pleasures in spectator sports (Morse 1983; cf. Brummett and Duncan 1989, 1990, 1992). However, they have nothing to say about how the casual viewer of *Rear Window* becomes a Hitchcock fan, who collects his body of work, watches, shares and discusses it with friends, or how the viewer of a sports event passionately follows his or her team week after week, and the pleasures and fantasies that are generated through such forms of regular, sustained consumption. While desires or fantasies are clearly important emotional dimensions of fandom, they cannot be isolated from their behavioural context. It is not so much in the particular details of primal fantasy, castration anxieties or voyeurism, then, that Freud's work is of benefit to the study of fandom, but in his general conceptualization of the self between desire and culture.

More promising for our purposes here are unconscious fantasies, which can be verbalized through the therapeutic process, and in particular conscious fantasies. Having said this there are obvious methodological and ethical difficulties in asking participants to formulate their inner fantasies and desires, and only a few empirical studies of fans have focused on conscious fantasies in the form of as if-scenarios and daydreaming as integral aspects of fan experiences.

Yet, we easily find numerous clues and indicators of the importance of fantasies in fandom, and many such fantasies and their related pleasures are, in their directly or indirectly sexual nature, in line with Freud's conceptualization of the self. First, fans' textual productivity and, in particular, various forms of fan fiction give witness to the sexual pleasures and their related fantasies articulated in fandom. As Jones (2002: 81) notes in her analysis of the sexual fantasies of fans of television cult stars from shows such as *Xena*, *The X-Files*, or *Buffy the Vampire Slayer*: 'television inspired erotic literature [...] spans every gender combination and almost every sexual practice'. Similarly, Penley (1992: 291) identifies an outright 'pornographic force' in many slash stories. In less explicit manner, slash stories develop themes of intimacy and nurture through directly or indirectly sexual fantasies:

> In a great many stories the discovery of mutual love occurs as one partner recognizes and satisfies a basic need of the other – physical (warmth, food, care during illness) or emotional (reassurance) – and, more or less explicitly mothers them.... although not specifically sexual in themselves, warmth and food are eroticized because they give a physical dimension to the closeness of the bond between the partners and lead to, or become part of, an intimacy that also has a sexual component. (Cicioni 1998: 163)

While fan fiction draws on fictional genres and, primarily, television programmes, studies of fan fantasies focusing on popular icons such as celebrities and pop stars are also illustrative of such themes. While the relationship between fan and object of fandom cannot be reduced to sexual pleasure and attraction alone, sexually motivated fantasies clearly constitute a significant aspect of the pleasures of fandom. Much as Rojek (2001: 74) argues that 'fans are attracted to celebrities for a variety of reasons, with sexual attraction, admiration of unique personal values and mass-media acclaim being prominent', the various fantasies collected by Vermorel and Vermorel (1985) highlight forms of sexual pleasures in fandom. These accounts of the fantasies of fans of pop stars and actors of the 1970s and 1980s, such as David Bowie, Michael Jackson, Nick Hayward, Sheena Easton or Boy George, oscillate between romantic daydreams revolving around potential encounters between star and fan to full-fledged fantasies of sexual acts and intercourse. The following extract contains the less explicit parts of Lucille's favourite fantasy about Robert Plant:

> Many times I've thought about how passionate Robert Plant of Led Zeppelin looked. So many times I had sat in the middle of my room (which is covered with pictures of him) and imagined that he was lying between my legs, with his lovely blonde locks covering my stomach. ... Soon neither of us can bear it any longer, groaning

with yearning he rolls on top of me. He thrusts cruelly into me, whilst biting my neck, my nails tear at his back ... He's like a huge, golden Lion conquering me. (Lucille, quoted in Vermorel and Vermorel 1985: 27–8)

Illustrative as such accounts are, it is important to acknowledge that the degree to which fandom functions as a space for the articulation of sexual fantasies varies from fan culture to fan culture and from fan to fan. The forms of interaction with their favourite text of *Inspector Morse* fans which Thomas (2002) observes bear little resemblance to the sexual themes that dominate the *Inspector Morse* slash stories which Cicioni (1998) discusses. Similarly, the pleasures and passions in sport, often based on an intense relationship and identification with a given team or club, cannot be explained in terms of sexual pleasures and fantasies, although even here elements of an erotic gaze persist as some athletes, such as tennis player Anna Kournikova (Brookes 2002) or footballer David Beckham (Cashmore 2002), have become popular icons who in their sexualized representation are comparable to the 1980s pop stars in Vermorel and Vermorel's collection (1985). While, for reasons that we will explore later, producers of popular culture seek to represent objects of fandom in as open terms as possible, fostering fans' fantasies and desires appears a key concern of commercial cultural production. The visual representation of celebrities such as pop stars, actors and actresses, and athletes has long been marked by an emphasis on the female and, increasingly, also male body. By the same token celebrities have often sought to conceal their own relationships or marriages to maintain a façade of potential availability, or alternatively have aimed to invite fan fantasies by meticulously publicizing the details of their relationships. Similarly, television shows which have attracted substantial fan following, from *Dallas*, *Dynasty* and *Beverly Hills 90210*[3] to recent popular programmes such as *Buffy the Vampire Slayer*, *Friends* and *Sex and the City*, have cultivated fan fantasies through sexually explicit visual and narrative representations. If fans' (sexual) pleasures and fantasies outside areas of their own textual productivity, as in slash writing, remain nevertheless an underexplored area of fandom, the reason lies primarily, as Hills indicates, in the profoundly uncomfortable nature of this discussion for both researcher and researched:

Although I have included Gillian Anderson as one of my fan 'objects', I have refrained from discussing this until now, perhaps

> through a class-based sense that issues of sexuality are not a
> 'proper' topic of discussion. I remain highly uneasy about
> professing that any element of sexual attraction enters into my
> appreciation of female cult celebrities. This unease may stem from
> an investment in a broadly feminist academic position which
> disagrees theoretically with the objectification of women while
> continuing to practise practically these 'bad' cultural mechanisms.
> (Hills 2002: 87)

While the reasons for the reluctance to deal with sexually explicit
fan fantasies are thus easily understandable, we must nevertheless
avoid pasteurized representations of fandom and its underlying
mechanisms – not least because the sexual desires and fantasies
that underlie fandom and audienceship are of course utilized by the
media industry.

The following case of Chloe, an 18-year-old university student,
who recalls her daydreams about the early eighties pop ensemble
The Police, taken from Vermorel and Vermorel's above-mentioned
rich collection of fan fantasies (1985; see also 1992) further
illustrates how fans' pleasures and fantasies are formed between the
sexual drives of the id and the cultural constraints on sexuality
through the super-ego. In a ten-page letter Chloe recounts her
frequent daydream about the band. In this fantasy she is usually 'at
a disco or concert where I'm such a fabulous dancer that Stewart
[the band's drummer] joins me and we dance and chat. Then he
takes me home' (Vermorel and Vermorel 1985: 158). In the car on
the way home Chloe masturbates Stewart, and they arrange to
meet again. Following this first encounter, Sting, the lead singer,
visits the school where Chloe works, and, impressed by her skills
with children and how well she gets on with his son, asks her to
work as a nanny for his family. When Chloe meets Stewart for the
arranged weekend, she quizzes Stewart about his girlfriend.
Reassured of the girlfriend's absence, Chloe agrees to stay with
Stewart. At his flat they soon engage in sexual acts which Chloe
describes in great detail, including the sudden appearance of Sting
at the scene. After this encounter Chloe loses touch with Stewart,
but soon finds out that she is pregnant and decides to keep the
baby, while getting a court order to prevent Stewart from ever
seeing the child. Months later she starts work at A & M studios,
the record label of The Police. Unlike Stewart, Sting recognizes her
and asks her again about working for his family. He finally visits
Chloe and finds out about her son, whom she has kept secret from
Stewart. Subsequently he seduces Chloe, and she again engages in

a detailed fantasy of her sexual encounter with Sting. The next morning Sting rushes out in a panicky mood, stating that the previous night should not have happened. Soon afterwards Chloe finds out that she is pregnant again, and meets Sting while asking for maternity leave:

> I run out before he can catch me. I hide in a cafe but he finds me and tries to talk to me. I realise that he wants to adopt the baby. But I won't let him. He tells me not to worry about the money – he will pay for everything, So I let him. The baby, Philip is born on 22nd October. A few days later, I leave the hospital. I quit my job and move to another part of London where Sting and Stewart cannot find me. (Chloe, quoted in Vermorel and Vermorel 1985: 161)

From this point Chloe ponders different outcomes, but remarks that 'usually my fantasy never has an ending' (Vermorel and Vermorel 1985: 161). In its clear sexual motivation, Chloe's fantasy reflects a self which is fuelled by fantasies subject to its inner drives and libido. Chloe recounts the sexual excitement she gained from this and similar fantasies following her first attendance at a Police concert (ibid.: 162), and there is no doubt that her fantastic relationship with the band is structured through sexual desire. Yet, it is also reflective of the cultural constraints on Chloe's drives, which in Freudian terms we can describe as a form of repression. Chloe's fantasy here can usefully be compared to the fantasies of Elvis Presley fans analysed by Hinerman (1992). Hinerman focuses on the cases of Elvis fans reported by Moody (1987) who, confronted with different challenging situations – such as the death of a family member or the trauma of adolescence – resort to their Elvis fantasies not only as a refuge but also as an active coping mechanism. In one such case, Vanessa becomes an avid fan of the singer during her high-school years and maintains her fandom after getting married. When in 1977 she first learns that she is infertile, she and her husband plan to travel and see Elvis perform. When, soon afterwards, Elvis and then Vanessa's younger stepsister die, she falls into periods of severe depression. During this time she has recurring daydreams in which Elvis becomes a conversational partner who is increasingly integrated into her everyday life. These fantasies, according to Hinerman (1992: 122), form a site of negotiation which allow Vanessa to maintain mental stability: 'Around the prohibition of death (and earlier, sexuality), Elvis provides a way for desire to find some satisfaction and still allow her to function in a non-fantasy world.' On this basis Hinerman describes the function of fantasies as follows:

> Fantasies are ... one way humans have to negotiate a troubling situation. They bridge the gap that is created when desire is prohibited but the longing for full satisfaction is still there. Fantasies allow us to 'close the distance' between what we need or want and what we can have. When the unconscious desires and the ego prohibits, throwing open questions of identity and the self, fantasies step into the breach. (Hinerman 1992: 115)

While Hinerman's emphasis on fans undergoing particular traumas carries the risk of reinforcing a victimization perspective of fans, Chloe's Police fantasy illustrates that what Hinerman describes as trauma also includes the common and inevitable tension between inner drives and cultural taboos – in particular, yet not exclusively, during the teenage passage from childhood to adulthood. Chloe's intense fantasies and daydreams began when she first saw the group on stage at the age of 14 and continued until the age of 16 (we will return to the reasons for the breakdown of her fandom later). During this period her fantasies became a source of daily, often orgiastic pleasure; pleasures articulating aspects of her sexuality that were and continue to be socially and culturally prohibited to a teenage girl. As Chloe recalls:

> I didn't really want to [meet him]. I was afraid the reality wouldn't be like the fantasy.... I was a virgin then.... I had met a guy on holiday and we swam together in the nude.... But I preferred my fantasies to reality because they were safer. I also had my reputation to think of because being at an all-girls school if they found you were sleeping with anyone it was murder. You were branded. (Vermorel and Vermorel 1985: 164)

Chloe's fantasies thus offer a third space in which she safely negotiates conflicting cultural pressures and internal drives and desires. Fans' fantasies and daydreams are, then, no simple form of escapism or withdrawal from 'reality', but a meaningful engagement and balancing of conflicting forces between self, fantasy and culture. Chloe's case thus also functions as a marked point of contrast to the notion of 'subversive pleasures' in the fandom of the same socio-demographic group, teenage girls, in Fiske's work (1989b). What early fan studies have described as empowerment may in fact be an attempt of the ego to balance the opposing demands and pressures of culture and super-ego, on the one hand,

and drives and id, on the other. This, however, is not to say that such fantasies do not hold the potential to impact on social and gender relations. As Cicioni (1998: 160) argues in her exploration of slash writing with reference to Russ (1985) and Lamb and Veith (1986), 'in representing the move from friendship to deeper intimacy, women — socialized not to initiate sexual relationships — express at the same time a sexualization of their conditioning and their own needs'.

Yet, our exploration of fan fantasies here, drawing on a Freudian conceptualization of self, demonstrates that such challenges to existing norms and power relations are a by-product, not the source, of fan pleasures. As Jones (2002: 81) notes regarding the same subject matter of slash stories as Cicioni, the great 'variety of sexual fantasy, both within and outside the slash genre, attached to cult television characters suggests that there is something about their construction that both invites and tolerates such diversity of use, and which is not adequately accounted for by the "incorporation/resistance paradigm" that has dominated and conditioned studies of audiences, fans and slash fiction'. Yet, as much as fan fantasies point to the need to move beyond notions of power and resistance, they already indicate the limitations of Freudian psychoanalysis in the examination of fans' motivations and pleasure. As fantasies are a simultaneous form of externalization of internal desires and internalization of external texts and images, there is no simple starting or end point of fantasies in a primal scene or in external objects, or in the fan's self. Fantasies are instead formed in the dynamic interaction between text and reader, or, in psychological terms, between self and object world. We therefore need to turn to psychoanalytic approaches that account for the sustained interaction between self and its social and cultural environment.

Introjection and projection in fandom

One such less static concept of self can be found in the school of post-Freudian psychoanalysis that has become known as 'object relations theory'. While different approaches to fan theory have begun to draw on various aspects of the diverse body of work of object relations theory, I will focus here on the work of Melanie Klein and D. W. Winnicott, who both, in different ways, have lastingly shaped the field of psychoanalysis. The key concepts of

Kleinian psychoanalysis that have attracted attention in fan studies (Stacey 1994; Elliott 1999; Hoxter 2000) are the processes of introjection, projection and object splitting, which in turn reflect what Klein describes as 'paranoid-schizoid position'. At their root lies the relationship between the pre-oedipal child and its first relational object, the mother and her body. Klein returns to the Freudian understanding of the self and the id that I outlined above as structured in the field of tension between the libidinal forces of Eros and the inherent death drive, Thanatos. The important difference from Freud's work, however, lies in Klein's concern with how the self negotiates this tension in relation to its environment. The emotional engagement with 'objects' – such as other humans – surrounding the self is thus reflective of the inner anxiety experienced by the child, which 'arises from the operation of the death instinct within the organism, [which] is felt as fear of annihilation (death) and takes the form of fear of persecution' (Klein 1946/2000: 132). At this point Klein moves from an understanding of the self as largely self-contained and organized around internal desires, as in Freud's work, to conceptualizing the self as a socially related object. In an attempt to deal with his or her immense fear, the child seeks to dislocate elements of the death drive from the self to its surrounding objects, notably various parts of the maternal body, and the mother's breast in particular. The mother's breast takes on a split meaning, as gratifying and nurturing object in its stimulation of oral libido, while equally signifying the externalized death instinct and hence persecution. This double (good/bad) meaning of the object is reflective of the ego split between libidinal and destructive drives. Herein lies what Klein identifies as the 'paranoid-schizoid position'. This position is maintained through processes of projection, in which the internal 'bad' feelings are channelled and assigned to the external object, and introjection, which allows the child to integrate 'good' aspects of external objects into the split self.

The benefits of notions of projection and introjection in developing a meaningful alternative to Freudian conceptualizations of spectatorship are evident in Stacey's (1994) study of female cinema-goers in 1940s Britain, which formulates an outright challenge to the orthodox Freudian understanding of the constitution of pleasures in psychoanalytic film theory. Stacey observes such processes in the building of an emotional bond between fan and star. Projection in Stacey's description becomes a process reminiscent of our earlier discussion of consumption as a form of communication, as spectators 'make choices between competing definitions of desirable femininity in relation to their feelings about themselves and about particular stars who embody such definitions' (Stacey 1994: 230). In turn, the idealized representations of stars in Hollywood cinema suggest that processes of projection in fandom evolve around 'good' objects – in other words, fans project what they see as desirable dimensions and qualities in themselves. Yet, as Klein (1946/2000: 134) notes, 'idealisation is bound up with a splitting of the object' – while the 'star-as-good-object' constitutes the dominant mode of the fan–star relationship, stars also function as projected 'bad object'. As Stacey (1994: 230) argues, 'female stars are often set narratively in opposition to each other, and the transgressive or rebellious character is often more popular than the caring or nurturing one'.

However, it is not only the fan who shapes her object of fandom, but the object of fandom which shapes its fans. Stacey identifies devotion/adoration, worship, transcendence, aspiration/inspiration as the main cinematic 'identificatory fantasies'. These fantasies are mirrored in fans' memories of their affection for particular stars. In an example combining elements of transcendence, worship and adoration, Deanna Durbin fan June Thomas remembers how 'film stars ... seemed very special people, glamorous, handsome and way above the ordinary mortals' (quoted in Stacey 1994: 142). In addition, and in marked contrast to previous psychoanalytic approaches to cinema spectatorship, Stacey highlights the importance of the social, cultural and economic framing of the object of fandom by formulating four extra-cinematic identificatory fantasies: pretending, resembling, imitating and copying. These in turn are reflective of processes of projection and introjection, the latter necessarily preceded by projection – unless we argue that qualities of 'good' and 'bad' are objective categories – which following the recognition of the star as good object, allows for the adoption of particular aspects of the representation of the star in the presentation of the fan's self by replicating physical appearances or a distinct habitus. In particular, fantasies of resemblance allow for this simultaneously projective and introjective relationship between fan and object in which the star is first realized as good object and subsequently integrated into the self through introjection:

> Bette Davis – her eyes were fabulous and the way she walked arrogantly ... I have dark eyes, those days I had very large dark eyebrows ... and my dad used to say ... 'Don't roll those Bette

Davis eyes at me young lady ...' now Doris Day, that's a different thing – we share the same birthday. (Patricia Ogden, quoted in Stacey 1994: 162)

Yet processes of projection and introjection are not only based on the relationship between fan and star, but also draw on the commodity system in which the star is embedded. As Stacey (1994: 231) notes, 'a part of the star image thus metonymically symbolizes the desirable form of femininity which can be introjected by the spectator through consumption'. Such forms of introjection are evident in accounts of copying and imitation:

Now Doris Day ... I was told many times around that I looked like her ... I bought clothes like hers ... dresses, soft wool, no sleeves, but short jackets, boxey type little hats, half hats we used to call them and low heeled shoes to match your outfit. (Patricia Odgen, quoted in Stacey 1994: 168)

Their make-up was faultless and the fashion of the forties platform shoes, half heads with rows of curls showing at the back under the hat.... we used to call the shoes 'Carmen Miranda' shoes. ... I felt like a film star using Lux Toilet Soap, advertised as the stars' soap. (Vera Barford, quoted in Stacey 1994: 170)

The meticulous attention to detail and particular products displayed in these retrospective accounts of fan consumption is illustrative of the emotional significance that the object of fandom acquires through acts of introjection, thereby tying the fan to existing conditions of production and thus dominant social, cultural, economic and technological systems. Similar processes of introjection exist across the spectrum of fandom: fan meetings and conventions of popular television shows or subcultural gatherings allow for a carnivalesque introjection through dresses and make-up, while in sports replica shirts signify the membership to one's object of fandom.

Fan violence

Yet processes of projection and introjection in fandom can not only manifest a bond between the fan and the object world (and its dominant social system), but can equally function to construct a hated 'Other'. Klein herself describes the projective control and fantasies of power and omnipotence as the prototype of aggressive object relations. Klein (1946/2000) labels the dislocation and containment of 'bad' parts of the self through imagined control over the object of projection as 'projective identification', a process whereby the boundaries between self and object are increasingly blurred. This notion is taken up in Anthony Elliott's (1999) analysis of the relationship between media stars and their audience. Elliott identifies fantasy as the key realm through which the affective relationship between fans and their object of fandom is structured. Yet, this emphasis on projective identification provides a considerably starker account of the psychological roots and consequences of fandom than Stacey's application of objects relations theory. Elliott illustrates strategies of projective identification in the case of John Lennon biographer Albert Goldman. Goldman's infamous posthumous biography of Lennon draws an unflattering picture of the ex-Beatle: a paranoid and self-destructive man obsessed with cleanliness and scared of physical contact, a violent and aggressive drug-user who maintains a façade of public deception. Goldman finds the reasons for Lennon's alleged disturbed personality in his perverse, misogynistic sexuality, reflecting repressed, even paedophilic desires. To Elliott (1999: 26), this portrayal of Lennon is reflective of the author rather than Lennon himself: 'Goldman, as biographer, makes his subject, Lennon, in and through unwitting repetitions of unconscious fantasies.' In this act of projective identification, Lennon becomes 'the carrier for a range of fantasies about desire and sexuality, fantasies which, once projected onto Lennon, can be represented as dangerous, threatening, and disturbing'. Thus Goldman 'unleashes his fantasies on Lennon in order to both "know" his subject and establish control' (Elliott 1999: 26). If in this analysis of Goldman's biography, which Elliott (1994: 26) describes as 'the second assassination of Lennon', the projective processes in the relationship between (anti-)fan and star are associated with aggression and mental instability, Elliott's subsequent exploration of the first assassination of Lennon is even less unambiguous about fandom as a form of psychological dysfunction. Elliott identifies the obsession of Lennon's killer, Mark Chapman, as projective identification, in which Lennon ultimately fails to live up to the violent idealization in Chapman's projective fantasies. Chapman engaged in a range of introjective processes in imitating and copying Lennon, such as growing his hair, learning to play the guitar, and even marrying an older Japanese-American woman. However, when Lennon seeks to align his public image with the transformations in his personal life and makes a series of statements regarding music, religion and politics that run against Chapman's values and reading of Lennon, he can no longer accommodate Chapman's projective fantasies. As a result, the fragile stability of Chapman's ego collapses as he loses control over the external, projected object, and his dislocated 'bad' elements return in force. While Elliott (1999: 139) seeks to balance his account by stating that 'fandom can enrich the emotional development of the self and may contribute significantly to an individual's sense of the interpersonal world', the thrust of his argument points in the opposite direction. Drawing on Klein, Elliott comes to a decidedly bleak assessment of fandom's potential consequences:

> In the process of identifying with the celebrity, the fan unleashes a range of fantasies and desires and, through projective identification, transfers personal hopes and dreams onto the celebrity. In doing so, the fan actually experiences desirable qualities of the self as being contained by the other, the celebrity. In psychoanalytic terms, this is a kind of splitting: the good and desirable parts of the self are put into the other in order to protect this imagined goodness from bad or destructive parts of the self. There is, then, a curious sort of violence intrinsic to fandom, a violence that forces the other to symbolically fulfil the dreams and desires of the self. The relation of fan and celebrity is troubled because violence is built into it. (Elliott 1999: 139)

Elliott's claims thus expand well beyond the particular psychological profile of Mark Chapman. There are no structural factors in his account that distinguish the fatal fan projection in Chapman's case from cases of 'normal' fandom. The difference between Chapman and other fans, in this interpretation, is one of degree rather than kind. 'Sometimes', as Elliott notes (1999: 140), 'the pain of disillusionment is simply too much.'

While there are indisputable strengths to Kleinian approaches to fandom – notably that they recognize the fantasies fostered in fandom not as mere reflections of inner drives and impulses but as part of the relationship between the self and the object world that forms the ego, and thus as constitutive rather than reflective of self-identity – Elliott's assumption of an inherently violent dimension of fan identifications highlights the difficulties arising out of these approaches. In contrast to Stacey's (1994) and Elliott's (1999) use of her work, Klein identifies the processes of splitting, projection and introjection indubitably as a *stage* of early childhood development that is left behind in the passage to a stable, unified ego in later life. The paranoid-schizoid position is followed by the depressive position, during which the splitting of objects is increasingly overcome, and which thus 'makes for an increased understanding of psychic reality and a better perception of the external world' (Klein 1946/2000: 139). In this sense the continuation of the paranoid-schizoid position into adulthood, which is implied by Stacey and Elliott, functions as a marker of failed ego development and even schizophrenia. While fan-related violence has spasmodically surfaced, particularly in sports fandom, claims regarding psychological dysfunction as a general condition of fandom seem difficult to sustain.[4] It is, as Hills (2002) argues, of limited analytical value to conceptualize as common a practice as fandom as an individual psychological dysfunction. Nor does Kleinian object relations theory, as Stacey (1994: 232) correctly observes, enable us to 'delineate any variation, change, resistance or indeed deviation' in the relationship between fan and object of fandom. The main benefit of its adaptation to the study of fandom, therefore, does not lie in its capacity to provide a fully-fledged theoretical framework of fandom, but in its illustration of some of the important processes that underlie the relationship between fan and object of fandom. Given how easily a Kleinian understanding of self as a form of continuous containment lends itself to an inherently conservative position with regard to the balance of self and society (Elliott 1996), this may be a comforting insight. However, to the extent that we separate psychological processes (introjection and projection) from their psychological condition (paranoid-schizoid position) in the analysis of fans, we confirm the need for a post-Kleinian framework in which both these can be meaningfully conceptualized.

Fan objects as transitional objects

Contemporary psychoanalytic approaches to fandom have increasingly drawn on another branch of object relations theory, in which the affection in which we hold our object of fandom is explained in the same terms as how we first, as infants, develop a strong emotional bond to our first possessions, such as blankets, toys and teddy bears. In their study of soap opera fans, Harrington and Bielby (1995: 135) argue that 'the nature of the soap genre lends itself to intense viewer attachment and involvement, more than any other televisual form'. Yet, they remain dissatisfied with the explanations of pleasures in soap fandom as a form of resistance, repetition or ritual (Modelski 1983; M. E. Brown 1987; Brundson 1989; Geraghty 1991) or as rooted in the generic structure of soap texts (Kielwasser and Wolf 1989), as 'they focus on pleasure as an entity and largely ignore the *process* by which the pleasure is created by fans' (Harrington and Bielby 1995: 133). Among the alternative conceptualizations of pleasures in soap viewing, the one of particular interest here is the suggestion that pleasures are rooted in the fact that the interaction with the object of fandom allows fans to 'challenge the boundaries between internal and external realities' (ibid.). In this context Harrington and Bielby, in line with its growing popularity in social sciences (Giddens 1991) and the study of television in particular (Lembo and Tucker 1990; Silverstone 1994), draw on the notion of the transitional object in the work of D. W. Winnicott.

In contrast to Klein's strict distinction between internal and external objects, Winnicott (1951/2000) identifies a realm between inner self and external object world, arguing that the relationship between the self and the object world forms a third, intermediate area of experiencing 'to which inner reality and external life both contribute' (Winnicott 1951/2000: 151). This area constitutes 'a resting-place for the individual engaged in the perpetual human task of keeping inner and outer reality separated yet interrelated' (ibid.). Like other object relations theorists, Winnicott thus accounts for an initial sense of wholeness and omnipotence experienced by the new-born child, in which there is no distinction between object and subject and which is re-enacted in the autoerotic experiences of early infancy and later life. He thus accounts for the motive of 'lack' (a lost sense of wholeness) in the formation of the self. Yet this lack is 'managed' through the mediating use of objects. Winnicott (1951/2000: 152) observes how in the early autoerotic activities such as thumb-sucking children hold on to or suck external objects such as blankets, clothes or napkins, activities he describes as 'transitional phenomena'. The material focus of these transitional phenomena – 'perhaps some soft object or other type of object [that] has been found and used by the infant' (Winnicott 1951/2000: 153) – is what Winnicott calls 'transitional objects'. They are transitional in that they allow for fluctuation between inner reality and outer world. The transitional object is experienced as a 'not-me object' and hence acknowledged as belonging to an external reality. The object becomes a source of emotional warmth because it has a 'texture' or 'reality of its own' (Winnicott 1951/2000: 154). At the same time, however, the infant exercises illusory control over the transitional object. The transitional object, whether it is a teddy bear, a doll or a favourite blanket, must not be changed unless by the child him or herself, and most of us will be able to recall a situation witnessing the emotional distress caused to infants – including ourselves – when their control over the transitional object is broken through loss or interference by others. The transitional object thus becomes an important device in building relationships, by assisting the integration of internal and external realities. Drawing on Winnicott's observation that children and adults alike continue to negotiate the boundaries between internal and external reality, and soap operas' inherent dialogue between real and fictional, Harrington and Bielby (1995) thus argue that soap opera fandom constitutes a transitional realm.

There are obvious analytical benefits to describing fandom as a transitional realm, or, as Hills (1999, 2002) has done since, objects of fandom as transitional objects. In contrast to fantasy-based processes of projection and introjection, the unified sense of self in relation to the object world is maintained, rather than threatened, in the intermediate realm of illusion and fantasy surrounding the transitional object. A long way from Elliott's troubling depiction of fandom as inherently aggressive, Winnicott provides a theoretical framework that allows us to conceptualize fandom within conventional, non-aggressive psychological processes. Moreover, the emotional bond in an intermediate space between self and object world is evident in many studies of audiences and fandom, well beyond those that have made explicit use of Winnicott. Barbas (2001: 114), for example, describes the relationship between movie fans and their favourite stars of pre-war Hollywood cinema as follows: 'although fans raved about their star's dramatic ability and spoke passionately about her face or his physique, what drew them most to their idol, they claim, were the qualities of warmth, sincerity, and compassion'. Like the soft and inviting surface of teddy bears or blankets, these qualities constitute what is experienced as the 'texture', the external reality of the object. Through this texture, as in the case of the first infantile possession such as a doll or a teddy bear, the object of fandom is acknowledged to belong to an outer, 'not-me' reality. This interaction between the self and external reality through the transitional object has been interpreted as a source of play in fan studies (Hills 1999, 2002) and of security in wider sociological perspectives of everyday life (Giddens 1991). Both interpretations highlight important qualities of fandom.

Giddens (1991) focuses on the role of transitional objects in establishing and maintaining what Winnicott calls 'basic trust'. To Giddens, transitional objects allow for the gradual distancing of the infant from its prime caretaker. By containing an emotional investment and as a means of reality testing, transitional objects aid the passage from initial omnipotence, based on the physical presence of the caretaker, to abstract relations in time and space – the faith or trust that a relationship between self and caretaker will continue even in the caretaker's absence. This basic trust derived in transitional space thus becomes the basis of managing individual security and anxiety within abstract systems, allowing for a 'protective cocoon' (Giddens 1991: 40) through which we generate a sense of trust and security in everyday life. In this context Giddens (1991: 39) highlights the role of particular routines with which transitional objects 'are virtually always connected' as 'both defences against anxiety and simultaneously links with an emerging experience of a stabilized world of objects and persons'.

While Giddens underplays the libidinal foundation and the erotic pleasures derived in the illusory experience of the transitional object, as it enables the infant to pass 'from (magical) omnipotent control to control by manipulation (involving muscle eroticism and co-ordination pleasure)' (Winnicott 1951/2000: 155), his emphasis on the transitional realm as source of ontological security opens a new perspective on the role of fandom in everyday life beyond discourses of resistance. The particular affection for a given actor, singer or writer, the lifelong support of a sports team, the ritual viewing of one's favourite television show, or even fan activities focusing on seemingly mundane tasks such as home-making (Mason and Meyers 2001), help to maintain a 'protective barrier' (Giddens 1991: 40) which brackets off risk and anxiety from the self and thus enables the formation of self-identity on the basis of trust – an emotional capacity that is indispensable in an industrialized and technology dependent, phantasmagoric world which is at constant risk from the very technologies it has created (cf. Beck 1992, 1999). In this sense fandom as a transitional space offers a strategy that addresses the anxieties of fans described thus by Cavicchi (1998: 185-6): 'fans [. . .] are concerned with how to get through each day and how their participation in performance helps them to understand the fluctuating and contradictory experience of daily life and to make connections with other people around them'.

Beyond their function as a source of security, initial infantile transitional objects such as teddy bears are as much, and maybe more so, objects of play – of play that, according to Winnicott (1951/2000), becomes a developmental means in itself, regardless of its content. This notion of the transition object as an object of play is taken up by Hills (1999, 2002), whose work constitutes the most comprehensive application of Winnicottian psychoanalysis to fandom to date. Hills in particular addresses the problem of how a psychoanalytical model of childhood development can be meaningfully applied to adult media consumption. In response to Harrington and Bielby (1995), Hills argues that transitional objects according to Winnicott are both created and found, an assessment that is confirmed in the many accounts of how fans first 'discover' their object of fandom, a term often used by fans themselves (see, for example, Radway 1987; Cavicchi 1998; Sandvoss 2003). Highlighting this importance of fans' agency in finding the object of fandom, Hills (2002: 107) rejects the link that Harrington and Bielby construct between particular modes of production and textuality of soaps and their adaptation as transitional objects by fans as falling 'back into a model of theoretical over-rationalization'. Related to this is the wider problem of how to conceptualize the difference between actual transitional objects of early childhood and the cultural field within which fandom is constructed.

While Winnicott emphasizes 'that the task of reality-acceptance is never completed, that no human being is free from the strain of relating inner and outer reality, and that relief from the strain is provided by an intermediàte area of experience which is not challenged (arts, religion, etc.)' (Winnicott 1951/2000: 158), he also argues that in healthy development, transitional phenomena are gradually 'decathected' as they 'have become diffused and spread out over the whole intermediate territory between "inner psychic reality" and "the external world as perceived by two persons in common", that is to say, over the whole cultural field' (Winnicott 2000: 154). On this basis Hills distinguishes the 'proper' transitional object (such as a child's toy or blanket) and the secondary transitional object which is constituted in and through the cultural field in adulthood. There are, then, two ways to conceptualize fandom. Either we argue that objects of fandom are proper transitional objects. Given that transitional objects are associated with a particular developmental stage of childhood, they therefore – as Silverstone (1994: 14) argues in relation to television viewing – 'must offer a regressive experience'. Or we abandon the notion of fandom as a transitional object and describe fandom instead as a transitional space that finds its points of reference in the cultural field at large, and as such is part of the continuing, non-regressive 'task of reality-acceptance'. With regard to the latter, we should of course note that material objects of fandom, such as collections of posters, artwork, prints, records or replica shirts, can equally function as transitional objects. These various fan memorabilia then constitute transitional objects that create a common realm between the fan and the star, while the star remains the primary object of fandom. Hence physical objects of fandom such as records, autographs or photos function as second-order transitional objects – the physical transitional objects inside transitional objects – that function as intermediate spaces between the self and the actual (transitional) object of fandom which itself is absent. Hills (1999: 111), by contrast, emphasizes the textual nature of fan objects as he remains adamant with regard to the inadequacy of conceptualizing post-infantile fandom as proper transitional object (pto), arriving at the following definition of fan cultures:

> A fan culture is formed around any given text when this text has functioned as a *pto* in the biography of a number of individuals; individuals who remain attached to this text by virtue of the fact that it continues to exist as an element of their cultural experience. Unlike the inherently private but also externally objective *pto*, this 'retained' object must negotiate its intensely subjective significance with its intersubjective cultural status. It is this essential tension which marks it out as a *secondary transitional object*. (Hills 2002: 108)

Drawing on Phillips (1998), Hills traces the theoretical difficulties here back to the vagueness of Winnicott's original work with regard to the actualities of the progression from transitional object to a wider engagement in the cultural field. By the same token, however, the strict division between original proper transitional object and secondary transitional fan object that Hills proposes is, I think, not fully convincing: the proper transitional object is not inherently private; nor is the object of fandom experienced as fully intersubjective. In Hills's argument the transitional object enters and is constituted through the cultural field, and thus becomes non-regressive. By contrast, my own reading of Winnicott is such that both the emotional quality and the potential regressiveness of the transitional object lie not only in its private nature or lack of integration into an intersubjective cultural field, but in its re-enactment of the initial relationship between self and primary caretaker, and therefore in a lost sense of wholeness. Consequently, we cannot assume a fundamental structural difference between a textual and a material transitional object, and thus that we can meaningfully distinguish between an initial and a secondary transitional object.

Nevertheless, conceptualizing the object of fandom as transitional object usefully illustrates the origin of fandom in childhood. The fact that a fan text may function as a transitional object during childhood is already highlighted in Hills's definition of fan cultures. This assumption seems further confirmed by the range of fan texts that are popular among children, from stories of action heroes to science fiction and comics. Brooker (2002), for example, documents how *Star Wars* fandom often originates during childhood. In the words of Brooker's 11-year-old interviewee Frazer, when asked if music is more important to him than *Star Wars*: 'Star Wars is definitely more important, I like it more than anything else. ... I've already liked it for a long time, four years. I'll probably like it forever' (Brooker 2002: 236). Equally, the product range of toy manufacturers witnesses to children's intense interest in their first textual possessions, with *Lego* featuring an extensive *Star Wars* range in its current programme. *Star Wars* and other popular stories, films and television shows, then, are the first beloved set of characters, the first narrative possession, and as such fulfil the characteristics of a transitional object, although such textual possessions depend on a certain degree of literacy and hence are not accessible to children until a later age than physical transitional objects.[5]

Not all objects of fandom are 'found' during childhood, of course, and there are many examples of fan cultures with a substantial share of adult participation that have emerged around texts within a few years or even months of the initial entry of the object of fandom into the market-place, including those fan texts that have been subsumed under the above-discussed label 'cult'. Yet, I have already argued that any definition of cult cannot be rooted in generic qualities alone, but that cult – like the transitional object – is found and created by fans. While this constitutes no conclusive definition, it seems to me that the use of fan texts as original transitional objects during childhood is one determining factor in what leads us to consider texts as 'cult'. The premiss of the object of fandom as an infantile transitional object is of course that such texts are available during fans' infancy. It therefore is no coincidence that the notion of cult has become increasingly popular since the 1990s, with the emergence of fans and scholars as part of the first generation, then in their thirties and early forties, to whom television was an everyday life childhood experience. Furthermore, the importance of the potential availability of cult television programmes as transitional objects during childhood is underlined in the varying selection of such television programmes across different cultures or, more to the point, 'broadcast areas'. Television programmes tend to become cult or objects of fandom only to certain audience groups to which they were available during their childhood. In other broadcast cultures, we find descriptions of cult television shows virtually unknown to English-speaking audiences. German-language websites dedicated to cult television, for example, include Germany's first science fiction television series *Raumpatrolie* (1966), the Japanese-produced cartoon *Captain Future* (1978/1980), which also enjoys popularity in France (*Capitaine Flam*), Italy (*Captain Futuro*) and Venezuela, the German-Czech co-production drama *Pan Tau* (1965), and Boy Lornsen's adventure novel turned-TV show *Robbi, Tobbi und das Fliewatüüt* (1972) as among the most frequently listed and most intensely discussed programmes. These differences and diversity in televisual cult fandom are set to be gradually eroded through the emergence of transnational television networks and cable channels (cf. Herman and McChesney 1997; Hesmondhalgh 2002), many of which are dedicated to children's programming, such as Nickelodeon, Fox Kids or the Disney Channel.

Yet, in contrast to Hills (1999), who argues that the affection for childhood media texts is a form of 'nostalgia' rather than fandom, in lacking the necessary active involvement in and with the texts – this, I think, suggests that these objects of fandom as transitional objects are often maintained, rather than reconstituted, in secondary transitional objects. It is primarily texts 'which appeal from the very beginning to both children and adults' (Hills 2002: 109) that serve as potential transitional objects and later objects of fandom (cf. Brooker 2000). Having said this, there is no doubt that the context of fan consumption, whether in childhood or later life, matters. This includes questions of how the texts one consumes are regarded by others, as much as the above-discussed questions of when, to whom, and how texts are available as transitional objects and therefore as later objects of fandom. This context of fan consumption is also technological. When Silverstone identifies television in both its form and its content as possible transitional object, he also unveils its intrinsically suburban form as part of a (domestic) technological system of mobile privatization (Williams 1974), with all its socio-cultural implications of the self-contained home and a decentralized and literally fenced-in relationship between television as a transitional objec source of ontological security, and rationalized, suburbar Silverstone's argument is no coincidental one, r psychological and sociological conditions of televi~i~ii ai necessary premises to each other. Ultimately, the confusion over the degree to which the integration into a cultural field changes the nature of the object of fandom as transitional object (cf. Hills 2002; Silverstone 1999) is indicative of the ambiguous status role of modern mass media between private and public and between the self and the object world.

Hence, we must not too quickly dismiss the possibility that a continuation of transitional objects in later life constitutes a regressive, though not pathological, experience (Silverstone 1994), which can be intensely pleasurable precisely because of its return to pre-separation wholeness in childhood, fostering a most radical sense of belonging and *Heimat*. In light of the specific social, textual and technological conditions of the fan text through which it functions as a transitional realm, I believe that we cannot shift our attention fully from the object of fandom to the activity of fandom, as Hills suggests when he argues with regard to the question of whether transitional objects in fandom are retained, 'that it is whether or not our "stuckness" can act as a personal space for effective play that is significant, and not whether or not we or our interests are "stuck" *per se*' (Hills 2002: 112). While it is an important element of fandom, the focus on play inevitably privileges fan performances and activities over their social and cultural conditioning. Yet, the tendency to neglect questions of structure in a focus on agency is not restricted to Hills (2002), who in fact provides a more balanced account of structure and agency in fandom beyond the question of fan objects as transitional objects. Instead, it is an inherent feature of Winnicott's work and its various adaptations. Craib (2001) suggests that Winnicott's popularity derives partly from the congruence between his theory and contemporary ideological tendencies within social sciences and beyond: in contrast to Freud and Klein, Winnicott does not portray the outer struggles between the self and the outside world, between the self and repressive structures, or the inner struggles of the torn, ambivalent or even schizoid self. To Winnicott human development compares, rather, to 'a bud opening into a flower' (Craib 2001: 126), corresponding to predominant contemporary discourses on childhood development. As Craib (2001: 125–6) warns: 'the contemporary tendency to idealize children, to see them as doing no wrong except that which comes to them from the outside (see A. Miller 1987), is responsible not only for some of Winnicott's popularity but also for some of the ways he is misread or misunderstood.' It is important to avoid equally one-sided interpretations of fandom by exploring the interdependence of psychological motivations of fandom on their social, cultural, textual and technological framing. In the remainder of this book I thus turn to developing a theoretical perspective based on this interplay of self, text and society.

Summary

I have outlined three psychoanalytic perspectives on the motivations and pleasures of fandom. Freudian approaches demonstrate inherent pleasures and desires articulated in fandom that cannot be reduced to particular social and cultural contexts. Whereas the emphasis on unconscious and primal fantasies in psychoanalytic film theory fails to account for the processual nature of fandom as an everyday life activity, Freudian concepts of self nevertheless provide a useful starting point to explore fan fantasies constituted in the field of tension between id and super-ego. Yet Freud's original work insufficiently explores the role of external objects in the constitution of such fantasies. Kleinian approaches to fandom, by contrast, enable us to conceptualize the particular bond between fan and object of fandom arising out of their continuing interaction through processes of projection and introjection, whereby the object of fandom becomes an extension of aspects of the fan's self, as well as vice versa. Yet, as is particularly evident in Elliott's work (1999), projection and introjection reflect a paranoid-schizoid position which is not only latently aggressive but also carries the traits of psychological dysfunction in adult life, and thus invites the pathologization of fans. While Winnicott's concept of the transitional object is equally derived from an analysis of early infancy, it underlines the important function of fandom as a realm of negotiation between inner and external realities, and thus as a source of both pleasure and security. The emphasis on play in the discussion of objects of fandom as transitional objects, however, needs to be counter-balanced by an analysis of the content and the framing of such play.

5

FANDOM AS EXTENSION OF SELF: SELF-REFLECTION AND NARCISSISM

Juxtaposing fans' fantasies and pleasures in their interaction with their object of fandom with the social and technological distance between fans and their object of fandom, we are confronted with a seemingly paradoxical situation. On the one hand, fandom is based on a strict separation and distanciation between fan and object of fandom. Objectively, from the position of the outsider, this division is obvious. There is a definite communicative, social and economic distance between, say, Madonna or Manchester United and their fans. On the other hand, psychoanalytic approaches to fandom emphasize the intense emotional bond between fans and their objects of fandom through processes such as projection and introjection or the intermediate function of the object of fandom located between the spheres of self and object world as transitional object. In the following I will argue that these conflicting subjective and objective dimensions of fandom are not only the source of many of the discourses that have dominated the study of fandom, but in fact are necessary premises of each other. In conjunction, they form the socio-psychological basis of fandom against which its social and cultural consequences need to be assessed.

Far away, so close: fandom and self-reflection

Researchers concerned with the subjective, intrapersonal experience of popular culture in fandom have often found it difficult to establish meaningful boundaries between fans and their objects of fandom. As, for instance, Hills notes, 'it is almost as if you can't find the distance between text and reader that is required to think about them in the conventional cultural studies way' (Hills and Jenkins 2001: 1–2). Equally, fans themselves often fail to acknowledge any such boundaries. Fans of team sports often choose the pronoun 'we' when referring to their favourite club (Miller and McHoul 1998). Similarly, fan performances of impersonation and imitation (Spigel 1990; Fiske 1993; Stacey 1994) are aimed to eradicate the visual distinctions between fan and object of fandom, and to function 'as a sign of itself' to the fan community (Nightingale 1994: 13).

The theoretical challenge here is to account for the dual function of the object of fandom as experienced not in relation to the self, but *as part of the self*, despite constituting an external object. The basic premise of my argument, then, is that the object of fandom, whether it is a sports team, a television programme, a film or pop star, is intrinsically interwoven with our sense of self, with who we are, would like to be, and think we are. To some extent I have already highlighted such processes in the discussion of fan communities and fan consumption as a form of communication. However, the relationship between fans and objects of fandom goes beyond forming a symbolic basis for fan communities and functioning as a signifier of our socio-cultural or subcultural position. The case of sport fans is particularly reflective of the degree to which the object of fandom becomes part of the self. Michael, fan of the West London soccer team Chelsea, struggles to explain his emotionally intense relationship to his object of fandom:

> It's difficult, it is very difficult. It is just very personal to me. What other people think about it isn't important to me ... I was there when there were only 6,000 people there, week in and week out. Now I see 30,000 and they are not real supporters. They are here because it's fashionable. It's very personal, to me. It's the club I was brought up with. This is my life, basically. (quoted in Sandvoss 2003: 32)

The perception of the external object as part of the self is in turn based on the recognition, consciously or unconsciously, of aspects of the self in the external object. Any extension of the self is thus based on *processes of self-reflection*, which in both sociology and psychology have been summarized under the heading of narcissism. Various accounts of fans and audiences have drawn upon the many interpretations of the Narcissus myth. Psycho-analytic film theory has often been anchored in a Lacanian understanding of narcissism, in which narcissistic reflection provides the key to understanding the identification between spectator and text. Broader social and cultural accounts of celebrity culture and consumerism have equally drawn on notions of narcissism in analysing the increasingly privatized, self-centred nature of consumption in late twentieth-century capitalism (Lasch 1979/1991; Postman 1985; B. King 1992), arising out of, in Weber's terms, the 'disenchantment' of an increasingly rational world. However, where one approach remains too narrow in its sole focus on the text, the other is too general in its broad-brush discussion of culture to provide a meaningful assessment of forms of narcissism in the interaction between fan and object of fandom.

An empirically grounded conceptualization of audiences and fans drawing on notions of narcissism, by contrast, is proposed by Abercrombie and Longhurst (1998). I have already outlined Abercrombie and Longhurst's useful analysis of the nexus between spectacle and performance. They argue that narcissism arises out of the ongoing performance of media consumption: 'narcissism involves an imagined performance in front of others who constitute an audience which is focused on the narcissistic self' (Abercrombie and Longhurst 1998: 93). Narcissism, according to Abercrombie and Longhurst, constitutes a consequence as well as a premiss of the cyclical interaction between production/spectacle and consumption/performance. The proliferation of the production and distribution of popular culture leads to the constitution of what they describe as 'diffused audiences' (ibid.), which in a media-saturated environment engage in media-related performances in all everyday life situations. Fans and audiences, then, search out their own audiences for their performances of media texts, and the individual partly constructs itself through its object of fandom and its performative display. Indeed visual signifiers of fan consump-tion, such as particular dress styles, stickers, buttons, posters or replica shirts, have become part of the performance structure of our everyday lives. The degree to which the boundaries between spectator and performer have been blurred, and mundane everyday life performances have themselves entered popular culture, is illustrated by the rise to stardom of the college student Jennifer Ringley, who from 1996 onwards embarked on an unedited, 24-hour live transmission of her dorm life via webcam – much of which Ringley spent watching television or consuming other mass media herself. Ringley's website attracted a substantial online fan community, drawing up to 100 million hits a week.[1] To Rojek (2001: 98), writing before the closure of the website in 2003, Ringley's case is illustrative of Lasch's notion of a culture of narcissism, in which 'narcissism is associated with the hyperinflation of the ordinary'. At the same time it serves – alongside the rise of various shades of reality TV, ranging from fly-on-the-wall documentaries to the 'game-docs' discussed above – as a powerful example of how the rise of spectacle and the media infiltration of all areas of everyday life has induced narcissistic performances. Abercrombie and Longhurst's 'spectacle/performance paradigm' thus ties elements of narcissism necessarily to public performance. On the basis of their own typology of fandom, we are more likely to find such performances among organized fan groups such as the soccer enthusiasts showing more interest and concern about how their singing, chanting and rehearsed displays are represented on television, than in the game itself (Sandvoss 2003).

Yet, there is a second form of narcissism in fandom, more closely linked to forms of self-reflection, which does not presuppose that fan texts are performed in front of an actual audience of friends, acquaintances or strangers. This form of narcissism also applies to fans lacking the tighter social networks of cultists or enthusiasts. While these fans may still in one form or another communicate their fandom in everyday life talk, and thus engage in enunciative productivity, the hesitation of, for example, female horror fans to publicly acknowledge their fandom (Cherry 2002) illustrates the fact that the public performance of fandom is a common but not necessary characteristic of fandom. Rather, the first and foremost audience for the performance of fans is the fan him- or herself.

I am thus proposing a model of fandom as a form of narcissistic self-reflection not between fans and their social environment but between the fan and his or her object of fandom. My starting point in this endeavour lies neither in the psychoanalytic nor the sociological interpretations of narcissism, but in the conceptualization of the media as an extension of the self in the work of Marshall McLuhan. To McLuhan (1964), electronic mass media such as radio and television expand our perceptory senses in that they extend our vision and hearing beyond our immediate surroundings. In light of this consideration, McLuhan (1964) interprets the Narcissus myth, in which Narcissus detects his mirror image in the water while drinking from a river and subsequently falls in love with the image unaware that it is his own reflection, as an analogy to the consumption of electronic mass media. According to McLuhan (1964: 45), the importance of the myth lies in 'the fact that men at once become fascinated by any extension of themselves in any material other than themselves'. Much as the boundaries of Narcissus's body are extended in space through his mirror image in the water, electronic mass media, according to McLuhan (1964: 47), extend ourselves in time and space: 'with the arrival of electronic technology, man extended, or set alongside himself, a live model of the central nervous system itself'.[2] However, the body is unable to sustain the physical stress resulting from this extension of the self, and its only possible reaction lies in what McLuhan calls 'self-amputation', much as Narcissus is numbed in his perception as his intense interaction with the mirror image anaesthetizes him. Similarly, modern media consumers are unable to process the unprecedented volume of information with which they are confronted through their extended nervous system, and likewise react with a strategy of 'auto-amputation', in which they block such information received by the offending organ. This may explain why the emergence of highly networked and interconnected societies has coincided with a rise of anxiety and political apathy. Yet, for our purposes here, it is important to note that from the sense of narcosis inherent in narcissism – and herein, according to McLuhan, lies the shared etymological root of both terms – also follows a situation in which the extension of the self through the external object gains far-reaching command over the self, to which I will turn below.

Before further pursuing the consequences of narcissism, I want to explore forms of self-reflection of fans and fan objects. So far I have discussed various accounts of fandom that emphasize the claims of ownership over the object of fandom by fans: *Beauty and the Beast* fans (Jenkins 1992) clearly have a sense of textual ownership. Similarly, Elliott (1999) illustrates how fans seek to exercise control over their object of fandom in processes of projection and introjection. Nightingale (1994: 9) has even gone so far as to suggest that fans through performances of impersonation 'strive to be instantly identifiable as the "loved object"'. From this identification with the object of fandom also derives a greater degree of control: 'Where the star, by definition, was more than the image but less controllable – always threatening to prove the image false by a bad performance, weight gain, drug addiction – the impersonator is less than the image but more amenable to regulation' (ibid.). Here, I want to take such arguments to their conclusion and suggest that in the intense interaction between self and object of fandom, acknowledgement of the object of fandom as an external object disappears. Rather than as a transitional realm between the self and an external world, the object of fandom forms part of the self, and hence functions as its extension.

This self-reflective interaction between fan and fan object in which the latter comes to function as an extension of the former is evident on a number of levels. First, despite the communal context of a significant proportion of fan consumption, many fans emphasize the centrality of their object of fandom to their sense of self, and entertain a highly personal relationship with their fan object. As mentioned above, sport fans, for instance, often resort to the pronoun 'we' when talking about a favourite team (cf. Miller and McHoul 1998; Sandvoss 2003). Moreover, they often emphasize the personal and private nature of their fandom (Sandvoss 2003), on occasion going so far as to privilege their fandom over any other form of social interaction. As Benny, a football fan from London, puts it: 'I feel a lot more than I let out ... I know if it comes to choosing between my wife and football, Chelsea, there would only be one winner' (quoted in Sandvoss 2003: 32). Similarly, David, a Bruce Springsteen fan quoted in Cavicchi's (1998: 49) study, reflects on the breakdown of a relationship with a former girlfriend at the time of Springsteen's 'Human Touch/Lucky Town' album: 'for reasons beyond my control, that was the last time I was friendly with this girl, although some part of me thinks that when the album came out, I had something personal and private that I no longer needed as badly from a relationship (especially her)'. The point here is not to imply that Benny or David lack compassion for their partners or are unable to build relationships. If they privilege their object of fandom over actual personal relationships, then this is illustrative of the degree to which their object of fandom functions as an extension of self and is constitutive of their identity. Benny's and David's accounts are comparable to other articulations of the erosion of distance between fans and object of fandom. Doss (1999) reports how many Elvis fans think of Elvis as a close friend or family member. The various (sexual) fantasies of fans drawn from Vermorel and Vermorel's work (1985) all involve a projective quality in which inherent aspects of the self in the form of drives and fantasies are articulated through the object of fandom which functions as its extension. Conversely, various fan groups resort to textual productivity, in which fans' authorship of the fan text further indicates the need of the object of fandom to fulfil a set of expectations formulated with regard to the fan's self. In all these cases fandom becomes an integral part and extension of the fan's self, rather than a mere textual possession. As Cavicchi concludes in his discussion of Springsteen fans: 'while fans' feelings may fluctuate, connecting with Springsteen means that he becomes a part of each fan, a continuing presence to which they may turn again and again. On the whole, fandom is not some particular thing one *has* or *does*. Fandom is a process of being; it is the way one *is*' (Cavicchi 1998: 59, original emphasis).

The object of fandom in this sense is not so much a textual possession; nor does it only define the self. It is part of the fan's (sense of) self. For the object of fandom as an external object – whether it is Bruce Springsteen or, say, *Star Trek* – to be experienced as part of the fan's fabric of self, fans need to build an intense identification with their object of fandom. This identification is reflected in the aforementioned 'we' used by sport fans. Yet, even if less obvious on a rhetorical level, intense identification with an object of fandom is not limited to sports. It is worth recalling some of the studies I discussed earlier. The adamant manner in which female fans of *Beverly Hills, 90210* in McKinley's study (1997) attack the figure of Lucinda as antagonist to the show's lead character Kelly cannot be explained in terms of the hegemonic framing of the show alone. It is not a simple reflection of the ideological positions of *90210* fans – in which case the show would, contrary to McKinley's claims, only reflect rather than reinforce or shape the ideological position of its fans. Rather, it is reflective of the extent to which fans identify with Kelly, who, as the object of fandom, becomes a narrative extension of the fan's self in the show. Reflecting on the many instances 'when viewers drew explicit parallels – or contrasts – between themselves and the characters', McKinley (1997: 100) argues that fans of the show construct a close community between themselves and the characters. This is further highlighted in the way female fans interact with the second female lead, Donna:

> the most interesting example of the way this community worked was the following comment by a college student, expressed to a chorus of delight from her sorority sisters: 'If Donna and David have sex – (laughter) – that's like – I would be in heaven with that.

No kidding (ovation). I would think I'm having sex.' Light-hearted, casual, and transient — nevertheless, this talk worked to construct, maintain, and defend a close community, even intimacy with Donna and David. (McKinley 1997: 100)

What McKinley describes as a close community between the fan and her fan object is rooted in the intense identification between the fan and the object of fandom that blurs the boundaries between the two. For all the patterns of fan identification, which, as we will see, are far from predictable, it should be noted that cultural producers often undertake concerted efforts to invite and encourage such identification. Brooker's (2000) analysis of the introduction of *Robin* as youthful sidekick to comic superhero *Batman* lucidly illustrates this point. Brooker reports how one of the comic creators, Bob Kane, saw the introduction not only as an additional narrative device in which *Batman* was given a conversation partner (as intended by his co-writer Bill Finger), but as a chance to provide a point of identification for the comics' young male audience. Kane 'imagined that young boys reading about Batman's exploits would project their own images into the story and daydream about fighting alongside the Caped Crusader as junior Batman. I thought that every young boy would want to be like Robin' (quoted in Brooker 2002: 56). Notably, Kane links the form of fan identification he sought to encourage with forms of projection and the interjection of the fan's image into the story. The assumed identification of the adolescent comic book fan with Robin, or the case of the above-quoted *90210* fan demonstrate that the relationship between fans and their object of fandom goes beyond mere identification: Donna or Robin are not simply points of identification — they are extensions of the fan's very self.

Objects of fandom as extensions of self

The role of the object of fandom as textual extension of the self is further manifested on a third level: the assumed congruence between fan and object of fandom, which is based on processes of self-reflection. What I mean here by 'congruence' is the active construction of parallels, identity and 'identicality' between fans and their object of fandom. Again, some of the previously discussed studies are already indicative of such tendencies. Remember, for example, Stacey's (1994) discussion of how fans emphasize the resemblance between themselves and film stars, as in the above-quoted case of Bette Davis fan Patricia Ogden. Such an assumed resemblance is equally evident in fans' identification with fictional characters. What qualifies fans' emphasis on the resemblance between themselves and their object of fandom as a form of self-reflection is that such assumed parallels are not objectively verifiable, but based on the particular meaning which fans construct in their reading of the fan object. An interesting point of contrast emerges, for example, if we juxtapose the various studies of *Star Trek* fandom and return to the comparison of the interpretations of the series by the MIT students whom Jenkins interviewed (Tulloch and Jenkins 1995) with the female fans organized in fan circles in Bacon-Smith's (1992) study. The fantasy and fiction of these female fans often evolved around the figure of Spock, who became the focal point of narratives of sexual encounters which radically reworked gender relations and sexual conventions in reference to the needs, desires and convictions of these female fans. In their stories, Spock becomes the reflection of their own struggle against a disenchanted, emotionally impover-ished and discriminating world. Compare such readings, which are profoundly critical of rational, technologically driven modernity, with the reading of Spock by an MIT student in Jenkins's study:

> I always wanted to be like Spock. I suppose I was like him − an outsider. He was an alien in the ship and I was an outsider in my town. I grew up there but I didn't belong. He was in science and things like that. He would solve all the problems. He was someone I looked up to at the time. (John, quoted in Tulloch and Jenkins 1995: 233)

Spock thus accommodates diverging readings as the imagined resemblance and communality between fans and their object of fandom functions as a reflection of the fan's self. Fans like John therefore make, in the words of another *Star Trek* fan whom Jenkins (1991: 192) quotes in his earlier work, '*Star Trek* uniquely our own'.

While various accounts of fans reveal their self-reflective readings by emphasizing parallels between themselves and their object of fandom, narcissistic self-reflection remains a process that is both conscious and unconscious. It is of course conscious to the extent that we are aware of our intense fascination with our own extension. Herein also lies the source of the above-described numbness. Narcissus is so preoccupied with his mirror image in the water that he fails to engage meaningfully with his social environment, represented by the nymph Echo, who, constrained to endless repetition, turns to stone in unfulfilled love for Narcissus. It is this meaning of narcissism that has been picked up on in most sociological, but also popular, discourses on narcissism. However, narcissism does not equal self-love, as there is a second, unconscious dimension to narcissistic self-reflection. While we are fascinated by our mirror image, this fascination is based on our failure to recognize the image as our self-reflection. As McLuhan (1964: 45–6) notes: 'the wisdom of the Narcissus myth does not convey any idea that Narcissus fell in love with anything he regarded as himself. Obviously he would have had very different feelings about the image had he known it was an extension or repetition of himself.' We may then be aware of parallels between ourselves and our objects of fandom, and even actively seek to foster and construct these, yet self-reflection is always based on a misrecognition of the external object. Our fascination with the object of fandom does not arise out of the fact that, objectively, it is like us, but is instead based on the projection of our own image. The object of fandom, like the river in the Narcissus myth, is the coincidental medium of self-reflection, whose true quality lies in its reflective capacity.

Beyond identificatory fantasies of resembling or imitating (Stacey 1994), (the key indication of fans' self-reflective reading of their object of fandom then lies in the way in which they superimpose attributes of the self, their beliefs and values systems and, ultimately, their sense of self on the object of fandom.) To return to our earlier discussion of the role of religion and fandom, Brooker (2002) documents the wide variety of readings by *Star Wars* fans, in which their relationship to their object of fandom is fundamentally structured through their own beliefs. Consider, for instance, the following account by a 21-year-old *Star Wars* fan from New York:

> Its message is so positive and optimistic, making us all feel special .. like we belong to something much bigger than ourselves.... *Star Wars* represents my own personal beliefs of religion and spirituality ... Sure, we may not be able to lift droids, rocks or X-Wings, but we could 'use the force' in other ways such as helping, loving, caring and supporting, and be our own personal Jedi. (quoted in Brooker 2002: 5-6)

Again, what separates objective resemblance and self-reflection is the subjective reading position through which the fan finds his or her values and beliefs in the fan text. This self-reflective interpretation of the object of fandom discloses itself in the sheer range of varying, and frequently contradictory, readings of the same object of fandom by different fans and fan groups. Brooker (2002) documents this wide spectrum of interpretation in *Star Wars* fan culture, illustrative of fans' socio-demographic background, such as, most notably, fans' age, and their different reading positions, reflecting their values and beliefs. The extent to which the meaning of the object of fandom is constructed with reference to the fan's self is also illustrated in the diverging and opposing readings of fans of sport teams. In my study of football fandom (Sandvoss 2003: 27-8), I illustrated such divergent readings with the example of two fans of Chelsea Football Club:

> I think Chelsea stand for success. We have so many brilliant players. We also have a very successful past, winning the FA Cup and the European Cup in 1970/71. There were some dire years in between, but today the main attribute of the club is success, fortunately. (Karen, Chelsea fan)

> Nobody could ever give [success] as a reason for supporting Chelsea, because Chelsea have never been successful. Chelsea have always been almost successful, and fucked it up, which is possibly why a lot of people support Chelsea ... There are people who have been almost successful in their life who support Chelsea. They have all the right attributes, but never quite succeed ... maybe that reflects Chelsea fans' lives. (John, Chelsea fan)

As in the above examples, the contrary construction of meaning in these readings again corresponds with the socio-demographic position of these two fans (Sandvoss 2003). More importantly, however, beyond their class position, the readings correspond with the sense of self and self-image of both interviewees: Karen, a businesswoman in her late thirties from Surrey, happily identified with formal rational formulations of success, whether they are in the form of monetary rewards or of trophies. By contrast, to John, a freelance writer from Brixton, the formal rational goals of winning and (economic) success were marked absences in his own life. The opposition between these two accounts hence echoes how Karen's and John's appropriation of their object of fandom serves as an extension of their sense of self. Their statements tell us less about the text (Chelsea Football Club) than about its readers. Both construct distinct meanings of the object of fandom that reflect their image of self and which they adamantly defend against other readings. Among other Chelsea fans, all sharing the same object of fandom, I encountered many further interpretations, again sometimes diametrically opposed. For some fans the club became a symbol of their own cosmopolitan, urban life-style; others found in what they saw as 'London's last white club' refuge for their right-wing convictions. Yet others opposed what they interpreted as 'political' readings of their object of fandom, although, as in the case of Tulloch's study of *Dr Who* fans who rejected particular readings of the programme, 'it was not "politics" as such which fans objected to, but "politics" attached to *another reading formation*' (Tulloch and Jenkins 1995: 172, original emphasis). In all such cases the club functioned as a reflection of the fans' selves articulated through superimposed values and beliefs.

The case of football fandom also demonstrates how fans, failing to recognize their own reflection, are unable to fully and rationally account for their own fandom.[3] The emphasis on (self-reflective) readings over textual substance explains the frequently coincidental starting points of fans' interest in their object of fandom. A Chelsea fan from South Africa, for instance, stated that his interest in Chelsea began with little more than seeing the name printed in the newspaper: 'I . . . noticed the word Chelsea amongst the teams. There is a suburb close to where I lived which was called Chelsea. Who Chelsea were, where they played, who played for them, I didn't know, but I decided that, because I knew the Chelsea nearby, I would support the team' (quoted in Sandvoss 2003: 38). Similarly, the editor of a Chelsea fanzine was surprised by the seemingly random and coincidental reasons that many fans give for their original choice of object of fandom:

> We just ran a questionnaire in some pages and there was this question, 'Why do you support Chelsea?'. And a lot of people have written in, 'because they played in blue'. And a lot of others use idiosyncratic reasons, and fewer people than expected have been ticking because my mum and dad did. (James Edwards, editor of the *Chelsea Independent*, quoted in Sandvoss 2003: 34)

The fact that fandom can evolve around as initially minimal semiotic configurations as the colour of a particular sports team's shirt confirms Jenkins's (1992: 284) aforementioned dictum that fandom revolves around 'not exceptional texts but rather exceptional readings'. Yet, to the extent that the fan text plays an ever more subordinate role in the construction of meaning, reading, as a form of interaction between text and reader, gives way to self-reflection. Leaving spectator sports behind for the time being, consider the very personal meaning that the fans in Cavicchi's (1998) study find in Springsteen songs. As one fan remembers, 'I remember when I first ... listened to ... "I Wish I Were Blind" ... I said, "Oh that's my theme song!" I mean that's – you couldn't have written a more perfect song.... how did you know I was thinking that?' (Cavicchi 1998: 135). Cavicchi concludes:

> Fans' 'listening', then, is not simply hearing and interpreting a song but an ongoing process of deepening the connection between their hearing and their lives. Fans always have the feeling that Bruce is reading their minds because 'their minds' are active elements in constructing and interpreting the music. (Cavicchi 1998: 135)

It is, then, not so much Springsteen who is reading fans' minds, as a form of inner dialogue through the object of fandom. In this sense the specific meanings constructed by fans move beyond subjective readings reflective of the reader's socio-demographic position and become meanings whose point of reference is not to be found in the texts (their object of fandom) but within the reader him or her self. Hence, they are a form of self-projection and reflection. What Cavicchi (1998: 59) earlier describes as a 'complex relationship with Bruce Springsteen through his work, a dramatic opening of oneself to another's experience', then is in fact an opening to an externalized image of self.

Accounts in which fans seek to explain the particular importance of the object of fandom emphasizing the way in which the object of fandom speaks to them, further confirm the self-reflective quality of fandom. The reflections of film critic Mark Kermode (2001: 126, original emphasis) on being a horror fan reveal a self-projective reading position similar to the above example of sport, television and music fans: 'I felt from the outset that beyond the Gothic trappings these movies had something to say to *me* about *my* life. I just didn't have any idea what.' Notably, the same passage is interpreted by Hills as an example of 'a moment where the subject *cannot* discursively and "rationally" account for its own fan experience, and where no discourse seems to be available which can meaningfully capture the fan's opening ... to a mediated text' (Hills 2002: 7, original emphasis). While, as I have pointed out, it lies in the nature of narcissism that fans do not recognize their self-reflection, fans' insistence on the particular importance of their object of fandom, as displayed by Kermode, points to the self-reflective nature of fandom. The different meanings constructed in the reading of fan texts are thus shaped through fans' self-recognition in the text, rather than through any inherent semiotics of the text itself. The text thus functions as a mirror.

The degree to which fan texts incorporate self-reflective readings is also evident in the debates regarding the relationship between academia and fan cultures, and the role of the fan as scholar, and vice versa (see Hills 2002; Tulloch and Jenkins 1995; Hunter 2000; Tulloch 2000). These are debates led by academics who, as fans, have to reconcile their readings of the mass-circulated fan texts with the critical distance to consumer capitalism that most academics in the field share. As Hunter notes in his discussion of Verhoven's film *Showgirls* (1995):

> For me, as an unmethodological (if not very inspired) fan, *Showgirls* has been an invaluable cultural resource. As I thought, talked and wrote about it I worked through whatever obsessed me at the time: the double life of the academic fan; the sexual thrills of consumer culture; the inevitable triumph of capitalism; the agreeable way that irony legitimizes an addiction to trash culture; and so on. It was a means of revising what Rorty [1989: 72] calls one's 'final vocabulary': 'the words in which we tell, sometimes prospectively and sometimes retrospectively, the story of our lives'. (Hunter 2000: 201)

Much as the teenage Madonna fans construct a reading of their favourite star reflecting their ambitions and idealized self (Fiske 1989a), so academics appropriate and rework fan texts to suit their own self-understanding as critical media consumer. Hills (2002) recognizes four distinct positions in explorations of the relationship between fans and academia. First, academic accounts portray the interpretative practices of fans as largely identical to rational academic discourse (Jenkins 1992: McLaughlin 1996). Secondly, they privilege fan discourses over academic discourses for precisely the lack of such rationality (Hills ranks his earlier work in this category). Thirdly, scholars such as Hunter or Hartley (1996) retreat to their supposedly superior academic position. Or, fourthly, they abolish academic conventions and subjectivity altogether (Green et al. 1998; Brooker 2000). Yet, in contrast to Hills, I would argue that it is not so much the point which of these interpretations enforce a form of moral dualism. Instead, the proliferation of this debate among scholars working on fandom is in itself illustrative of the personal need to meaningfully position scholarship and fandom in relation to each other in a form that allows the continuing self-reflection of the fan as scholar in the object of fandom.

In this context I have already discussed the various strategies that scholars employ to legitimize their own fandom relating to the notion of cult. Indeed, in many respects the reflection of fans' vision of self and the subsequent communication of such a vision not only to oneself but also to others through fan performances confirms the structured and structuring qualities of consumption that Bourdieu (1984) analyses so poignantly. However, there is a crucial discrepancy regarding the sign value of objects of fandom and Bourdieu's analysis. In Bourdieu's multi-dimensional class system, particular practices and commodities can be associated with corresponding socio-demographic groups. Equally, in the adaptations of Bourdieu's work to fan cultures, the cultural logic of the class system is shown to be temporarily subordinated to new organizational principles such as 'hipness' (Thornton 1995). Yet, each fan's hipness as subcultural capital can nevertheless be assessed through external signifiers, such as white label records or knowledge of underground rave events. In the above cases, these universally recognized denotations of the object of fandom have disappeared. As fan texts come to be 'interpreted' from different, on occasion diametrically opposed positions, they lose any objectively realized meaning independent of the interpretative position of the reader. I will return to the profound semiotic and textual consequences that follow from this in the next chapter. For now, I want to turn to the wider social and cultural implications arising from the interpretation of the relationship between fans and their object of fandom as a form of self-reflection.

Servo-mechanisms and limits of appropriation

Beyond Bourdieu's (1984) sociology of consumption, conceptualizing the relationship between fans and objects of fandom as a form of self-reflection also bears close parallels to another approach to the study of fandom introduced earlier: projection and introjection as psychological processes through which fans interact with their fan object. However, as with the notion of the habitus, there is an important difference between fandom as a form of projection/introjection and self-projection. Elliott (1999) in particular argues that the relationship between fan and object of fandom based on projection and introjection is one in which the fan seeks control over the object of fandom. John Lennon's murder at the hands of Mark David Chapman is the extreme example of reinstating one's control over the fan text. The shots fired at Lennon were Chapman's response to a changing object of fandom.

Now, for all the insights that Elliott's analysis of Chapman offers, Chapman's need to exercise this control over the object of his fandom – his need to model the world in accordance with himself – is undoubtedly a clinical, pathological exception. By contrast, conceptualizing fandom as a form of self-reflection allows us to account for the reverse process in which the object of fandom exercises a degree of control over the fan and thus enables a continuing relationship between fan and object of fandom despite changes to its symbolic basis. If we look carefully, we find that many objects of fandom undergo profound transformations during their lifetime. Spectator sports, and none more than soccer, but also baseball, American Football, Formula One or even snooker, have all undergone substantial changes since the introduction of multi-channel television. Not only John Lennon, but other pop stars and bands who have succeeded in remaining in the public eye over long periods of time, such as Madonna, Peter Gabriel, Depeche Mode or Michael Jackson have continuously refined their style, image and appearance. New *Dr Who* episodes following a twenty-year intermission, mark yet new directions to a series which underwent substantial changes during its first two decades (Tulloch and Jenkins 1995).

Yet all these objects of fandom have succeeded in maintaining and building fan communities. The reason for this is again illustrated by the myth of Narcissus: the relationship between self and extension of self is such that the latter is not a mere reflection of the former, but also assumes the appropriative power over the self. In its most radical formulation, Narcissus responds to the realization of his self-reflection with his own transformation and disappearance – as his tears drop into the water and his mirror image thus vanishes, he melts in vain, for a flower since carrying his name to spring up in this place. For fans' self-reflection in the object of fandom, this means that it is not just the fan who appropriates the fan texts, but that the text assumes the power to appropriate the fan. While the object of fandom is subject to a radical reworking and appropriation into a reflection of the fan him- or herself, the fan text gains structuring influence over the fan. The burden of maintaining the self-reflective relationship between fan and object of fandom falls not on the mirror image alone, but equally on the fan him- or herself. Through fans' self-reflective reading, the object of fandom, the fan text, becomes a narrative focal point in the construction of life narratives and identities. As Spigel observes in her study of Elvis impersonators:

> The impersonators ... delight in characterizing Elvis as the ultimate working-class hero, using that characterization as a point of identification with their idol. ... Along the way, their own life stories become intertwined with their recountings of the Elvis myth, in other words, their historical narratives provide the stage for their self-representation. (Spigel 1990: 185–6)

Yet, like any stage, it is a stage that shapes the performances which take place on it. Moreover, as the object of fandom becomes part of our fabric of self through processes of self-reflection, fans actively maintain this stage of self-performance and projection. Fans thus seek to emulate and emphasize parallels between themselves and what they recognize as external qualities of the object of fandom. Cavicchi (1998), for example, observes how fans stress commonalities between themselves and their fan object which are reminiscent of our earlier discussion of resembling and imitating. Fans from New Jersey, for instance, are keen to stress how they share a home state with Springsteen; others find such parallels in emotional experiences, or what they perceive to be Springsteen's very own interpretation of patriotism. Similarly, Mason and Meyers (2001: 813) observe how in the case of some Martha Stewart fans their 'friends and co-workers tease them by nicknaming them Martha and commenting on every Martha Stewart like-thing they did', indicating how Stewart as their object of fandom had become part of the publicly performed self. Yet, beyond resemblance and imitation, the actual origin of meaning in either the fan object or the fan becomes unclear. In fans' self-reflective relationship with their object of fandom, we cannot allocate the origins of personal beliefs and attitudes in either the fan or the fan object. As Laurie, a female Bruce Springsteen fan contemplates:

> I have learnt a lot from Bruce! I think I probably – I don't know which came first: maybe I had this philosophy and I didn't know about it and that's why I liked Bruce. But it could be the other way, that my philosophy came from Bruce. Which is certainly possible. But I don't want to give him too much credit for my entire existence. (Quoted in Cavicchi 1998: 134)

The content of fans' self-reflection – in other words, the image of self which they recognize in the object of fandom, would of course be of secondary importance if the object of fandom were a true mirror to the fan's self. In this case the fan and his or her reflection would always be identical. But, as I have noted above, objects of fandom are subject to ongoing transformations. Like the fragile reflection of Narcissus in the water, they are at risk of external interference. In this situation the object of fandom as extension of self is privileged over the self. As the fan object becomes fans' focal point of identity-sustaining self-narratives, fans are prepared to adjust to changing external textual characteristics of their object of fandom, even when they are understood to be in opposition to the fan's world view and self-image. The case of sports fandom is again illustrative here. The globalization of the labour market in sports (cf. Arabena 1993; Lanfranchi and Taylor 2001) has led to an increasingly international composition of club teams around the world. This internationalization is often at odds with the partisan, nationalistic and ethnocentric beliefs of a substantial number of fans. Yet, while a minority of fans finds it increasingly difficult to sustain their fandom of such clubs, many others adapt their values and beliefs to such changing situations (Sandvoss 2003). As one German fan of the Bundesligateum Bayer Leverkusen, who had initially stated his dislike of Dutch people, conceded regarding the team's regular forward Dutch striker Erik Meijer: 'Erik plays here and that's all right then' (Sandvoss 2003: 52).

Similarly, McKinley (1997) does not assume that female *90210* fans necessarily subscribe to the dominant ideological positions inscribed in the programme prior to its consumption. Yet beyond its seemingly polysemic textual surface, McKinley argues, the programme carries a singular meaning, which is enforced through fans' identification with the show's lead characters. Regardless of whether we pinpoint the inherent meaning of objects and fandom as McKinley does in production structures – thus implying a profound degree of ideological control over popular texts that is, I think, questionable – or in the social and cultural structures of contemporary life beyond the control of particular interest groups, fans are shaped and appropriated by their object of fandom in the way in which McLuhan (1964: 45) describes Narcissus's relation to his mirror image: 'this extension of himself by mirror numbed his perception until he became the servomechanism of his own extended or repeated image.'

It is, then, precisely because objects of fandom can be so radically appropriated by fans to service their own self-reflection, that they gain the ability to profoundly shape the fan. The fan text as the fan's extension of self thus positions the fan within social, cultural, economic and technological macro structures and transformations of contemporary life, such as globalization, rationalization and commercialization. From this follows the question as to whether fandom as a form of narcissistic self-reflection inherently ties us to an existing socio-cultural system.

Fandom and narcissism and the logic of capitalist exchange

In this context it is useful to conceptualize fandom as a form of self-reflection in the broader discourses surrounding narcissism in cultural and social theory. This is a dual process in which not only discourses on narcissism inform our understanding on fandom, but the self-reflective relationship between fans and their object of fandom also helps us to assess the validity of contemporary discourses on narcissism.[4]

Being a fan is of course not a universal human condition. It is based on forms of consumption and a separation between actor and spectator that are inherently intertwined with the rise of capitalism and industrial modernity and, more specifically, with twentieth-century mass consumerism. It is these historic epochs which have been linked with the proliferation of narcissism and social theory. The latter forms a particular background to Christopher Lasch's (1979/1991) still powerful critique of the promotion of narcissism in American consumer capitalism. Lasch portrays the self-reflective relationship between consumers and consumer goods, the heightened emphasis on the improvement of self and body, and the instantaneous need for ultimately unachievable gratification as a manifestation of a narcissistic cultural disposition. As part of this narcissistic order of contemporary culture, he identifies media consumption and fandom as a key pillar:

> The mass media, with their cult of celebrity and their attempt to surround it with glamour and excitement, have made Americans a nation of fans, moviegoers. The media give substance to and thus intensify narcissistic dreams of fame and glory, encourage the common man to identify himself with the stars and to hate the "herd", and make it more and more difficult for him to accept the banality of everyday existence. (Lasch 1979/1991: 21)

This striving for fame and success, according to Lasch, sets an unobtainable goal in the external reflection of the self. When the fan, placing himself in the media universe of fame and success, finally realizes 'that he can live not only without fame but without self ... he experiences this discovery not merely as a disappointment but as a shattering blow to his sense of selfhood' (Lasch 1979/1991: 22). Yet, the question here is how exactly one embarks on one's search for fame and extraordinariness. Lasch suggests that objects of fandom provide points of aspirational identification when he quotes from Frederick Exley's *A Fan's Note* (1968: 131) that half-back Frank Gifford, the focus of Exley's admiration, and Gifford's team, the New York Giants, 'sustained for me the illusion that fame is possible'. The thrust of Lasch's argument is then directed at those who seek to cross the divide between spectator and actor and to become famous in their own right. Fans on occasion strive to become petty producers (cf. Abercrombie and Longhurst 1998; Brooker 2000; Thornton 1995) and thus to gain (at least subcultural) fame. Ironically, though, it is precisely through processes of self-reflection that fans are able to put themselves into the media frame of fame and success without ever having to become media performers in their own right. The motivations and dreams of unknown contestants queuing up in their thousands to participate in casting or 'reality' shows, on the one hand, and of fans of popular icons and texts, on the other, may all be fuelled by a search for the extraordinary. Yet, through their ability to find the enjoyment of the glamorous and the outlandish, of fame and glory in their object of fandom as a reflection and thus extension of themselves, fans take a more subtle route to addressing such desires. In this sense fan consumption not only, as Lasch proclaims, fosters narcissistic desires but it also offers strategies for their fulfilment (even though such fulfilment is rarely complete). Paradoxically, then, the particular investment in an external object at the heart of narcissistic self-reflection does not lead to self-love but to the privileging of the external image and the object that embodies this image over the self. There are thus two conflicting forces within narcissism: self-centredness and self-love, on the one hand, and the partial abandoning of the self in favour of the external object of reflection, on the other. Sennett's work usefully highlights the first of these elements in narcissism. If what we are attracted to in the fan object is in fact our own image, then the object of fandom is always read and interpreted against the framework of the self. Everything is seen, as Giddens (1991: 170) paraphrases Sennett, in the light of 'what this means to me'. Hence 'nothing new, nothing other, ever enters the self; it is devoured and transformed until one thinks one can see oneself in the other – and then it becomes meaningless' (Sennett 1977/1992: 325). The Tocquevillean political vision that underscores Sennett's work here in his insistence on maintaining rigid distinctions between public and private life has been rightly attacked by Lasch (1979/1991). Yet, despite their ideological differences, Lasch and Sennett are unified in their emphasis on self-centredness and the decline in meaningful interpersonal communication, which in turn is associated with particular social and economic systems (see also Kovel 1980).

While I pursue these themes further when turning to fan texts in the next chapter, we equally need to examine the dimension of narcissism that these approaches overlook. Fans' motivations and performances provide rich evidence for this second dimension of narcissism as an extension of self through self-reflection. Through their fascination with their extension of self, fans, wittingly or not, withdraw themselves from the formal rational logic of capitalist exchange. It is because the object of fandom functions as an extension, and hence becomes part of one's identity and self, that fans engage in practices that evade, to use Weber's term, formal rational considerations.[5] The distinction between formal and substantial rationality in Weber's work is partly reflected in the difference between use- and exchange-value in classic as well as Marxist economic theory. Capitalist exchange, as the term indicates, is based on exchange-value, which is formed in the market-place between supply and demand, and can thus be expressed in monetary terms. Use-value, by contrast, is based on the actual benefits of a certain object, whether physical or textual. Now, through market factors of demand, use-value would always be reflected in exchange-value were it not for the possibility of capital accumulation through monetary exchange. In the Marxist analysis of capitalist exchange, it is through exchange-value that producers can create surplus value, leading to ever greater capital accumulation, further deepening the divide between those holding the means of production and those who do not, culminating in the inevitability of social uprising (so far, we should remember, of course, that only the final part of this equation has failed to hold true). The logic of capitalist exchange is based on the assumption that objects of exchange are recognized precisely as that: as external objects which can be evaluated in formal rational terms and exchanged through the standardized medium of money. Yet, this premiss is broken as the object of fandom comes to function as an extension of the self. Through fans' affective attachment, the use-value of objects of fandom thus spirals out of relation to their exchange-value. By making their object of fandom into extensions of themselves, fans give their consumption an inherently private and personal nature that removes their object of consumption from the logic of capitalist exchange. The cost of, for example, cinema tickets for the long-awaited latest instalment of *Star Wars*, a Bruce Springsteen album, one's favourite television show on video or DVD, will often stand in no relation to the pleasures and intense emotional involvement that fans derive from these purchases. At the other end of the spectrum, the immense costs of travel over hundreds or thousands of miles to see one's favourite sports team play an away game or to spend a couple of hours at Graceland seem to bear no justifiable correlation to any intersubjective exchange-value. As objects of fandom come to function as extensions of the self, they cannot meaningfully be related to exchange-value as the organizational logic of capitalism.

This is not to argue that fan consumption necessarily subverts capitalism. Indeed, the escape from the logic of exchange-value in fan consumption is short-lived, as ultimately any use-value is articulated through demand and thus reintegrated into exchange-value. In the first instance, media industries continue to generate profits through the sale of CDs, DVDs, magazines and by selling their audiences to advertisers. Even in the niche markets of fan consumption use-value is quickly correlated with exchange-value: at street markets, fan conventions, car boot sales or, more recently, on eBay we find fan memorabilia being sold at a price greatly multiplied from the cost of its initial purchase. Equally the desperation of the fan outside Boston's Fenway Park (see figure 5.1), willing to pay almost any price to watch his beloved Red Sox, which at the time had not won the World Series for 81 years, play the New York Yankees in a division play-off that featured the return of former Red Sox great Roger Clemens to Boston in Yankee uniform, illustrates how quickly use-value, however it is formed, is reflected in exchange-value. As Hills (2002) concludes in an insightful discussion in which he juxtaposes Jenkins's (1992) de Certeauian emphasis on appropriation through playful consumption with an interesting entry from Adorno's (1978) *Minima Moralia*:

> The fan's appropriation of the text is therefore an act of 'final consumption' which pulls this text away from (intersubjective and public) exchange-value and toward (private, personal) use-value, without ever cleanly or clearly being able to separate out the two.

Figure 5.1   Fans outside Fenway Park, Boston, in October 1999

> It is for this reason that fan 'appropriations' of texts or 'resistances'
> to consumption can always be reclaimed as new instances of
> exchange-value. (Hills 2002: 35)

We may take comfort from the fact that this process of reclamation
is not without its own pitfalls. It may be in the true spirit of Adam
Smith's invisible hand of the market economy that tens of
thousands of dollars will have ended up being pocketed by ticket
touts following the above described game between the Red Sox

and the Yankees. Yet the formation of such a black market economy is clearly not in the interest of the official institutions of the capitalist state. Moreover, not all attempts to gain monetary profit from fans' personal use-value of their object of fandom are successful: an episode of the BBC consumer programme *Watchdog* in 2003, for example, featured numerous complaints of British fans of *Buffy the Vampire Slayer* and *Angel* who had paid up to £79 to attend a one-day convention at which they were promised the opportunity to meet David Boreanaz, the actor behind the vampire protagonist of both shows. Predictably, the convention organizers had fallen pitifully short of fulfilling fans' expectations: fans complained that the convention was hurried, that the actor arrived late, and that they 'were told by stewards no touching, no talking'[6] during the brief time they were given with Boreanaz on an individual basis. Needless to say, none of the dialogue or spark they might have hoped for developed. In short, the convention organizers were never able to fulfil fans' expectations of what meeting *Angel* would be like, and thus to confirm the self-reflective appropriation of the object of fandom from which these fans derived their actual use-value of *Buffy* and *Angel*. While this rather naïve participation in a commercially organized convention is in sharp contrast to the social networks and conventions that have turned fandom into a social and cultural institution, it nevertheless neatly illustrates the fact that through our self-reflective investment in the external object of fandom, our consumption gains a dimension that can be fully integrated but never truly addressed in the capitalist logic of exchange on which the culture industries are built. This again echoes Hills (2002: 35), who concludes that 'the fan-based "use-values" interact with systems which belong to the economy proper, meaning that the existence of a market place for media-related collectibles is underpinned by the lived experiences of fandom'. Self-reflection and narcissism not only feed, but simultaneously interrupt a system based on intersubjective value and formal rationality through a projected sense of self.

Narcisissm and libidinal cathexis

There is, then, a sense of self-reflection bearing a kernel of social and economic change. In this context Herbert Marcuse's (1956/ 1987) initially widely publicized but increasingly neglected work on narcissism is particularly useful. Marcuse (1956/1987: 166) acknowledges elements of narcissism as a withdrawal from human interaction in the prelude to the myth: 'To be sure, Narcissus appears as the *antagonist* of Eros, he spurns love, the love that unites with other human beings, and for that he is punished by Eros.' However, Marcuse argues that those interpretations of narcissism emphasizing self-love, and death as its inevitable consequence, have failed to account for the particular relationship between Narcissus and the environment that contains his self-reflection. Through Narcissus's fascination with the external object that reflects his unrecognized image of self, 'the opposition between man and nature, subject and object, is overcome' (ibid.). Marcuse qualifies the singular link between repression and civilization in Freud's work, by distinguishing between 'basic repression', which is necessary in managing basic forms of human interaction, and 'surplus repression', which arises out of the patterns of domination and inequality that mark modern industrial societies, to which the performance principle of capitalism introduces a logic of exchange and standardization in which the individual becomes objectified. Narcissus thus becomes a symbol of a 'non-repressive erotic attitude':

> His silence is not that of dead rigidity; and when he is contemptuous of the love of hunters and nymphs he rejects one Eros for another. He lives by an Eros of his own, and he does not love himself ... . And when he dies he continues to live as the flower that bears his name. (Marcuse 1956/1987: 166–7)

Narcissus is thus unified with nature through the total integration of his libido in the environment that, as Marcuse notes, goes beyond autoeroticism and in Freudian terms constitutes a form of primary narcissism. In the same way as Narcissus is integrated into nature, fans' self-reflective reading of the object of fandom meaningfully integrates them into their respective cultural environment. For fans such self-reflection then constitutes a form of narcissism, that in Marcuse's words 'engulfs the environment, integrating the Narcissistic ego with the object world' (Marcuse 1956/1987: 168). Such narcissism thus forms a constitutive element in the construction of reality, rather than a neurotic symptom, and even a catalyst of social progress:

> The striking paradox that narcissism, usually understood as egotistic withdrawal from reality, here is connected with oneness with the universe, reveals the new depth of the conception: beyond

all immature autoeroticism, narcissism denotes a fundamental relatedness to reality which may generate a comprehensive existential order. In other words, narcissism may contain the gem of a different reality principle: the libidinal cathexis of the ego ... may become the source and reservoir for a new libidinal cathexis of the object world. (Marcuse 1956/1987:169)

In other words, by interjecting the object world with our self-reflection, which in turn reflects and expresses the ego's libidinal basis, we counteract surplus repression. In fandom the self-reflective meanings constructed through and from the object of fandom thus carry the utopian dimension of a different reality principle. As fans temporarily segregate use and exchange-value they juxtapose the objectification of the subject with the subjectification of the object. The fan fantasies surrounding a given celebrity or the self-reflective reading of television shows thus provide a starting point for a 'libidinal cathexis of the object world'. Nowhere is this more evident than in the realm of fan fiction and slash writing, where fans, in order to accommodate a self-reflective meaning, resort to textual productivity. The erotic relationship between Kirk and Spock, Batman and Robin, or Xena and Gabrielle that fans imagine and consign to paper in slash stories are self-reflective reformulations of gender relations and norms of sexuality. Interestingly, the intensely personal relationship between fan and object of fandom that is indicative of the way in which the object of fandom comes to function as a self-reflective extension of self is already identified as the basis of the progressive potential of slash writing in Jenkins's (1992) account:

Slash represents a particularly dramatic break with the ideological norms of the broadcast material ... slash poses complex and fascinating questions about the nature of female sexual desire, about erotic fantasy, and its relationship to media narratives; slash clearly speaks on a highly personal level to the women who read and write it. (Jenkins 1992: 221)

However, the question remains whether self-reflective reformulations of gender relations reach beyond the libidinal and sexual, and challenge the social, technological and economic principles of organization of modern societies. Jenkins (Tulloch and Jenkins 1995) indeed suggests so in his analysis of the work of fan writer Jane Land. Marcuse's conceptualization of narcissism, of course, rests on the premiss that through self-reflection a libidinal cathexis that overcomes divisions between the erotic, cultural, social, technological and economic becomes possible. Yet, since the publication of *Eros and Civilisation* in the mid-1950s, the overthrow of sexual repression has been largely confined to sexual liberation and has not affected the broader social realm (Foucault 1979; see also Miklitsch 1998). As Elliott (2001: 70–1) notes with regard to the decreasing attention paid to Marcuse's work after the 1960s, 'the psychoanalytic theorem which equates modern culture with high levels of sexual repression ... seems misguided at best in an age of sexual diversity'. Yet, we are, I think, misreading Marcuse (1956/1987: 166) when we equate the processes that have been described as 'sexual liberation' over the past half-century with the narcissistic practice that 'unites man and nature so that the fulfilment of man is at the same time the fulfilment, without violence, of nature' that Marcuse envisions. The reference to nature here, as his parallel discussion of Orpheus illustrates, is not only to human nature, but to nature as a whole, as our pre-technological, natural environment. And it is a part of this nature, the river over which he leans down to drink, which serves Narcissus as a medium of self-reflection, and through which he overcomes the opposition between man and nature. Hence, the medium of self-reflection will fundamentally shape its form (cf. Baudrillard 1993a). Contemporary fan texts, from cult films to sports teams, from television shows to comics, could hardly differ more from Narcissus's river in their technological and economic framing. In exploring the social and cultural consequences of narcissism, we thus need to analyse not only the self (or in our case, the fan), but equally the medium of self-reflection (here, the object of fandom). It is this investigation with which I want to conclude this book.

Summary

In this chapter I have argued that the relationship between fans and their objects of fandom is based on fans' self-reflective reading and hence narcissistic pleasures, as fans are fascinated by extensions of themselves, which they do not recognize as such. The notion of fandom as self-reflection describes the intensely emotional involvement between fans and their object of fandom portrayed in a wide range of fan studies. Such self-reflections are manifested on a number of levels: in fans' failure to recognize boundaries between themselves and their object of fandom, in a range of identificatory fantasies of resemblance or imitation, and in the construction of readings of objects of fandom that move from a characterization of the fan text to the characterization of the fan him- or herself. Drawing on McLuhan (1964) the chapter demonstrates that self-reflective readings nevertheless do not give fans full control over their object of fandom, but that, instead, fans are perceptible to function as servo-mechanisms to their own reflected image, incorporating changes to the object of fandom in their beliefs and performances.

However, the narcissistic dimension of fandom must not be equated solely with notions of self-centredness and lack of interpersonal engagement, as in the work of Lasch (1979/1991) or Sennett (1977/1992). It equally bears the potential to challenge forms of existing social organization, as the discussion of the reformulation of use-value through fans' self-reflection and of Marcuse's conceptualization of narcissism as a potential starting point for libidinal cathexis demonstrates. The degree to which this challenge might be successful in turn depends not only on the process of self-reflection but on the fan text as its medium.

6

FAN TEXTS: FROM POLYSEMY TO NEUTROSEMY

In the past four chapters I have explored different conceptualizations of fans, their practices, pleasures and performances. What unifies all these approaches – such as Fiske's conceptualization of popular culture as anti-hegemonic means of empowerment, Jenkins's de Certeauian notion of fandom as textual poaching, the various approaches linking fandom with forms of cultural and subcultural capital, Abercrombie and Longhurst's spectacle/performance paradigm, Stacey's and Elliott's use of Kleinian object relations theory, Hills's definition of fan objects as transitional objects, and my exploration of fandom as a form of self-reflection – is that they share related assumptions regarding the textual and semiotic structure of objects of fandom. In describing the multiple ways in which fans intensively rework the texts upon which their fandom is built (what I will call 'fan texts' hereafter) through interpersonal and intrapersonal processes, these approaches all imply that texts allow for a multiplicity of readings and uses – that they are 'polysemic'. In this penultimate chapter I thus return to the notion of polysemy by exploring the social, technological and textual premisses, which allow for fan texts to be read and appropriated in a multiplicity of ways.

Polysemy and neutrosemy

Given that the notion of polysemy constitutes a key premiss of the various approaches to fandom listed above, it is surprising that it has – with the notable exception of McKinley (1997; see chapter 2) – received relatively little critical attention since the first wave of fan studies, and John Fiske's (1989a, 1989b) work in particular. This is reflective not of a diminishing significance of polysemy to our understanding of fans and popular culture, however, but of a near-universal acceptance of the validity of the notion throughout the field. The fundamental assumption that (popular) texts are *open*, open to different interpretations and to different meanings constructed in the process of reading and by different readers, has rarely been challenged, not least because there is no *monosemic* text. Polysemic texts can of course have a clear and distinct meaning to an individual reader. Yet, from this it does not follow that any popular text can ever be 'closed' by its readers or its producers. Brooker's (2000) analysis of Batman in his different textual forms, from the first appearance of the capped superhero in comic books in the late 1930s to the 1960s television show and his appearances on the big screen in the late 1980s and early 1990s provides a useful example here. Following widespread public concern in the late 1950s over the possibility that the all-male household of Batman, his younger sidekick Robin, and his butler Alfred could be interpreted as an idyllic wish dream of homosexual partnership, which was propelled by the particular reading of the Presbyterian anti-comics campaigner Frederic Wertham, in *Seduction of the Innocent* (1955), editors at DC Comics introduced heterosexual love interests in the form of *Batwoman* and *Batgirl*. Medhurst (1991: 154) claims that this eradication of spaces of erotic speculation marked the beginning of an era in which *Batman* became a 'closed text', 'immune to polysemic interpretation', only to be salvaged by the colourful and in many interpretations distinctly camp television series in 1966. In doing so, Medhurst walks straight into the analytical pitfall of mistaking his own reading for the only possible interpretation. However clear the meaning of the Batman comics in question is to Medhurst, and however much producers of the comic have made truthful or seeming attempts to close down interpretations of the relationship between Batman and Robin as homoerotic, the *Batman* of the period in question remained a polysemic text. As Brooker (2000: 152) explains: 'It is surprising that Medhurst, who champions reading "against the grain", sees only one possible interpretation of the Batman story he cites. Why does Batman gulp when Batwoman offers to soothe him, if he has been transformed into an unproblematic heterosexual?' In the following, Brooker offers a very different interpretation of the story which Medhurst describes as 'closed', in which Batgirl's and Batwoman's admiration of Batman's masculine power and 'Batman's slightly pouty look out "to camera" as Batwoman flutters her eyelashes at him' (Brooker 2000: 153) appear as a parody and mockery of heterosexual romance. To falsify Medhurst's claim of a 'closed text', it is immaterial whether Brooker's reading is any more or less correct than Medhurst's interpretation (or whether, as we will discuss below, there are any criteria by which we can judge the accuracy of their readings). The simple fact that it exists contradicts the thesis of a text that can fully eradicate alternative readings. Instead, Medhurst's reading is a perfect example of how a particular reading – incidentally, much like Wertham's reading – is reflective of a particular socio-historic and professional position. Neither then, as Brooker poignantly highlights, is Wertham quite the homophobe reactionary he may at first seem; nor is Medhurst's reading of Wertham as free of prejudice as one might hope.

However, whether Medhurst has or 'has not really researched widely before making his assertions' (Brooker 2000: 153), he does his course no favours by resorting to an either/or dichotomy of open or closed texts. What transpires from this discussion is that *all* texts are polysemic. We cannot distinguish between closed texts, as for example the late 1950s Batman comics, and open texts, such as the 1960s television series. The determined researcher – in this case Brooker – will always be able to find evidence contrary to the assumption of a single interpretation. Instead, the key question is one of degree: of just how many and how easily different readings can be constructed from a given text – whether we are confronted with an unconfined play of signifiers or the different clusters of readings which Morley (1994: 255) describes as 'structured polysemy'. Polysemy, then, is constructed on two different levels. First, in qualitative terms, the text presents the reader with a multiplicity of possible interpretations which are consciously realized by the reader. It is the absence of this dimension of polysemy, to which I will turn later in the chapter, that Medhurst misinterprets as an indication of a closed text. Medhurst's misinterpretation is based on his rather curious oversight of the second quantitative dimension of polysemy that is otherwise dominant in Media and Cultural

Studies: that the polysemic text allows for different readings by different readers.

It is this question of the degree to which the same text offers different meanings to different readers to which I want to turn first. The quantitative degree of polysemy – in other words, how many different readings we find for any given text – carries significance not only with regard to questions of cultural hegemony that Medhurst (1991) or McKinley (1997) pursue, but also to the way we conceptualize the relationship between fan and fan object. The more that approaches to fandom emphasize the element of the reader's self in the construction of meaning, the greater the degree of polysemy they imply. This is taken furthest in my claim of a self-reflective relationship between fan and object of fandom. From such a self-reflective reading it follows that texts allow not only for a multiplicity of meaning, but for *any* meaning. Only if fan texts function as a mirror, can fans find their reflected image in the object of fandom. Having stated that all texts are polysemic, because they cannot carry a single, definitive meaning, this supposes that at the end of the spectrum polysemic texts allow for so many different readings that they can no longer be meaningfully described as polysemic. The notion of self-reflection in fandom suggests that some texts come to function as a blank screen on which fans' self-image is reflected. These texts are *poly*semic to a degree that they become *neutro*semic – in other words, carry no inherent meaning. By 'neutrosemy' I describe the semiotic condition in which a text allows for so many divergent readings that, intersubjectively, it does not have any meaning at all.

While this does not aid one in the effort to introduce a new notion, I need to admit that, strictly speaking, neutrosemy is a theoretical impossibility. If we were to divide a text by its number of readings, then a monosemic text (if it were to exist) would have an absolute value of 1. The more readings we find for a given text, the smaller the quotient of this division becomes (0.5 for two readings, 0.01 for 100 readings, and so on). Now, we can of course not measure polysemy practically with this crude formula, most of all because we will never know the number of possible readings spread over both space and time. What it shows, however, is that as the quotient decreases, it ever further approaches, but never equals, zero. Even if divided by an unlimited number of readings, the value of this equation would only be virtually, yet never actually, zero. Much as Baudrillard (1997: 27) concedes that true hyperreality and simulacra are ultimately impossible because 'there is no place for both the world and its double', so there are no texts

– objects of fandom or otherwise – which can be read in any and every way. Yet, much like 'simulacra' and 'hyperreality', the notion of neutrosemy provides us with a useful analytical tool in conceptualizing profound cultural changes. It equips us to explore whether, in the practice of fan consumption, texts are emptied of meaning and take on a mirror-like function. Or, to return to the above example, the question is whether Brooker (2000: 25) – after reviewing different interpretations of Batman as a creature of the night, a lonely bachelor, a re-creation out of tragedy through God's grace, Robin's lover, or a racist in a Klan-like costume – rightly broadens the title of Pearson and Uricchio's (1991) anthology in concluding: 'There is, I would argue, potentially no limit to the many lives of Batman.'

The suggestion that fan texts such as *Batman*, Manchester United or *Friends* are neutrosemic and contain no inherent meaning may nevertheless conflict with the personal experiences of many readers. However, it is important that we do not repeat Medhurst's mistake in substituting our reading for any other reading. In qualitative studies of fan cultures, we often encounter unexpected readings which are in opposition to the meanings we construct from the same text. Before further exploring the premises and consequences of different degrees of polysemy and neutrosemy, I want to illustrate this with a further example taken from Brooker's (2002) study of *Star Wars* fans.

Not being a *Star Wars* fan myself, and based on my rather vague memory of the initial trilogy, I would, if asked to summarize its plot, describe *Star Wars* as a story of 'David versus Goliath', of human struggle against both the inner and the outer forces of evil. I can equally imagine other interpretations emphasizing romance or fantasy. In no case, however, would I have interpreted the rebels' fight against the Empire as an analogy to the armed forces of the world's only remaining superpower. Yet, this is precisely the parallel which a fan in Brooker's study (2002: 22) draws: 'As a *Star Wars* fan I have always been partial to the Hoth battle scene in Empire ... I always imagined taking part in something like that, given my chance to fight against a tyrannical government and system. I think part of my decision to join the US Army, rather than the Navy, is part of those ideals', thus potentially seeing himself like 'the rebels fighting against an evil empire with an all-encompassing state and no tolerance for other lifestyles'. While Brooker (2002: 22) notes that this comparison of 'the US Army to a progressive, guerrilla force battling to overthrow a totalitarian empire would seem questionable to some', the point, again, is the possibility and actuality of such readings.

The limits of interpretation

If the endless lives of Batman, the most surprising interpretations of *Star Wars*, and fans' ability to construct self-reflective readings all point towards a degree of polysemy that is best described as neutrosemic, the question arises as to what distinguishes fan texts from other, less polysemic texts. A useful starting point for such a comparison lies in Umberto Eco's work on textuality and interpretation (1981, 1994, 2000; also Collini 1992). In his early influential contributions to the debate on the reception of art and literature, Eco (1962/1989) confirms our assumption of an open text, by emphasizing openness to different interpretations as a key aesthetic category. More recently, however, Eco has sought to balance his notion of the open work with further-reaching claims which dispute the possibility of a scholarly correct interpretation of art as such. Fortunately we are spared the question of the extent to which popular texts constitute art by the broad nature of Eco's argument concerning all forms of signs and language regardless of their potential artistic merit. Eco (1994: 33) argues against the 'deconstructionist drift' in the work of Rorty and Derrida that 'to affirm that a sign suffers the absence of its author and of its referents does not necessarily mean that it has no objective or a literal linguistic meaning'. He illustrates this claim with an episode taken from John Wilkins's *Mercury* (1641/1707), in which an Indian slave is asked by his master to deliver a basket of figs. The basket is accompanied by a letter written by the master in which he explains that he sends the enclosed 30 figs as a present. The slave, having eaten most of the figs on the way, is then queried over the whereabouts of the lost figs, yet adamantly denies the evidence of the letter. Being sent back with another basket of figs and an accompanying letter again specifying their number, he hides the letter under a stone before eating the figs, making sure he cannot be seen. Now even more strongly accused than before, he confesses and admires the divinity of paper. According to Eco, the master's letter contains information which ultimately is beyond interpretation and negotiation. Conceding most unlikely scenarios in which 'the original slave was killed and replaced by another slave, belonging to a different person, and even the thirty figs, as individual entities, were replaced by twelve other figs' (Eco 1994: 3), Eco argues that even under these circumstances the reaction of the addressee would always be that someone sent him or her a particular quantity of figs which is now less than described in the letter:

> Even when separated from its utterer, its arguable referent, and its circumstances of production, the message still spoke about some figs-in-a-basket. I wish also to suggest that, reading the letter, and before questioning the existence of the sender, the addressee was in the first instance convinced that a given Figs Sender was in question ... I do not think there can be somebody eager to say that it means that Napoleon died in 1821; but to challenge such a farfetched reading can be a reasonable starting point for concluding that there is at least something which that message cannot positively say. (Eco 1994: 4-5)

While Eco acknowledges the difference between the letter in Wilkins's story and modern works of literature, which 'cast doubt on even the supposed commonsensicality of Wilkins example',[1] he remains adamant that 'we cannot disregard the point of view of the slave who witnessed for the first time the miracle of texts and of their interpretation' (Eco 1994: 6). There are important differences and similarities between different forms of textuality. For once, the sign always signifies something, even if only, in the last instance, its own existence.[2] Yet, if fan texts had powers of singular signification similar to the master's letter, the fan text as object of fandom could not possibly be appropriated in the multiplicity of ways outlined here. It is therefore important to identify the factors under which texts lose their objective, 'everyman' (Eco 1994) meaning and become a space of self-reflective meaning construction.

Let us briefly return to the divergent readings of football clubs outlined in chapter 5. In contrast to Eco's example of the inappropriate Napoleon interpretation of the master's letter, neither of the readings by John and Karen are incorrect. Karen could easily point to a number of competitions such as the European Cup Winners' Cup won by Chelsea in the late 1990s. On the other hand, John's reading seems supported by the fact that Chelsea, despite one of the highest investments in players at the time and what was generally considered to be an abundance of talent, consistently failed to win the Premiership or to qualify for the Champions League. Ultimately, even a fan of Real Madrid, the most successful football team in the world, described his club as 'potential unfulfilled' (Sandvoss 2003: 30). Similarly, Chelsea appeared distinctly cosmopolitan in its recruitment of a large number of players of European, African and Latin American origin, while still carrying connotations of attracting a right-wing and racist following arising out of a history of fan disturbances in the 1970s and 1980s.

Sports teams of course engage in multiple performances, which have a variety of 'authors', including athletes, managers, owners, television and radio commentators and summarizers, newspaper columnists and fans themselves. Similarly, to return to our example above, Brooker (2000) documents the multiplicity of different texts surrounding Batman, which reflect their different producers, from the comic's creators, actors and television executives to Hollywood studios and directors. Objects of fandom, such as comic heroes, sports teams, rock bands or television shows, do not constitute a single text like the letter in Eco's example, but a wide array of different signs and symbols in different forms of visual representation, written or spoken texts distributed through various channels of communication, ranging from electronic mass media such as television and radio to everyday life talk among fans, out of which fans privilege some and disregard others. No two fans will have read, in Eco's analogy, the exact same letter. Nor does a fan text resemble the textual coherence of a letter. Narratives of popular culture still include information which in its clear denotation – like the number of figs in the slave's basket – can hardly be interpreted in different ways. There is little room for negotiation in the scoreline New York 3, Boston 1, the fact that John Lennon was shot in December 1980, or that the final episode of the *X-Files* was titled 'The Truth'. However, the way in which such information becomes contextualized within the object of fandom is subject to the fan's appropriation and construction of meaning. Consequently, given this role of the reader in the constructing and shaping of meaning, questions of polysemy and neutrosemy are dependent on the reception context rather than the text itself.

Eco's example, despite his insistence on a single, correct reading of the master's letter, already points to the two key factors constituting different reception contexts, which are instrumental in allowing popular texts to be appropriated as objects of fandom: the boundaries of the text and its distance from the reader. As Eco argues, a reader finding the letter after decades or centuries will still understand much of its original, non-allegorical meaning, yet 'could start from that anonymous message in order to try a variety of meanings and referents' (Eco 1994: 5). One of the first strategies of the contemporary interpreter of the letter would be to establish the context of the letter, depending on which it could entail a whole variety of meanings. By the same token, specific events or information within fandom, such as the above-mentioned sports result or the narrative of a television programme, may bear apparent denotations if taken in isolation, yet become subject to a wider variety of readings depending on the reception context. What I have called a 'fan text' here, the narrative structure of the object of fandom, then, is not a single text comparable to the letter given to the slave.

Textual boundaries

The definition of textual boundaries forms a key strategy that allows fans to construct a self-reflective reading of the object of fandom. It is a simultaneous process of inclusion and exclusion. On the one hand, the discriminative power of fans serves to maintain the object of fandom as a space of self-reflection. The *Beauty and the Beast* fans in Jenkins's (1992) study, for instance, draw specific boundaries around their object of fandom, which include some story-lines, but exclude others, particularly those taken from the controversial third series in which the show's plot – the number of figs in the basket – did not match fans' expectations. Instead, these fans turned to alternative narratives authored by themselves or other fans. Similarly, the account of the following fan who saw in Chelsea Football Club a reflection of his right-wing convictions is illustrative of the selective exclusion of particular signs and representations in fan texts: 'now they have got blacks, they play for Chelsea, we try just to see the shirt' (quoted in Sandvoss 2003: 31). The determination with which some fans uphold the boundaries of what they recognize as their object of fandom is documented in the case of a fan of Fleetwood Mac vocalist Stevie Nicks that Rodman (1996) reports. Shocked by Nicks's appearance on a late night talk show, the fan is in disbelief that 'this beautiful woman could look so worn' (quoted in Rodman 1996: 15). His reading and appropriation of Stevie Nicks as his fan object no longer matches the text he is confronted with. Remembering a programme on photographic proof with regard to the identity of Nazi war criminals, he finds a strategy through which to exclude the particular episode of Nicks's appearance on the late night programme from his 'fan texts':

> What I did was to measure the distance between the left and right anterior temporal bone and then divide that by the distance from the right interior temporal bone and the tip of the gap in the two upper maxilla teeth. I then performed the measurements on some older Stevie Nicks videos ... The measurements from the Letterman show DID NOT match the earlier videos ... I conclude that the individual on Letterman was not Stevie Nicks. (Quoted in Rodman 1996: 15)

While few fans resort to such drastic methods, this case vividly illustrates how not all that is associated with the object of fandom (even an appearance of the actual person behind the fan text) is recognized by the individual fan as part of their fan text. The object of fandom thus always consists of a textual hybrid, a meta- or super-text composed of many textual episodes whose boundaries are defined by the fan him- or herself. The reader, then, does not, as Rorty suggests, beat the text into a shape which will serve his or her own purposes (cf. Eco 1994), but cuts his or her own text out of all available signs and information like a figure out of a seemingly endless sheet of paper. The rise of new forms of textuality in computer games, which have attracted substantial fan cultures in recent decades (cf. Brooker 2001), corresponds to the needs of fans to define the boundaries of the fan text. As Jenkins (Hills and Jenkins 2001: 3) notes with regard to *The Sims*, one of the most popular computer games, 'perhaps something like 60% of the content ... will be generated by the audience' as players not only control the characters (and thereby strictly speaking select rather than create content through game play) but can also draw on a plethora of characters, settings, situations and artefacts created by themselves and other players and made available via the world-wide web. Such games spell out the narcissistic self-projection otherwise implicit in the relationship between text and reader: the reader/player controls the narrative universe as in *The Sims* or projects the self into the text as evidenced by the popularity of first-person sports simulations or 'ego shooters'.

The shaping of textual boundaries by fans is theoretically and methodologically significant. Popular texts thus function as spaces of self-reflection, not only through the individual interpretation of particular signs, but also through a selective process of which signs are part of the fan text in the first place. Consequently, methodological approaches to fandom which study a singular text or the audience of a singular text, such as a given episode of a particular television programme, misconstrue fans' object of fandom as well as underestimate fans' appropriative power.[3] It is difficult to imagine a fan of a single baseball game rather than a team, or a single episode of a television series rather than of the whole show. Even among committed cineastes, it seems, it is more difficult to find fans of a single film rather than a particular genre, actor (Stacey 1994) or director (Mendik and Harper 2000a). Out of the sum of the various narratives evolving out of the object of fandom, fans privilege particular signs and texts while disregarding others. As Tulloch describes such selection processes among *Dr Who* fans:

> Fans are thus far from being uncritical or sycophantic about their show. Rather, they establish an aesthetic history of 'classics' and 'worst ever' episodes which they circulate through the fanzines. This aesthetic is articulated quite self-consciously in their discourse about 'continuity' and 'programme structure'. (Tulloch and Jenkins 1995: 147)

The self-selected fan text as meta-text is in turn dependent on a narrative universe which allows for the meaningful connection of individual narratives and episodes through a number of industrial and technological conventions. The seriality of fan texts that seems crucial to this process in Tulloch's assessment is, not withstanding its commercial imperative (Eco 1994), particularly important in television and popular fiction as a device to erect a narrative umbrella beneath which fans build their own fan text from different episodes and narrative strands. Harrington and Bielby (1995: 177) describe how this narrative umbrella in turn corresponds to the everyday life framing of fan consumption as soap fans 'construct their own narratives by blending their viewing histories, memorable moments in the story-lines, personal friendships, celebrity encounters, inside information with significant events in their real lives'. Elements crucial to the qualities of the fan text corresponding to its everyday life consumption, such as regularity and repetition inherent in television series, are also evident in other textual realms of fandom, such as team sports with their weekly or even daily schedules or popular music with its cycle of tours, single and album releases, and its daily availability on radio and music television. In a broader perspective, the ability of fans to determine the boundaries of 'their' fan texts also relates to different accounts of the cultural logic of postmodernity. Jameson (1991) identifies intertextuality, which in turn allows fans to relate different popular texts to each other in processes of inclusion and exclusion, as the predominant cultural consequence of consumer capitalism, and hence as a premiss of a postmodern cultural order. Conversely, the increasing lack of external signification value and referentiality of mediated texts, which have therefore been described, as mentioned above, as 'hyperreal' and 'simulated' (Baudrillard 1983), has enabled fans to appropriate such texts to their own systems of (self-reflective) referentiality.

Fan texts as myths

The connotative fog that surrounds objects of fandom is equally highlighted in the description of fan texts as myths. While myth has formed a key concern of semiotics, and in particular the work of Roland Barthes (1957/1993), it is particularly useful in illustrating the amorphous connotative nature of fan texts as well as the preceding problem of what is part of the fan texts in the first place. Both these distinct characteristics of fan texts are highlighted in Rodman's (1996) analysis of the myths surrounding Elvis Presley. While a link between myth and the fictional texts may be apparent for the less verifiable nature of fiction, Rodman illustrates that fan texts based on real-life persona such as Elvis equally evade verification. He refers to the case of the so-called shoe shine myth. Drawing on biographies and other sources on Elvis, Rodman encounters numerous versions of Elvis's alleged slur against Afro-Americans, ranging from 'all I want from blacks is for them to buy my records and shine my shoes' to 'the only thing niggers are good for is to shine my shoes' (Rodman 1996: 35); yet the original source of the story remains unknown. So does the answer to the question of whether Elvis ever said such words, with a number of sources, including Elvis's friend James Brown, denying such accusations. As Rodman (1996: 36) notes: no 'fact-checking ... seems possible ... as none of the story's innumerable versions provide any clues as to who Elvis was speaking with when (and if) he made this statement'. Yet, precisely herein lies the particular nature of the fan text as myth:

> what I mean by myth ... is a narrative (or, perhaps, a cluster of related ideas) that people collectively believe (or believe in)

independently of its 'truth' or 'falsity' .... One of the things that distinguishes 'myth' from 'fact', then, isn't that the latter is true and the former isn't, but that the truth value of facts can be readily verified, while the truth value of myths isn't necessarily subject to straightforward proof or disproof. (Rodman 1996: 30–1)

In this inherently mythic nature of popular texts, which in turn results from the multiplicity of possible sources, interpretations and media (cf. Chin and Gray 2001), lies a further difference between the neutrosemic fan text and the letter specifying the number of figs in the basket in Eco's example. In popular fan texts there are no simple 'truths', no figs to be counted, and no accompanying letter gives the game away. Fan texts thus lack precisely the limits of interpretation which Eco insists upon in the scholarly study of literature. Instead, facts become relative within the meta-narrative of the myth, which in turn is reflective of the fan's values, beliefs and image of self. It might be a fact – even though racial categorizations can also be deconstructed – that Elvis was 'white'. However, whether this fact is interpreted within the myth of Elvis as an early symbol of racial integration, a white man making black music, or whether it is appropriated within the myth of an 'all-white Elvis', 'who corresponds to [fans'] nostalgia for an American culture that never really existed' (Doss 1999: 181) and whose image proudly shines from Confederation flags sold around Graceland, is ultimately not a question of the fan text (Elvis and his public representation), but of the fan's self-reflection in Elvis as fan object. As Rodman (1996: 38, original emphasis) notes, *'which* facts matter – and *how* they matter – ultimately depends more on the nature of the myths they are bound up with than on the facts themselves'. And these myths – Rodman (1996) also points to myths concerning sexuality, class and the American Dream, while Doss (1999) explores myths of religion and faith in Elvis fandom – in turn reflect fans' individual and collective appropriation of the fan text.

Myths, of course, are not limited to specific cultural icons such as Elvis, as Rodman suggests, but instead are an intrinsic feature of all areas of popular culture that serve as objects of fandom. Remember, for example, the different, even contradictory readings of Spock by different fan groups (Bacon-Smith 1992; Tulloch and Jenkins 1995). As Brooker (2000) reminds us in his discussion of potential clues to Batman's homosexuality, textual ambiguities are actively encouraged by textual producers in their search for the widest possible audience. Similarly, many top division sports teams now constitute what Bale (1993) has labelled 'super clubs' — clubs constantly and transnationally mediated and distributed, that are largely freed of any intrinsic meaning and thus foster contextual myths comparable to those of Elvis.[4] In this sense fans do not, as Lehtonen (2000: 148) argues, 'often attempt to use texts for their own purposes, which can greatly differ from those intended', but instead use texts in which 'what is intended' neither matters particularly nor can be easily determined. In the absence of a recognizable *intentio auctoris*, there are no facts in fan texts such as films, romance novels, comic books or television shows, but only contextual myths arising out of the fan's appropriation (*intentio lectoris*). The mythic rather than factual nature of popular texts thus enables fans to determine the boundaries of their own fan text by contextualizing facts and positioning these within the self-reflective meta-narrative of their fandom.

By juxtaposing myth and neutrosemy in fan texts with Eco's insistence on the verifiability and limits of textual interpretation in the scholarly study of literature, I do not intend to invoke distinctions between highbrow and lowbrow art. The point is not that Elvis's work contains no inherent meaning, in contrast to the sheer unrealizable density of meaning in Joyce's *Finnegans Wake*. Degrees of polysemy are instead dependent on distribution and consumption contexts. Franz Kafka's *Amerika* is a good example of an open work which nevertheless maintains limits of scholarly interpretation, which, as many students of literature will know, are fiercely guarded by teachers and secondary literature alike. One may like or even cherish the book, but it seems difficult to imagine that we could find a fan of *Amerika*, corresponding to the definition of fandom as a form of continuous and emotionally involved consumption. However, to the extent that Kafka has become a cultural icon, his grave in Prague a site of pilgrimage, his name or image a familiar sight on T-shirts and other merchandise, his work and life subject to various filmic representations culminating in Stephen Soderbergh's *Kafka* (1991), which in best Hollywood tradition erases the boundaries between the two, we move from the polysemic novel to Kafka as a space of popular myths, and hence a possible (and actual) object of fandom. On the one hand, the root of neutrosemy lies in the positioning of individual texts within popular myths and fans' self-selected meta-texts, which I have outlined above. On the other, it is also a question of mediation: the patterns of distribution through which any given text is encountered by its reader.

Fan texts and textual distance

The communicative consequences of different forms of mediation are highlighted in Thompson's (1995) notion of 'mediated quasi-interaction'. According to Thompson, the mediated distance between text and reader creates a non-reciprocal consumption context that facilitates audiences' ability to shape their relationship with 'distant others' as objects of fandom, in terms of both temporal and spatial availability (when and where we engage in fan consumption) as well as content. In contrast to forms of mediated interaction such as telephone calls or letters, the intimacy created in mediated quasi-interaction is non-reciprocal. While the fan interacts intensely with a particular text, the text does not talk back. Thompson illustrates this with the example of Barry Manilow fan Joanne, a 42-year-old married with children, taken from Vermorel and Vermorel's (1985) collection of fan fantasies and testimonies. While her fandom becomes an integral aspect of everyday life, in which she imagines Manilow to be her romantic and sexual partner, it is precisely the textual distance between Manilow and Joanne that allows Joanne's 'ideal Manilow' to be called upon to satisfy her needs, wishes and desires. The, in our terms, neutrosemic state of the fan text is thus dependent upon the mediated distance between text and reader:

> The non-reciprocal character of mediated relationships does not imply that recipients are at the mercy of distant others and are unable to exercise any control; on the contrary, the very fact that others are not situated in the same spatial-temporal locales as recipients, and are not normally participants in face-to-face interactions with recipients, means that recipients have a great deal of leeway in shaping the kind of relationship they want to establish and sustain with distant others. (Thompson 1995: 220)

The greater the communicative distance, then, the lesser the text's denotative power and the greater the number of possible interpretations. In their study of the cultural reception of *Dallas*, Liebes and Katz (1990), for instance, demonstrate that the greater the geographical and cultural distance between viewers and the locus of the programme in Dallas, Texas, the more interpretations diverged from the routine interpretation of the programme based on generic, contextual knowledge of western audiences. Similarly, the spectator of a sports event inside a stadium encounters a series of signs and symbols: the stadium's environment, its architecture, and verbal and extra-verbal communication with fellow spectators. In such circumstances possible readings are comparatively limited. Sports crowds can, for example, be sexist and fiercely partisan. On television the game event is largely freed from such signifying practices. Here the encounters between two teams, distinguished by the colour of their shirts, are open to a whole new range of interpretations. The meanings attached to Manchester United in the context of Old Trafford thus fundamentally differ from the signification value of the club recognized in its televisual interpretation in, for example, South-East Asia. In television football, then, as Baudrillard (1993b: 80) argues, the actual event is enclosed in a referential vacuum: 'no one will have directly experienced the actual course of such happenings, but everyone will have received an image of them. A pure event, in other words, devoid of any reference to nature.' Far from signalling the end of passionate identification in football, however, the referential vacuum is filled through fans' self-reflective readings of their club.

The basis of the emotional involvement with the object of fandom is therefore not hindered, but aided, by the distance between fan and object of fandom. It is not the distance between text and reader that has disappeared, as Hills (2002) suggests, but the distance between reader and meaning. In turn, the erosion of boundaries between reader and meaning in self-reflective fan consumption becomes possible only through the neutrosemic condition of fan texts arising out of this communicative distance. In face-to-face interaction, the text (the other person's speech and extra-verbal communication) is territorially and socially close, and the communication context is reciprocal. In this situation the 'author' of the text is present and readily at hand to correct our interpretation if it diverges from the *intentio auctoris*. Let us imagine that we are, while travelling on a bus, asked by a ticket inspector to show our ticket. Let us further imagine that we misinterpret the inspector's request because we are travelling in a foreign country whose language we do not speak: the reaction of the ticket inspector would ensure that we understand that we misinterpreted his request, and he would continue to give us verbal and extra-verbal clues – probably of an increasingly threatening nature – until we finally produce our ticket. In this case the negotiation of meaning of the text can end only in the reader's realization of the author's intention. As the text is distanced from the reader, its signification value lessens. This distance enables the reader to construct a specific meaning reflective of his or her interpretative frameworks. Thus, the greater the distance between text and reader, the lesser the distance between reader and meaning.

The importance of this communicative distance in fandom is most evident in those instances where it is eroded. Like a *fata Morgana*, the object of fandom loses its reflective surface the closer we come. When Sting fan Chloe, whom I discussed in chapter 4, unexpectedly meets Sting in a London pub, her fears that her reading, fantasies and daydreams revolving around *The Police* do not correspond with the actual fan text from a close-up perspective, are realized:

> And then I met them. And that crushed it for me. … it was Sting and Stewart in a pub. And they were being so pretentious … I was really shocked at the time, really shaken. They were having a generally bitchy time: I'm so depressed, I'm so harassed – all that business … I suppose it just shook me because I'd built up this picture of him and he didn't fit this picture at all. I felt sad, disappointed. … All my fantasies about meeting him … they totally collapsed. (Quoted in Vermorel and Vermorel 1985: 166)

The varying distance between fan and text also explains the different choices of objects of fandom between different fan groups, as categorized by Abercrombie and Longhurst (1998). Fans following their object of fandom from a large communicative distance can relatively easily maintain a self-reflective reading of their object of fandom. Yet, the greater the knowledge that fans accumulate about their object of fandom, the more they communicate with other fans, the more they narrow the distance between themselves and the fan text. As they move ever closer to the *intentio auctoris*, it becomes increasingly difficult to maintain a self-reflective reading. The case of football fandom is again illustrative here. Enthusiasts who follow their team to every home and away game often display hostility towards 'their' team, ostensibly highlighting the distance between themselves and players (Sandvoss 2003). Such negative readings of the object of fandom by enthusiasts are related to the frustrations that occur in the intense contact of enthusiasts with their object of fandom. Through their routine interaction with officials, players and club stewards, these enthusiasts are deprived, like Chloe upon her encounter with Sting, of the textual distance granted in mediated quasi-interaction. Similarly, authors of alternative fan texts are often those left disillusioned by their particularly close reading of 'their' fan texts: the female fans of *Beauty and the Beast*, who come to realize that network executives have little regard for their reading of the show (Jenkins 1992), the gay or bisexual *Star Trek* fans whose hope in a character with an alternative sexual orientation is, while on occasion fostered in the textual frame, ultimately eluded (Tulloch and Jenkins 1995), or fanzine writers seeking to counter the corporate power that controls their football clubs (Sandvoss 2003; Haynes 1995). These enthusiasts have narrowed the gap between the text and themselves so far that the text is no longer neutrosemic – that is, it can no longer contain a self-reflective reading. Hence, these fans fail to recognize themselves in their close reading of the object of fandom. These fans then move to forms of textuality in which their self-reflective control over the text is reinstated through their own authorship: niche media such as fanzines, fan club activities, and their own textual productivity. They do what the slave carrying the basket of figs should have done. When the number of figs in the basket does not correspond with the number specified in the letter, they write a new letter.

Open texts and closed readers: fan texts and (lack of) aesthetic distance

This emphasis on neutrosemy, fans' authorship of alternative texts, and the self-reflective nature of fans' appropriation of the object of fandom appear to suggest that the fan text plays a marginal role in forming the social and cultural consequences of fandom. However, the fact that neutrosemic texts function as mirrors enables a specific dynamic between text and reader in which the text's influence is manifested not so much in the meanings that such texts incorporate but rather in the absence of such of meanings. I now want to turn to the qualitative dimension of polysemy – in other words, the way in which the multiplicity of meanings is constituted in the act of reading of the individual fan.

In this context it is helpful to revisit the approaches to polysemy and reception in the work of literary theory on aesthetic responses (*Wirkungstheorie*) and the aesthetics of reception (*Rezeptionstheorie*). In what has become known as the Constance School, the early work of Wolfgang Iser (1971) is particularly useful for our purpose in its sociological orientation, in comparison to the largely phenomenological basis of his later work (Iser 1978; cf. Holub 1992). Iser (1971) argues that literary texts cannot create or represent objects but can only represent the reaction to such objects. Hence, the realism of literary texts is constituted through the act of reading whereby the reader carries out the reactions offered by the text. While in the case of expository texts the reader has the ability to positively verify such reactions before the background of factual information, literary texts evade such verification. Thereby the literary text creates what Ingarden (1973) calls 'spots of indeterminacy' – textual figures which cannot be ascribed a single meaning and thus allow for a multiplicity of readings – which require concretization by the reader and so allow for a spectrum of different readings, and hence are polysemic. In this sense all fan texts, whether they are evidently fictional, as in the case of song lyrics, comics or television series, or seemingly factual, such as sports events, can be compared to literary texts in that they lack a factual framework against which their meaning can be verified.[5] To Ingarden, who is mainly concerned with the literature of the classical period, the concretization of 'spots of indeterminacy' can none the less be subjected to criteria of adequacy. The problem here, as Iser (1978) points out, is that such adequacy can be judged only in relation to the aesthetic value and metaphysical qualities of the work, categories which themselves elude easy description and formulation, as even Ingarden (1973) concedes by arguing that metaphysical quality must be grasped through empathy. Consequently, Iser addresses the polysemic structure of literary texts through the alternative notion of gaps and blanks (*Leerstellen*): 'an empty space which both provokes and guides the ideational activity' (1978: 194–5). As such blanks, by definition, do not have any determinate content of their own, the process of connecting and filling in such blanks by the reader cannot, contrary to Ingarden's position, be judged in relation to the text itself, and hence as adequate or inadequate. In this sense blanks are constituted within the rhetorical structure of the texts and are executed in the process of reading. On the level of the text, blanks arise out of the discrepancy between reality and textual representation which finds no empirical match in the former, but can only 'build' its objects progressively through a series of views, which Ingarden calls 'schematized aspects'.[6] Thus a framework of referentiality emerges, to which there is no end, in that every new aspect introduced to describe the object creates a new literary object which needs to be defined. Consequently, the relation between different 'schematized aspects', despite their importance in the creation of meaning, cannot be ordered within the text, which therefore contains textual blanks:

between 'schematized aspects' there is a no-man's-land which results precisely from the determinacy of this sequence of each individual view. Gaps are bound to open up, and offer a free play of interpretation for the specific way in which the various views can be connected with one another. These gaps give the reader the chance to build his own bridges, relating to different aspects of the object which have thus far been revealed to him. It is quite impossible for the text itself to fill in the gaps. In fact, the more a text tries to be precise ... the greater will be the number of gaps between the views. (Iser 1971: 11)

Here Iser's analysis of literary texts corresponds with the particular semiotic qualities of fan texts. As in the case of the literary text, the number of textual gaps and spaces of negotiation increases with the growing density of description and information. As the earlier discussion of Elvis fandom demonstrates, it is through the multiplicity of information and views promulgated in the formation of myth that fan texts contain ever more textual blanks which allow the fan to order these 'schematized aspects' as part of his or her textual interpretation. This ordering of aspects and views in blanks, in literary and fan texts alike, is undertaken in reference to the reader and his or her horizon of experience. Hence, the relationship between text and reader is necessarily projective. As Iser (1978: 197) notes, the first structural quality of the blank, then, is that it makes possible the organization of a referential field of interjecting projections. Constituted in this projective field, both literary and fan texts never gain finite determinacy – a circumstance which, as Iser (1975) observes, often creates a sense of a 'forced ending' in literary texts, whereas the fan text, through seriality and through the fans' ability to define its boundaries, often lacks any ending at all.

However, there is an important difference between literary texts and fan texts once we move our focus from their semiotic structure to the projective appropriation of blanks, and thus the actual act of reading. The crucial question in the relationship between text and reader, and thus of the external qualities of a text, is how blanks or gaps are negotiated by the reader. According to Iser the reader, running through the various perspectives and schematized aspects of a text, can only verify these against the background of his or her own experience. As the reader's experience is thus projected on to the text, a spectrum of reactions arises, resulting from the conflict between the actual experiences of the reader and the potential experience represented in the text. Iser describes the two extreme ends of this spectrum as follows: 'Either the literary world seems fantastic, because it contradicts our experience, or it seems trivial [banal], because it merely echoes our own' (Iser 1971: 8). Iser's expectations of the qualities of literary texts leave little doubt that to achieve their purpose literary texts have to be located towards the fantastic end of the spectrum. As he argues elsewhere: 'The literary text ... takes its selected objects out of the paradigmatic context and so shatters their original frame of reference; the result is to reveal aspects (e.g. of social norms) which had remained hidden as long as the frame of reference remained intact.' (Iser 1978: 109).

Literary quality is thus defined through a text's function within the reception context which in its ideal disposition amounts to a willingness 'to reflexively correct one's values and attitudes' (Iser 1975: 233).[7] The multiplicity of meanings in literary texts thus has a double function. In the first instance, it is reminiscent of the common interpretation of the notion of polysemy in media studies, in that it occurs in the different readings of the same text by different readers. There is, however, a second, qualitatively decisive dimension: the multiplicity of meanings within a given text experienced on the level of the individual reader, thus creating semiotic ambiguities and challenges to the value position of the reader, thereby invites a reflexive dialogue between reader and text. On this level of indeterminacy, literary texts differ fundamentally from fan texts. It is precisely these semiotic ambiguities and challenges that are lacking when the fan of a sports team can so easily project his values and beliefs on to the team, when the Bruce Springsteen fan finds her own philosophy readily represented in Springsteen's songs, or when the fan of *Star Wars* finds no difficulty in relating the fan text to his own military career and aspirations.

Iser (1971) does concede that readers also 'normalize' literary texts by seeking to create a congruence between the different schematized aspects that culminate in textual blanks and their own experience. Commonly, this is achieved through a transfer of the reader's horizon of expectations on to the text; yet, even when the fantastic potential of the text does not allow such a transfer and instead requires a reflexive reorganization of the readers' experience horizon, this constitutes a closure of the distance between text and reader, and therefore a 'normalization' of the text. Once the text's indeterminacy is 'normalized', as 'the gaps of indeterminacy can be filled in by referring the text to real, verifiable factors, in such a way that it appears to be nothing more than a mirror-reflection of these factors' (Iser: 1971: 9), it loses its literary quality. Yet this normalization is the very process which turns the text into a fan object, stripped of any ambiguity, wholly familiar. Fan texts are normalized and familiarized to a degree that the boundaries between text and reader are eradicated and the text itself functions as a reflection and extension of the self. It does not invite a reflexive dialogue with different norms and horizons, but recognizes, and consequently reinforces, the readers' 'horizon of expectations' (cf. Jauss 1982).

The affirmation of fans' experiences is considered a key quality of fan texts in the eyes of fans. Fans' experiences are reflected in a rigid set of expectations directed at the fan text. Radway (1987: 63), for example, notes how 'romances may not deviate too significantly if regular readers are to be pleased. They expect and, indeed, rely upon certain events, characters and progressions to provide the desired experience.' Similarly Willis (2003: 137), in his study of the martial arts television show *Shanghai Express*, observes a 'clear sense of fan expectation' which 'informed the design and creation of the show'. Thus the show reinforces existing horizons of expectation by its fans, as, for example, 'the premier episode neatly produces a popular programme that celebrates their taste' (Willis 2003: 145). Harrington and Bielby (1995) emphasize the particular familiarity and respective expectations which soap fans direct at their favourite show. Brooker (2002) documents in great detail the sense of betrayal and disappointment among *Star Wars* fans following the release of *The Phantom Menace* (1999), which fell acutely short of many long-standing fans' expectations.

It is important to note that in all these cases texts are turned into fan texts through a relative judgement following the fan's horizon of expectations, not any objective generic qualities. What comes to function as a fan text to one reader may still possess literary qualities to another reader. Thus popular texts such as daytime and prime time drama have taken on a new, and substantially different cultural function in a different consumption context outside their locus of production (D. Miller 1992; see also Skuse 2002). However, defining texts through their reception context only underlines the contrary functions of fan texts and literary texts. From the perspective of reception aesthetics, fan texts can never fulfil the inherent aesthetic task of literature and art. According to Iser (1971), texts in which the reader finds nothing but his or her own experience are 'banal'. Similarly, Jauss juxtaposes the challenges to readers' horizon of expectations (*Erwartungshorizont*) in literary art with entertainment art:

The distance between the horizon of expectations and the work, between the familiarity of previous aesthetic experience and the 'horizontal change' (*Horizontwandel*) demanded by the reception of the new work, determines the artistic character of a literary work, according to an aesthetics of reception: to the degree that this distance decreases, and no turn toward the horizon of yet-unknown experience is demanded of the receiving consciousness, the closer the work comes to the sphere of 'culinary' or entertainment art (*Unterhaltungskunst*). (Jauss 1982: 25)

Neither Iser nor Jauss focus on popular texts in further depth; yet, it is out of the implied opposition between literary text and fan text that the aesthetic and cultural consequences of their difference are made clear. While aesthetic distance enables the reader to engage with the textual Other, its eradication in a fan text signals the collapse of the reading situation as potential dialogue between self and world. Here the circle between the aesthetic condition of fan texts and the conceptualization of fandom as narcissism closes: as all experiences found by the fan in the fan text coincide with his or her horizon of expectations, the fan text takes on the role of a mirror, and thus becomes the banal object of a narcissistic perspective. This lack of (aesthetic) distance between fan and object of fandom mounts a fundamental challenge to most theoretical approaches to fandom. It forces us to shift our attention from the aspects that fan texts enable audiences to do − whether they engage in emancipatory practices, construct a sense of *Heimat*, or create a mediating object between themselves and the object world − to aspects that fan texts fail to enable audiences to do.

Behind the mirror: the meaning of fan text

The final question regarding the relationship between fans and their objects of fandom, then, is whether it matters if fan texts offer a space for self-reflection rather than worldly engagement − in other words, whether it matters if fan texts fail to broaden our horizon of experience. The answer to these questions depends of course on the extent to which one subscribes to a social function of art and popular culture.

The concern with aesthetic distance is one that has traditionally shaped bourgeois reception of (high) art and literature and which has therefore in itself become a signifier of cultural, social and educational capital. For Jenkins, herein seems to lie the primary function of aesthetic distance, and he therefore disputes its validity as an evaluative category:

> When you see that look of sublime pleasure on the face of someone listening to classical music, which is not about holding it at a distance, it's about being awash in it, being affected by it, that's when that classical music consumption is connected to fandom in a very real way. Fandom is not about Bourdieu's notion of holding art at a distance ... it's about having control and mastery over art by pulling it close and integrating it into your sense of self. (Hills and Jenkins 2001: 33)

The contrast between Iser's and Jenkins's conceptualization of art could hardly be more pronounced. In Iser's (1978) functional definition of art, art that is fully controlled by the reader, integrated or collapsed into one's sense of self, is no longer art at all. Its function is instead inherently negative; negativity becomes the premiss of comprehension, a necessary condition to create the distance between the reader's horizon of expectations and the text.[8] Without this distance the literary text becomes redundant: 'communication would be unnecessary if that which is to be communicated were not to some extent unfamiliar' (Iser 1978: 229). Jenkins's definition, by contrast, is necessarily text-based, as art (as fan text) can only survive its integration into one's sense of self if its value is not dependent upon its relation to the reader's self but rooted in its symbolic and textual structure. It thus constitutes a liberal challenge to the work of reception aesthetics, based on a belief in art enabling a 'moment of passionate transcendence' (Hills and Jenkins 2001: 33). While Jauss (1982) has conceded that the concept of negativity has little to say about pleasure and enjoyment, Jenkins's essentialist understanding of fan texts is, I think, problematic, not only on ideological grounds but also in light of our reader-based definition of fan texts. Fan texts do not exist generically, but are a result of the process of reading. We cannot therefore turn to generic qualities in formulating their aesthetic value.

There are, nevertheless, three important points we need to bear in mind when assessing the relationship between fans and fan texts through the lens of reception aesthetics. First, a wholly normalized, self-reflective reading of a fan text might still fulfil an important social function for the fan beyond mere enjoyment, even if not constituting a form of communication. To those fans who are otherwise given an insufficient symbolic basis for performance in the social and cultural arena, such as the romance readers in Radway's study (1987), fandom as an extension of self based on their self-reflective reading of the fan text represents their selves, identity and desires to others in the social environment – even though this representation may not challenge the broader social and economic structures on which these fans' disempowerment rests in the first instance.

Secondly, reception aesthetics provides us with a useful tool for analyzing the reading of fan texts. However, while the relationship between fans and their object of fandom is at the heart of fandom, it does not account fully for all aspects of fan performance and social interaction. Beyond fan texts as fan objects are many texts, conversations and forms of communication which form part of fandom, yet lack the neutrosemic quality of the fan text. While in the mediated quasi-interaction between fans and their object of fandom the fan text cannot intervene in the normalized, self-reflective meanings that fans construct, other fans and texts which we encounter in our fandom can. Secondary texts, including, of course, academic studies of fan texts, may challenge fans' normalized, self-reflective readings. Moreover, the interaction with other fans through *in situ* consumption, everyday life conversation, fan meetings and online communication potentially constitutes an array of challenges to fans' (self-reflective) interpretation of the fan texts, demanding forms of self-*reflexivity* not dissimilar to those that Iser ascribes to reading of literary texts. The challenge to fans' horizon of experience and expectation consequently does not lie in the fan object but in the experiences and interactions that surround the relationship between fan and fan text – in other words in fandom as 'interpretative community'. As Eminem fan Natalie told me in a recent conversation, 'when I went to the concert, sat on the grass, met all the other fans – that broadened my, well, my horizon.' This fleeting remark, however, also illustrates some of the limitations regarding the significance of alternative texts in fandom. As Abercrombie and Longhurst's (1998) typology reminds us, the regular interaction between fans or even tight social networks are found only among some fan groups (cultists and enthusiasts). Moreover, the question remains as to how different fans move between different degrees of social organization and interaction with other fans. It is not unreasonable to suspect that the interpretative communities of cultists, and especially enthusiasts, include only those fans whose initial reading of the object of fandom coincides with readings of fellow fans to a substantive degree, and therefore is largely unchallenged through the interaction with fellow fans. As all forms of fans' semiotic, enunciative and textual productivity are, in the last instance, rooted in their reading of the object of fandom, we must also wonder to what extent fans' interactions can substitute for the neutrosemic lack of challenges to the horizon of expectations in the fan object.)

Finally, it should be noted that the notion of textual blanks, on which my conceptualization of the qualitatively neutrosemic aspects of fan texts is based, has itself been challenged. Most prominently, Stanley Fish (1981) has attacked Iser's distinction between determinacy and indeterminacy.[9] Fish argues, I think correctly, that our interaction not only with literary texts but also with the world always takes place as a form of mediation. Thus there can be no *determinate*, universally recognized objects outside the frameworks through which we recognize them. In turn, this also means there are no *indeterminate* objects, since it is only through frameworks of perception that these objects can be encountered in the first place. The issue, as Holub (1992: 27) notes, is thus primarily an epistemological one, and on this level 'Fish has stacked his argument so that he cannot lose' – at first sight that is, since Fish, like any other critic who disputes the possibility of textual determinacy, finds himself in the rather peculiar position of having to justify why his own reading of another text should hold any validity: 'Fish's objections ... call into question ... any endeavour to come to terms with the reading process, including, one might add, his own' (Holub 1992: 34). Taking his argument to its logical conclusion, Fish thus needs to argue no less than that all texts are inherently banal, precisely because they can be comprehended. I have already summarized Eco's opposition to such claims in the above discussion of limitations of interpretation. Yet the empirical study of audiences in particular illustrates the fact that intense emotional investment and pleasures in fandom result specifically from confirmations of horizons of expectations and thus verify the need to account for differences in reading practices. Epistemological objections aside, it is thus analytically useful to differentiate between how comprehension and appropriation take place, and crucially whether they involve forms of reflection or reflexivity.

This is further illustrated in the ideological importance of negativity that Iser ascribes to aesthetic dissonance. Here Iser's position ties in well with the cultural critique of the Frankfurt School (cf. Fluck 2000) and particularly Adorno's analysis of the production and consequently reception context of the novel in industrial modernity:

> Nowadays, anyone who continued to dwell on concrete reality ... and wanted to derive his impact from the fullness and plasticity of the material reality contemplated and humbly accepted ... would be guilty of a lie: the lie of delivering himself over to the world with a love that presupposes that the world is meaningful. (Adorno 1954/ 1991: 30)

While it is important not to resuscitate the debates of fandom as 'good' or 'bad' object, which Hills (2002) rightly rejects, Adorno's assessment of the nature of (popular) representation in modernity underlines the need to analyse fan texts in light of their aesthetic value. Adorno's critique of the state of the novel in 1954 can equally be applied to the by now dominant forms of representation in popular culture. Fan texts, like all forms of communication, are inherently ideological even, or particularly, if they have nothing to say in themselves:

> Telling a story means having something *special* to say, and that is precisely what is prevented by the administered world, by standardization and eternal sameness. Apart from any message with ideological content, the narrator's implicit claim that the cause of the world is essentially one of individuation ... is ideological in itself; ... the tighter and more seamless the surface of the social life process becomes the more it veils essence. *If the novel wants to remain true to its realistic heritage and tell how things really are, it must abandon the realism that only aids the facade in its work of camouflage by reproducing it.* (Adorno 1954/1991: 32–3, original emphasis)

Consequently, banality of content, whatever the function of a text, matters. To the degree that the fan text reflects the fan's self, and hence has nothing new to say, it becomes part of the trivial façade that maintains the social *status quo*. The accusation that reception theory is unable to account for the enjoyment of texts is therefore, I think, misguided. It is not so much that Jauss and Iser are unable to account for the pleasures that arise when the reader/fan finds him- or herself in the text instantly and without challenge to his or her expectation horizon. It is merely that they cannot account for this enjoyment as being a meaningful engagement with otherness, and thus a premiss of social change if in fact it is self-reflective. They simply cannot square the circle of self-reflective enjoyment in fan texts, on the one hand, and discursive engagement with the artistic object through aesthetic distance, on the other.

However, there is a final challenge to conceptualizing the interaction between fans and object of fandom as a form of self-reflective non-communication, which lies not in the context of fandom but in fan texts themselves. Iser's and Jauss's work on reception aesthetics, which largely follows Gadamer's (1965/1996) hermeneutic approach to language as medium, can function only as heuristic momentum rather than empirical truths in the study of actual audiences (cf. Groeben 1977; Schmidt 1980). Like the notion of neutrosemy, the idea that any given text will ever fully meet the horizon of expectations of a given reader is a theoretical ideal that reflects an important tendency but that, like neutrosemy, does not find its full match in actual reading situations. However much Bruce Springsteen fans may feel that Springsteen's songs describe their emotions and experiences (Cavicchi 1998), however much sport fans feel that a particular team they support stands for their own struggles and convictions (Sandvoss 2003), or however much *Buffy* fans' everyday life experiences of growing up resonate in America's popular paranormal teenage drama (Bloustien 2002), all such fan texts contain a residue of textual blanks and combinations of 'schematized aspects' that will elude readers' horizon of expectations to some degree.

Commonly, this discrepancy – given the inherent textual distance of mediated quasi-interaction, as well as fans' need to maintain their relationship to the object of fandom based upon familiarity – will be kept at bay by the fan. However, different factors can trigger a decreasing textual, and hence growing aesthetic, distance between fan and object of fandom. First, the fan text is more complex in its boundaries over time and space than single literary texts. As dynamic texts evolving over time, fan texts cannot fully meet the fan's horizon of expectations, and thus remain truly banal. The departure of a lead character from a given television show, the increasingly international labour market in professional sports, the new artistic direction of a given musician or band, or the death of one's favourite star in this sense possess literary quality, in that they increase the aesthetic distance between text and fan. In these moments of rapture, the fan text assumes a quality similar to that proposed by Iser for literary texts, in that it evades attempts at normalization and thus demands a reflexive reaction. This reaction can take two possible forms, in line with Jauss's (1982) later addition that aesthetic experience cannot only create, but can also reinforce or reject existing social norms. In the first case the fan resolves the discord between his or her values and sense of self and the now altered fan text through rejection of the former object of fandom. The fan text thus loses its significance, and the respective fandom comes to an end. The relocation of professional soccer teams, such as the move of the English First Division side FC Wimbledon from south London to Milton Keynes, which saw stadium attendance decrease dramatically before the move was completed, or the above-mentioned consternation of many *Star Wars* fans following *The Phantom Menace*, are two of many examples of social and economic conditions – the rigid application of capitalist principles of formal rationality in a search for the possibly largest market – manifesting themselves in fan texts, yet being rejected by a majority of fans. Inevitably the industrial frame of cultural production and its accompanying social norms will continue to produce such breakages, and thus textual blanks. However, not in all cases will the widening of aesthetic distance lead to a breakdown of the projective relationship between fan and fan object. Fans also overcome dissonance and indeterminacy by reinforcing the norms encapsulated in the fan texts, thus refashioning the self in an attempt to conform with its changing reflection in what I have previously described as the fan's tendency to serve as servo-mechanism to the object of fandom. If textual blanks and aesthetic distance in the reading of fan texts, and subsequent processes of a reflexive readjustment of self, however, are created through the economic and social forces which already structure the conditions of modern industrial living, fandom cannot function as a space for the creation of new social norms; neither, then, can fandom reflexively challenge the macro parameters of the production of fan texts, which in turn are reflective of the economic and social *status quo*. It is this predicament, the question of whether fandom ultimately contributes to a one-dimensional society, that I will confront in conclusion to my analysis of fandom.

Summary

In this chapter I have explored the technological and textual premises whereby fan texts gain sufficient degrees of openness to accommodate the wide range of readings in fandom, including in their most radical appropriation the self-reflective reading of fan texts. To this end I have focused on the qualitative and quantitative degrees of polysemy, and have suggested the notion of neutrosemy to describe fan texts which accommodate the widest possible range of contradictory interpretations, such as *Star Wars*, Batman or sport teams. On a qualitative level, neutrosemy follows from fans' ability to draw textual boundaries in the process of reading. This ability, in turn, is reflective of the communicative distance of mediated texts in what (Thompson 1995) has described as 'mediated quasi-interaction'.

However, while popular texts have different meanings for different readers, the qualitative level of polysemy, such that the text itself evades easy normalization for a multiplicity of schematized aspects, is eroded in the non-reciprocal, intertextual consumption context of fandom. As meaning in fandom is constructed in ever greater distance from the text and ever closer to the reader, fans' reading privileges self-reflection and reaffirmation of horizons of experiences and expectations over a reflexive engagement with the text (and thus the world) as meaningful Other. While the fan text/object of fandom is contextualized through other forms of social interaction and secondary sources which potentially challenge its neutrosemic state, the question arises as to what extent these in turn share the social, cultural and economic frames through which the fan text and its reading are formed.

7

CONCLUSION: ONE-DIMENSIONAL FAN?

In his critique of industrial capitalism Herbert Marcuse (1964/1991) develops an account of a 'one-dimensional society' in which all possible alternatives to the existing *status quo* of social and economic organization are being eradicated. He portrays a society which based on 'technical progress ... creates forms of life (and of power) which appear to reconcile the forces opposing the system and to defeat or refute all protest' (Marcuse 1964/1991: p. xlii). The one-dimensional society thus becomes totalitarian, not in the way of a single ruling party or class, but as a 'non-terroristic economic technical' system (Marcuse 1964/1991: 5) from which there is no escape. As Adorno (1966: 366) notes in his study of negative dialectics that 'only when what is can be changed, what is, is not everything'. Contemporary society, however, 'seems to be capable of containing social change – qualitative change which would establish essentially different institutions, a new direction of the productive process, new modes of human existence. This containment of social change is perhaps the most singular achievement of advanced industrial society'. (Marcuse 1964/1991: p. xlii).

A key objection to Marcuse's dystopian analysis has been the claim that he insufficiently accounts for the potential for resistance and change which, following the original publication of *One-Dimensional Man* in 1964, manifested itself in the students' revolts of the 1960s and which has subsequently taken the form of social movements which, alongside feminism and ecological activism, also include the formation of particular groups in the consumption of popular culture, ranging from music subcultures to the fans of television shows, comics or films.[1] In this sense social and cultural theory are not only important reference points in the study of fandom, but equally, the study of fans becomes an important empirical test in the formulation of cultural theory. To conclude my analysis of fandom, I will sketch out the lines of a critical dialogue between the two by juxtaposing the conceptual perspectives on fandom I have explored here with Marcuse's critique of the one-dimensionality of modern life.

The study of popular culture and its fans has been assumed to falsify the Frankfurt School's cultural pessimism and its proposed need for negative dialectics. In the empirical analysis of the micro settings of media consumption, a very different picture from such dystopian visions emerged: one of audience activity and negotiation, of the utilization of media texts for the specific purpose of shaping one's identity and place in the world. Much of this analysis has been case-specific. However, in their sum such studies leave no doubt that fans intensely negotiate, appropriate and rework mediated texts, and herein lies the basis of my own conceptualization of fandom as a form of self-reflection as well as that of most other theorizations of fan activity. Yet the case-specificity of most fan studies has also led to a limitation of their conceptual framework. Fan studies have often sought a too narrow and immediate framework of analysis. Explicitly and implicitly, what can both chronologically and thematically be described as the first wave of fan studies, explored in chapter 2, took its conceptual basis from Stuart Hall's (1980) discussion of encoding and decoding, which was concerned primarily with the nexus between textual production and consumption. Yet, it did so only to refute the critical perspective on ideological influence of Hall's argument in favour of a celebration of fans' ability to evade linear ideological influences, without questioning the ideological purpose and strategy of popular texts. In neglecting the Marxist focus on structural context so pivotal to Hall's initial analysis, the scope of fan studies was limited to the narrow question of who exercises control over the text, a question perfectly suited to qualitative and ethnographic empirical research, but limited in its analytical relevance. Consequently, the first wave of fan studies assumed a simple dichotomy of power, with producers on the one hand and fans on the other. From this perspective the social and cultural consequences of fan texts are limited to the degree that producers exercise ideological influence over the consumers or, alternatively, to what extent such 'indoctrination' is rejected. This diametrical understanding of the polarities of power in contemporary societies is well illustrated in the wide adaptation of de Certeau's (1984) description of the power relations as a situation in which the 'strategies' of such powerful (producers) are countered by the small-scale 'tactics' of the disempowered (consumers). For all its benefits in helping to understand and legitimize such audience tactics as an aspect of contemporary power struggles, producers and consumers do not so readily represent the complex structures of power and repression in contemporary societies. It would be naïve to believe that repression and ideological control are exercized through popular culture, or even mass media, alone. Both are subject to a wider ideological apparatus, in which they occupy more diversified roles than simply cultivating or rejecting ideology. Consequently, the possibility of rejecting or radically reworking the ideological framework of a particular media text cannot by itself keep the integration into an ideological system at bay. Nor does it necessarily create a distance between the consumer and the system as a form of aesthetic distance through critical reflexivity, or translate into the power of initiating social change. Equally, the absence of any ideological meaning and the appropriative dominance of the fan over the text, which reflects a lack of aesthetic distance, become themselves factors in maintaining the subsistence of the social *status quo*.

None the less, even recently published work, which appears critical of the emphasis on the semiotic and textual power of fans in the first wave of fan studies, still follows this broad theoretical path and fails to conceptualize the question of power in fandom beyond the simple polarity of media on the one hand and fans on the other. Couldry's (2000) work, for example, goes a long way towards demonstrating the cultural power of mass media in the construction of symbolic boundaries marking an extraordinary realm of quasi-religious importance, that extends beyond the simple ideological analysis of media texts. Similarly, McKinley's study (1997) of *Beverly Hills, 90210* fans points to the persistence of hegemonic perspectives in popular texts which still profoundly shape fans' appropriation of the object of fandom. Both studies invite a critical re-evaluation of the balance of power between media, fan texts and fans; however, neither moves beyond a dichotomy of power between mass media and audiences.

More useful in this respect are the second and third waves of fan studies. A number of fan studies following the initial rise of the academic analysis of fandom, discussed in chapter 2, found a new theoretical focus in Bourdieu's sociology of consumption. The particular theoretical benefit of these studies lies in their adaptation of Bourdieu's detailed account of the complex and multi-layered distribution and maintenance of power in contemporary society and culture beyond the limitations of bipolar conceptualizations of power between media and audiences. In studies such as Thornton's (1995) investigation of rave culture, Thomas's (2002) research on *Inspector Morse* and *The Archers* fans, or Jancovich's (2001) work on cult fans, the semiotic activity of fans is analysed not only in relation to media texts themselves, but also in relation to the social context of reception. These studies highlight how on the level of organized fandom, as in the cases of cultists and enthusiasts, social hierarchies are constituted and fan activity becomes itself a form of distinction, discrimination and preservation of existing power structures within society. They reveal the inadequacy of attempts to associate fan cultures with particular socially disadvantaged groups and classes as in Fiske's (1989a) adaptation of Bourdieu. From sports (Erickson 1996; Sandvoss 2003) to *Star Trek* (Bacon-Smith 1992; Tulloch and Jenkins 1995), different genres of popular culture have attracted fans across the class spectrum. These studies also qualify Bourdieu's work in one important respect: while they still account for the complex power relations that are structured and structuring through the habitus, they also indicate a shift from consumption practices as a signifier of class position to a signifier of self-identity. In other words, while particular objects of fandom may attract socially diverse groups of fans, this does not prevent fans from finding their self-image reflected in the object of fandom. However, the reverse process no longer holds true: we cannot deduce a fan's class position from his or her choice of fan object. This crisis of signification has a profound impact on questions of power in fandom. As one's habitus and self-identity are divorced from representations of class in fandom, they can no longer be conceptualized as *a priori* resistance against the 'power bloc'. Rather than functioning as a practice of subversion, fandom, through the adaptation of existing social hierarchies in a subcultural context, further cements the *status quo* by undermining the role of class as a vector of social change. In this sense studies of fandom drawing on Bourdieu further corroborate the disappearance of class not as a category of social hierarchy, which still persists, but as a space of social resistance as outlined by Marcuse:

> If the worker and his boss enjoy the same television programme and visit the same resort places, if the typist is as attractively made up as the daughter of her employer ... if they all read the same

newspaper, then this assimilation indicates not the disappearance of classes, but the extent to which the needs and satisfactions that serve the preservation of the Establishment are shared by the underlying population. (Marcuse 1964/1991: 10)

For all its benefits, this second wave of fan studies, which develops a more complex understanding of power and illustrates the limitations of notions of empowerment in fandom, signals the need to progress beyond its own initial framework, which in its core is based on the assumption of a correlation between class position and consumption practices.

We therefore need to focus, not on the objective socio-demographic position of fans, but rather, on the role of fandom in constructing fans' identity, in order to understand its social and cultural implications. A first step towards this goal is the study of fan performances that are reflective of the importance of fans actively shaping a sense of self through the object of fandom. However, it is important to re-contextualize such performances and move beyond the ahistorical nature of performance studies as used by Lancaster (2001) and other work drawing on Goffman's (1959/1990) explorations of the presentation of self, as the symbolic resources through which such performances take place are inherent aspects of the existing social and technological system. As Thompson's (1995) notion of mediated quasi-interaction illustrates, such performances are for the majority of fans – the enthusiasts who engage predominantly in textual activity within a tight social network aside – constituted within a particular, technologically defined non-dialogical communication situation. In Marcuse's radical vision, it is through identity and its technological framing that the total integration of modern consumers into the existing social and economic system is maintained:

> The people recognise themselves in their commodities; they find their soul in their automobile, hi-fi set, split-level home, kitchen equipment. The very mechanism which ties the individual to his society has changed, and social control is anchored in the needs which it has produced. (Marcuse 1964/1991: 11)

Whether we agree with the conclusions Marcuse draws or not, his assessment illustrates the significance of identity in any discussion of the distribution of power in contemporary society. This, however, is not to dismiss his critical assessment out of hand. Abercrombie and Longhurst's work (1998) in particular demonstrates the interplay between fans' agency (performance) and social and cultural macro structures (spectacle) as a dialogical process and thus positions fandom firmly within the context of industrial consumerism. Fans' performances and productivity, whether they are semiotic, enunciative or textual, do not only originate in audience creativity alone, but are also an inherent articulation, to borrow Debord's phrase, of spectacle as accumulated capital-turn-image. Fandom thus becomes part of the aestheticization of everyday life that has collapsed the distinction between art and life and consequently the possibility of reflexivity through aesthetic distance.

Two further considerations follow: the first is the question of the extent to which performance becomes a narcissistic performance of self. The second concerns simulation (and mimesis). According to Debord (1995) the spectacle of late capitalism can function only as ersatz for genuine productive activity. The prominence of the notion of the copy coincides with concerns regarding the authenticity of experience and social and cultural life in super-mediated societies in postmodern thought, as the symbolic building blocks of identity in fandom are no longer fixed in place and face-to-face interaction. Many sites of fandom, ranging from the televisual representation of sport to theme parks, verify Baudrillard's (1983, 1993b) conclusions concerning the prominence of simulation and hyperreality in postmodernity. However, such notions of hyperreality and simulation necessarily fall short of the complexity of popular culture and fandom, in that they too focus on only one side of the interplay between structure and agency in fandom (cf. Nightingale 1996).

The question that remains is whether industrial modernity sets insurmountable boundaries to fan performances as inherently system-congruent. The limiting of all symbolic resources forming objects of fandom to aspects of industrial consumerism whereby consumers shape such identities would preclude the possibility of fandom as the space of social utopia that Aden (1999) encapsulates in his notion of 'promised lands'. It corresponds, however, to the notion of fandom as a form of *Heimat*, as fandom provides the symbolic ground on which individuals recognize themselves in the signs and symbols of fan objects as they may previously have done predominantly within the territorial locus of their everyday life. The recognition of the fan in the object of fandom is thus inevitably self-reflective, rather than a meaningful engagement with anything new or other. In light of the discussion of textual blanks and aesthetic distance, we can conclude that the particular emotional quality of fan texts in offering familiarity and security arises out of a reading of the object of fandom in which the fan's horizon of expectations is met and blanks are self-reflectively filled by the fan. Hence, engagement with the object of fandom constitutes an interaction with fans' own vision of self, rather than any new form of experience. This, of course, as I have pointed out in reference to Morley (2000), is by no means different from the general moral and social ambivalence of *Heimat* in industrial modernity. Furthermore, it leaves us with the aesthetic dilemma to which Adorno points in what he appropriately calls *Heimtkunst* (1996: 129), the art of *Heimat*[2] – an art or craft form which has nothing to say but the false illusion of a meaningful world.

Both the conceptualization of fandom as a self-projective reading arising out of an unchallenged horizon of expectations and experiences and Marcuse's notion of a one-dimensional society are at odds with interpretations of fandom as self-reflexive (Hills 1999, 2002; Tulloch 2000), rather than self-reflective. The difference here is whether we understand the object of fandom as Other, and thus as meaningful external entity against which fans can be reflexive, or as fans' extension of self in which no meaningful distinction between the fan and the object of fandom is maintained, and hence, in Marcuse's sense, the assimilation of the self into the system is complete. Ultimately, the question of the social and cultural consequences of fandom thus becomes a question of its psychological premises.

There is a second reason to turn to theories of fandom which have sought to utilize psychoanalytical thought. Neither Fiske's notion of the pleasures of fandom as arising out of resistance or subversion, nor the assumption that fan performances become embedded in a totalitarian system of spectacle or one-dimensionality, can fully account for the pleasures and enjoyment of fans without which their regular and dedicated consumption of their given object of fandom cannot be explained. In particular, the work on fan fantasy and approaches drawing on Freudian psychoanalysis highlight the importance of affect, sexual pleasure and libido in the relationship between fan and object of fandom. Freudian psycho-analysis thus illustrates how the appropriation of fan texts opens spaces of fantasy through which essential libidinal drives of the fan's self are articulated. However, it has little to say about how these drives are meaningfully related to the object world, and how objects of fandom are formed out of a multiplicity of texts within an intertextual field.

What are needed instead are psychological models which

account for the dynamic relationship between fan and object of fandom. The notions of projection and introjection drawn from Klein (1946/2000) usefully outline the processes in which the particular emotional relationship between fan and fan object is based. Beyond notions of affect, the range of emotions stimulated and addressed in these processes can range from security to frustration, corresponding with the complex emotional qualities of fandom, which, as may be best exemplified by sports fandom, are not limited to pleasure and enjoyment. In fans' projection, 'good' and 'bad' aspects are externalized and ascribed to the object of fandom. Herein lies the basis of the exceptional disappointment, frustration or aggression arising out of situations in which the object of fandom takes on a symbolic form that can no longer contain such projections. Introjection in turn highlights processes through which fans internalize and thus utilize the external object of fandom in their own making of self and identity. The symbolic resources through which fan identity is built are thus, as Stacey (1994) illustrates, firmly anchored within the particular historical context of fan consumption. Yet, it is in this linkage between socio-economic conditions and individual psychological processes that the particular difficulty of applying notions of introjection and projection to fandom lies. Klein's work, more than any other psychoanalytic theory applied to fandom, is rooted in the clinical analysis of individual pathology; introjection and projection as an articulation of an assumed paranoid-schizoid disposition of the individual fan thus not only carry the danger of pathologizing fandom, but are also at odds with the social and cultural context of fandom as a widespread phenomenon of contemporary consumption. The same consideration underscores Marcuse's assessment that the notion of introjection as a mechanism of existing social organization has become problematic, as it assumes an antagonism between self and object world that indeed constitutes a pathological exception rather than the rule. Accordingly he argues that in the one-dimensional society this antagonism, and hence the premiss of introjection, no longer exists:

> Introjection suggests a variety of relatively spontaneous processes by which a Self (Ego) transposes the 'outer' into the 'inner'. Thus introjection implies the existence of an inner dimension distin-guished from and even antagonistic to the external exigencies. ... The idea of 'inner freedom' here has its reality: it designates the private space in which man may become and remain 'himself'. Today this private space has been invaded and whittled down by

technological reality. Mass production and mass distribution claim the entire individual. ... The result is, not adjustment but *mimesis*: an immediate identification of the individual with *his* society, and through it, with the society as a whole. (Marcuse 1964/1991: 12)

Now, we must not, as Hills (1999: 198) warns, employ mimesis, the hollow repetition of the external, as a convenient 'scapegoat' as it has been throughout the history of Western philosophy. Yet, this is not to say that Marcuse's specific socio-historic analysis is incorrect. The question of the social and cultural premises and consequences of fandom is thus in the first instance the question of how we account for the non-conflictual relationship between self (fan) and object world (fan text). I will therefore briefly compare the two socio-psychological models that are, I think, best suited to answer this question: the object of fandom as transitional object, and as extension of the self.

The first, introduced into fan studies by Harrington and Bielby (1995) and further developed by Hills (1999, 2002), appears in marked opposition to notions of one-dimensionality or mimesis. Instead, fandom is interpreted as a playful engagement with the object world, as a form of popular learning. The particular affection for the object of fandom as bridge between the fan's self and the object world in this interpretation is a meaningful device in integrating internal and external reality, and is hence reflexive rather than reflective. The scope of Winnicott's original analysis of the transitional object and its adaptation in fan studies is fundamentally opposed to Marcuse's approach: the question is not how external reality appropriates or limits the self, but how the self meaningfully addresses external reality. It is, in its core, an argument about agency. In their emphasis on fandom as realm of play and security and of basic trust, these approaches to fandom echo Giddens's (1991) understanding of the modern self in its protective cocoon constructed through social interaction, whether it is face-to-face or mediated quasi-interaction. And, like Giddens's work, which dismisses claims regarding the proliferation of narcissism, self-identity in these approaches becomes a form of balancing and compensating for the structural forces and pressures of modern life. The problem here, from the perspective of one-dimensionality, is the same as with introjection: it supposes that the self is somehow independent of its social, cultural and economic conditions.

In a contrasting approach to fandom, Abercrombie and Long-hurst (1998) highlight the role of narcissism in the construction of fandom. While they identify narcissism primarily in fan performances and thus in fans' social interaction, I have emphasized the self-reflective relationship between fan and object of fandom. Like the notion of the transitional object, the idea that the object of fandom functions as a mirror to the fan helps to explain the intense emotional involvement of fans, which is based on, as McLuhan describes it, one's fascination with one's own extension. It equally explains the often fierce resistance of fans to transformations of their object of fandom up to the point that semiotic productivity is turned into textual productivity in order to maintain spaces of self-reflection. However, conceptualizing the fan object as a medium of self-reflection carries profound implications with regard to its social and cultural consequences. In self-reflection the link between self and object world is immediate; there is no inherent opposition between self and object world, as in the notions of fandom as introjection/projection or as transitional object. The fans' (unconscious) self-recognition in popular texts thus requires in the first instance the negotiation and appropriation of such texts in order to create a self-projective reading; but on a second level, it guarantees that the symbolic basis of fandom is found within the existing conditions of production and consumption. Therefore, fans are liable to function as 'servomechanisms' (McLuhan 1964) to macrostructural transformations such as globalization or commercialization which come to shape their object of fandom. However, Marcuse's optimistic account of narcissism reminds us that the extension of self that follows from the self-reflective relationship between subject and object is a dialogical process. As much as the external object as medium of reflection gains the ability to shape the reflected self, the ego reformulates the object. Self-reflection thus opens up spaces of utopian thought in what Marcuse (1956/ 1987) describes as libidinal cathexis. As I have illustrated, 'slash writing' is only the most prominent example of how fandom thereby opens up a space for the libidinal reformulation of social relations. Yet, Marcuse's earlier work on narcissism (1956/1987) correlates with his later exploration of one-dimensional society (1964/1991) in an interesting way. The form of narcissism that Marcuse envisions finds its reflection in nature, human or otherwise, and it is from this amalgamation of self and nature through self-reflection that the possibility of libidinal cathexis derives. The symbolic basis of self-reflection in fandom, however, is very different. To the degree that objects of fandom are rooted in existing systems of consumer capitalism, fans' narcissistic self-reflection neither overcomes oppositions to nature nor erodes surplus repression, but leads to the further integration of the self into a one-dimensional society. Thus it is not only in narcissism as a process, but in its symbolic basis, that its social and cultural consequences lie.

While both these theoretical approaches to fandom come with their own difficulties, in particular regarding the application of psychoanalytic concepts describing either particular developmental stages or psychological dysfunction to the analysis of media consumption, the key question here is an empirical one. Put simply, it is the question of whether the relationship between fan and object of fandom is more accurately described by the pronoun 'mine' or 'me'. It is the question of whether this relationship is primarily one of possession ('mine') or of extension ('me'). My reading of the variety of quantitative, qualitative, auto-ethno-graphic studies of fans discussed here in light of this distinction is that they reveal an immediacy of identification that goes beyond a mere possessive relationship between fan and object of fandom. The sports fan's favourite team, the favourite show of the dedicated science fiction enthusiast, or even the more casual music fan's favourite song progress beyond what these fans see as a possession and become an integral part of their identity and vision of self, as much as their perception by others, as the debates on spectacle and narcissism as well as fandom and distinction through taste have demonstrated. The question of the material and symbolic basis of contemporary, media-based culture also emerges, then, as a question of the degree to which popular texts have progressed from polysemy to neutrosemy. The intense semiotic productivity of fans, as well as the nature of popular texts within an increasingly intertextual field of popular myths which enables (and forces) fans to take an active role in defining the textual boundaries of the fan text, confirm the increasingly reflective nature of fan texts. The absence of disruptive textual 'blanks' (Iser 1971, 1978) and 'otherness' in the fan text that constitutes the qualitative aspect of such neutrosemy further underscores concerns over one-dimensionality. It should be noted that the critical assessment of the disappearance of aesthetic distance is not an attempt to verify bourgeois or elitist sensibilities against popular culture, as the role of fandom in this context is by no means exceptional. Marcuse (1964/1991: 67) notes how classical works of art which have become part of the liberal education canon are emptied of their artistic potential as they 'are deprived of their antagonistic forces, of the estrangement which was the very dimension of their truth'. The aesthetic problem of fan texts, then, is one of form and distribution – as a form of increasingly rationalized, mediated quasi-interaction within the framework of popular intertextuality – over content. Yet, we also need to remember that objects of fandom are not the only texts and symbolic forms we encounter as part of our fan practice. However much our object of fandom may fulfil our horizon of expectation, it can be equally challenged through the context of fandom in our interaction with fellow fans and others in the cultural field.

For this reason alone, it remains important to continue to explore differences between different fans on the level of media usage, social connectivity and textual productivity, even though there is no linear correlation between Abercrombie and Longhurst's (1998) fan continuum reaching from fans to enthusiasts and increasing or decreasing degrees of one-dimensionality. I hope then to have presented a unified, yet not singular, theoretical perspective on fandom. Different theories of fandom should be seen, as I have suggested in the introduction, as different kinds of maps. What I have sought to do in this book is to order some of the existing maps of fandom and set them in relation to a map of areas of fandom, which hitherto had remained largely uncharted. In fitting these diverse maps together, I have inevitably reduced them in scale. Most importantly, however, we need to bear in mind what type of map/theory of fandom serves what purpose. In this context it is crucial to distinguish between the *model* of the ideal (self-reflective) reading of fan texts by fans and the empirical *reality* of fandom in which objects of fandom as transitional objects, spaces of empowerment, performance, projection or narcissistic self-reflection are constantly at risk of breaking down as a result of the social, technological and economic macro context of popular culture, which forms *and* threatens the very basis of fandom. As Marcuse (1964/1991: p. xlv) notes, one-dimensionality vacillates 'between two contradictory hypotheses: (1) that advanced industrial society is capable of containing qualitative change for the foreseeable future; (2) that forces and tendencies exist which may break this containment and explode the society'. Fandom as social practice, rather than as analytical ideal, radicalizes these polarities. Precisely because fans enter an emotionally significant relationship with mass-produced texts and commodities in which these come to function as extensions of the self, and fans are themselves shaped through their object of fandom – in other words, precisely because the integration into existing socio-economic systems is so complete in fandom – the realization of the one-dimensionality of such systems is accelerated. It is in the 'little breakages' between fan and object of fandom in the relationship, which leave fans disillusioned and sometimes disenfranchized, that fandom's progressive negative potential lies. Fandom, in pushing the distinction between use- and exchange-value at the heart of industrial consumerism to its extreme, thus oscillates between affirmation and rejection of existing social and economic conditions; between affirmation of the *status quo* and protest against what is, as a form of, in Marcuse's (1964/1991) words, 'Great Refusal'.

While fandom reflects the conflicting forces of modern consumption — its importance as a symbolic resource in the formation of identity and in the positioning of one's self in the modern world, on the one hand, and the integration of the self into the dominant economic, social and cultural conditions of industrial modernity, on the other — it is, in every sense, a mirror of consumption. If we look closely, there is a lot to discover.

NOTES

Chapter 1 Introduction: Representing Fandom

1 Similar plots revolving around fans include Edward Bianchi's identically titled *The Fan* (1981), the West German *Der Fan* (1982) and Stephen King's *Misery* (1990).

2 Few cases illustrate this better than the press coverage following the Hillsborough disaster in April 1989, when ninety-six Liverpool fans were crushed to death in an overcrowded section of the ground. The British tabloid paper the *Sun* quickly blamed Liverpool supporters for the disaster, pointing the finger at Liverpool fans who were alleged by the paper to have kept drinking and even to have pickpocketed those injured and fatally wounded. The following public inquiry revealed that the disaster was in fact a result of policing errors, misguided practices of crowd management, such as fencing in spectators and years of substantial under-investment in ground facilities.

3 See for example Hills on Žižek's erroneous belief that *Star Wars* was directed by Steven Spielberg (Hills and Jenkins 2001).

Chapter 2 The Dominant Discourse of Resistance: Fandom and Power

1 Madonna and the contradictions within her public image have attracted particular academic attention (cf. Miklitsch 1998): see for example the anthologies by Schwichtenberg (1993), Sexton (1993), and Frank and Smith (1993), as well as sections dedicated to Madonna in the work of Tester (1994) and Kellner (1995). With few exceptions (Brown and Schulze 1990), such work

focuses on style and textual analysis, and thus touches only fleetingly on empirical audience research.

2 See also Evans (1990) on the problem of identifying oppositional readings if taking into account a particular group or subcultural context of audiences' readings.

3 While Bacon-Smith's conclusions need to be read against the particular socio-cultural climate of late 1980s American suburbia, Brooker's (2002: 133) recent study of *Star Wars* fandom indicates that the vast majority of slash writers still shun public disclosure: 'the slash authors, even the slash readers I corresponded with, all requested that I refer to them only by pseudonyms, for fear that their employers or families would discover their involvement in the genre'.

4 While such fans tend to fall outside the investigative scope of qualitative fan studies, given the methodological difficulties of recruiting fans beyond established fan communities and networks, my research on football fandom (Sandvoss 2003), in which I adopted a sampling strategy that included fans who do not engage in textual productivity or participate in fan communities, suggests that there is no correlation between degrees of affect or pleasure and textual or enunciative productivity.

5 Qualitative research on football fandom provides a particularly clear picture of the size of these different fan groups. A 2001 survey of the five largest European media markets – Germany, France, Spain, Italy and England/Wales – revealed that out of the 170 million viewers over the age of 14 who were said to be interested in football, 69 per cent watched football at least once or twice a week on television (Sportfive 2002), yet only 5 per cent had attended games regularly during this period, and a mere 3 per cent had been to more than twenty matches.

6 Hills also challenges Thornton's understanding of fan subcultures on the grounds that her own class position with regard to academic employment remains unexplored: 'the value system of the cultural studies academic is tacitly assumed but never subjected to the same analysis as that of her respondents' (Hills 2002: 54). Yet, Thornton (1995: 162) is aware that her own study, like any other sociological discourses 'reflexively restructure their subject matter' (Giddens 1990: 43), while a close analysis of cultural capital in the area of academic employment and publishing simply lies outside her subject matter.

7 Grant (2000) highlights the different classifications of *The*

Cabinet of Dr. Caligari (1919), which is identified as 'the cult film par excellence' by Hoberman and Rosenbaum (1983), while the same film finds no mention in other work on cult movies (Peary 1981).

Chapter 3   A Text Called Home: Fandom between Performance and Place

1 For a detailed discussion of such romanticized versions of pre-modern life in various critiques of modernity, see Morley and Robins (1995).

Chapter 4   The Inner Fan: Fandom and Psychoanalysis

1 Freud's work, and in particular his claims with regard to gender (Chodorow 1978; Mitchell 1974; Kristeva 1981), have attracted more critical attention than, perhaps with the exception of Marx, the work of any other modern theorist.
2 For easily accessible and concise introductions to Freud see Elliott (2001: ch. 1; 2002: ch. 2) and Craib (2001).
3 Compare also our earlier discussion of the depiction of physical beauty in *90210* by McKinley (1997).
4 In addition to the extreme cases reported by Elliott, see also the case of Nick Hayward fan Cheryl reported by Vermorel and Vermorel (1985).
5 The trend towards pre-literary television programming, such as the BBC's *Teletubbies*, might, for better or for worse, overcome the otherwise delayed entry of television programming into a transitional space for the child.

Chapter 5   Fandom as Extension of Self: Self-Reflection and Narcissism

1 See 'R.I.P. Jennicam' under 'http://news.bbc.co.uk/2/hi/uk_news/magazine/3360063.stm' (accessed 20 April 2004).
2 See also Eco (2000), who describes television as a 'magnifying prosthesis'.
3 It is important to distinguish between the *recognition* and *awareness* of one's self-reflection. Throughout fan studies we find examples of fans who are aware that their object of fandom has a self-reflective function for them – my own fandom of given sports teams included. Yet, being aware of the fact that this self-

reflection exists, does not mean that we consciously recognize ourselves in the object of fandom, as this recognition of the image of self would no longer allow us to maintain our fascination with the self not as self but in its externalized form – the form of recognition that seals Narcissus's demise.

4 Narcissism has also formed a key concern in psychoanalytic theory, from Freud's (1914/1984) analysis, in which narcissism compensates for the loss of self-unity and omnipotence, to Lacan's work on the mirror stage. While I will turn to Freud in relation to Marcuse's work on narcissism (1956/1987), Lacan's (1949/2000) work is limited in its potential contribution to the analysis of fandom. Lacan describes the process of misrecognition when the infant first discovers its reflection in the mirror and, confronted with his or her own motor inabilities, constructs an 'Ideal-I' which is inherently imagined. To Lacan there is then no connecting structure between the super-ego and the id, for there is no ego. With nothing left to analyse but the mirror through which the void of ego is filled, Lacan's unrivalled status as theorist-of-choice in text-centred cultural analysis is easily explained. Yet, there is no room in Lacan's work for the process of how and in what reflecting surface one finds a mirror. As Castoriadis (1989), in his critique of Lacan, observes, Lacan's account fails to conceptualize how the self recognizes the self in the mirror if it has no capacity to create meaning. Here Lacan's most famous interpreter, Slavoj Žižek (1989, 1991), more usefully argues that the inherent lack of self is supplemented through enjoyment and fantasy, which constitute a core of self in the absence of an ego.

5 Weber distinguishes between formal rationality and substantive rationality, the first reflective of micro, system-inherent considerations, the latter of the universal consequences of a given decision.

6 For a brief summary of the item see 'http://www.bbc.co.uk/watchdog/reports/holidays9.shtml'.

Chapter 6   Fan Texts: from Polysemy to Neutrosemy

1 Eco refers here specifically to James Joyce's *Finnegans Wake*.

2 As Eco (1994: 7) points out, 'even in the case of self-voiding texts ... we have semiosic objects which without any shade of doubt speak of their own impossibility. Let us be realistic: there is nothing more meaningful than a text which asserts that there is no meaning.'

3 Tulloch (Tulloch and Jenkins 1995: 126), for example, remarks that the episode chosen by Fiske (1983) for his analysis of *Dr Who*, 'The Creature from the Pit', 'regularly ranks in the fans' "all-time low" lists'; Tulloch therefore wonders whether, 'if these textual accounts focus on what fans see as the untypical, how can we be more sure that the audience interviews do not do the same?' (see also McKee 2001).

4 Teams such as the Glasgow Rangers, for example, have actively sought to overcome the confinements and limitations of market appeal arising from their intensely signifying history and have sought to reposition themselves as a club fostering a multiplicity of possible meanings and myths (Sandvoss 2003).

5 This is also illustrated in Brooker's (2000) brief discussion of Ingarden's and Iser's work in relation to the possibility of different readings of Batman. However, Brooker quickly moves on to Fish's (1980) conceptualization of the reading process, without acknowledging the contradiction between Iser's and Fish's work.

6 As Iser (1978: 170) points out, the word 'aspects' commonly used in English translations of Ingarden is somewhat misleading here. Ingarden's 'schematisierte Ansichten' is more accurately translated as 'views', 'as the reference is primarily to the presentation rather than to the existence of such aspects'.

7 Miller translates this passage as 'compelled to revise those preconceptions' (Iser 1971: 9), yet the notion of reflexivity is clearly emphasized in the original ('reflexiven Korrektur').

8 Despite accusations of political conservatism and 'liberal humanist ideology' (Eagleton 1983: 79; see also Lentricchia 1980), Iser's work here echoes the key aesthetic propositions of the Frankfurt School (Adorno 1966). Iser and Jauss have also been attacked for their lack of post-structuralist commitment and inability to account for the 'play' of the signifier (De Man 1982: p. xix). Yet, here it seems that De Man's argument holds true at best on the rhetorical level rather than the empirical, as the spectrum of reading outlined by Iser allows us to conceptualize precisely the variations of reading resulting from a crisis of signification.

9 For a discussion of the potential benefits of Fish's (1980) own work in the study of fandom, see Lindlof et al. 1998.

Chapter 7   Conclusion: One-Dimensional Fan?

1 For a detailed critical appreciation of Marcuse's work see Kellner (1984) as well as two recent anthologies edited by Bokina and Lukes (1994) and Abromeit and Cobb (2003). A useful summary of the critique of Marcuse's work – which to address in detail lies beyond the scope of my work here – is provided by Cobb, who focuses in particular on the critical objections of McIntyre, Foucault and Rorty. Yet, Cobb (2003: 185) argues that despite the hostility displayed by such critics – and many outside the academic system, such as Ronald Reagan during his time as governor of California and former vice-president Spiro Agnew – they strikingly leave 'Marcuse's devastating critique of contemporary capitalism ... untouched'.

2 The English translation here omits Adorno's original term in favour of the somewhat unfortunate 'local-color commercialism', implying a territorial focus of such art which in fact is often absent, in particular in the formation of the post-war art form *Heimatfilm* (see Kaes 1989).

REFERENCES

Abercrombie, N. and Longhurst, B. (1998) *Audiences: A Sociological Theory of Performance and Imagination*, London: Sage.

Abromeit, J. and Cobb, W. M. (eds) (2003) *Herbert Marcuse: A Critical Reader*, New York and London: Routledge.

Aden, R. C. (1999) *Popular Stories and Promised Lands: Fan Culture and Symbolic Pilgrimages*, Tuscaloosa and London: University of Alabama Press.

Adorno, T. W. (1954/1991) 'The position of the narrator in the contemporary novel', in R. Tiedemann (ed.), *Notes to Literature*, New York: Columbia University Press.

Adorno, T. W. (1966) *Negative Dialektik*, Frankfurt am Main: Suhrkamp.

Adorno, T. W. (1978) *Minima Moralia: Reflections from Damaged Life*, London: Verso.

Adorno, T. W. (1996) 'Standort des Erzählers im zeitgenössischen Roman', D. Kimmich, R. G. Renner and B. Stiegler (eds), *Texte zur Literaturtheorie der Gegenwart*, Stuttgart: Reclam.

Allen, R. C. (1995) *To Be Continued . . .: Soap Operas Around the World*, London: Routledge.

Anderson, B. (1991) *Imagined Communities*, rev. edn, London: Verso.

Anderson, J. A. and Schoening, G. T. (1996) 'The nature of the individual in communication research', in D. Grodin and T. R. Lindlof (eds), *Constructing the Self in a Mediated World*, London: Routledge.

Ang, I. (1985) *Watching Dallas: Soap Opera and the Melodramatic Imagination*, London: Methuen.

Arabena, J. L. (1993) 'International aspects of sport in Latin

America: perceptions, prospects and proposals', in E. Dunning et al. (eds), *The Sports Process: A Comparative and Developmental Approach*, Champaign, IL: Human Kinetics.

Ashmore, R. D. and Jussim, L. (eds) (1997) *Self and Identity*, Rutgers Series on Self and Social Identity, Oxford: Oxford University Press.

Augé, M. (1995) *Non-Places: Introduction to an Anthropology of Supermodernity*, London: Verso.

Bacon-Smith, C. (1992) *Enterprising Women: Television Fandom and the Creation of Popular Myth*, Philadelphia: University of Pennsylvania Press.

Bakhtin, M. (1968) *Rabelais and His World*, Cambridge: MIT Press.

Bale, J. (1993) *Sport, Space and the City*, London: Routledge.

Bale, J. (1998) 'Virtual fandoms: futurescapes of football', in A. Brown, (ed.), *Fanatics: Power Identity and Fandom in Football*, London: Routledge.

Barbas, S. (2001) *Movie Crazy: Fans, Stars and the Cult of Celebrity*, New York and Basingstoke: Palgrave.

Barker, M. (1993) 'Seeing how far you can see: on being a "fan" of 2000 AD', in D. Buckingham (ed.), *Reading Audiences: Young People and the Media*, Manchester: Manchester University Press.

Barker, M. (1998) 'Taking the extreme case: understanding of a fascist fan of Judge Dredd', in D. Cartmell et al. (eds), *Trash Aesthetics: Popular Culture and its Audience*, London: Pluto Press.

Barker, M. and Brooks, K. (1998) *Knowing Audiences: Judge Dredd: Its Friends, Fans and Foes*, Luton: Luton University Press.

Barthes, R. (1957/1993) *Mythologies*, London: Vintage.

Baudrillard, J. (1983) *Simulations*, New York: Semiotexte.

Baudrillard, J. (1990) *Fatal Strategies*, ed. Jim Fleming, New York: Semiotexte.

Baudrillard, J. (1993a) *Symbolic Exchange and Death*, London: Sage.

Baudrillard, J. (1993b) *The Transparency of Evil: Essays on Extreme Phenomena*, London: Verso.

Baudrillard, J. (1997) 'Aesthetic illusion and virtual reality', in N. Zurbrugg (ed.), *Art and Artefact*, London: Sage.

Baudry, J. L. (1986) 'The apparatus: metapsychological approaches to impression of reality in cinema', in P. Rosen (ed.), *Apparatus, Ideology: A Film Theory Reader*, New York: Columbia University Press.

Baym, N. K. (1998) 'Talk about soaps: communicative practices and a computer-mediated culture', in C. Harris (ed.), *Theorizing Fandom: Fans, Subculture and Identity*, Cresskill, NJ: Hampton Press.

Baym, N. K. (2000) *Tune In, Log On: Soaps, Fandom, and Online Community*, Thousand Oaks, CA, and London: Sage.

Beck, U. (1992) *Risk Society*, London: Sage.

Beck, U. (1999) *World Risk Society*, Cambridge: Polity.

Becker, H. S. (1963) *Outsiders: Studies in the Sociology of Deviance*, London and New York: Free Press and Collier-Macmillan.

Bell, D. (1979) *The Cultural Contradictions of Capitalism*, 2nd edn, London: Heinemann Educational.

Berger, J. (1972) *Ways of Seeing*, London: Penguin.

Bloustien, G. (2002) 'Fans with a lot at stake: serious play and mimetic excess in *Buffy the Vampire Slayer*', *European Journal of Cultural Studies*, 5 (4), 427–49.

Blumer, H. (1969) *Symbolic Interactionism: Perspective and Method*, Englewood Cliffs, NJ: Prentice-Hall.

Bokina, J. and Lukes, T. J. (eds) (1994) *Marcuse: From the New Left to the Next Left*, Lawrence, KA: University Press of Kansas.

Bourdieu, P. (1984) *Distinction: A Social Critique of the Judgement of Taste*, London: Routledge & Kegan Paul.

Brailsford, D. (1991) *Sport, Time and Society – The British at Play*, London: Routledge.

Brooker, W. (2000) *Batman Unmasked: Analysing a Cultural Icon*, London: Continuum.

Brooker, W. (2001) 'The many lives of the jetman: a case study in video game analysis', *Intensities, the Journal of Cult Media*, 2, < http://www.cult-media.com/issue2/Abrook.htm > .

Brooker, W. (2002) *Using the Force: Creativity, Community and Star Wars Fans*, London: Continuum.

Brookes, R. (2002) *Representing Sports*, London: Arnold.

Brower, S. (1992) 'Fans as tastemakers: viewers for quality television', in L. A. Lewis (ed.), *Adoring Audience: Fan Culture and Popular Media*, London: Routledge.

Brown, J. A. (1997) 'Comic book fandom and cultural capital', *Journal of Popular Culture*, 30 (4), 13–31.

Brown, J. D. and Schulze, L. (1990), 'The effects of race, gender, and fandom on audience interpretations of Madonna's music videos', *Journal of Communication*, 40 (2), 88–102.

Brown, M. E. (1987) 'The politics of soaps: pleasure and feminine empowerment', *Australian Journal of Cultural Studies*, 4 (2), 1–25.

Brown, M. E. (1994) *Soap Opera and Women's Talk: The Pleasure of Resistance*, London and Thousand Oaks, CA: Sage.

Brummett, B. and Duncan, M. C. (1989) 'Types and sources of spectating pleasure in televised sport', *Sociology of Sport*, 6 (3), 195–211.

Brummett, B. and Duncan, M. C. (1990) 'Theorizing without totalizing: specularity and televised sports', *Quarterly Journal of Speech*, 76, 227–46.

Brummett, B. and Duncan, M. C. (1992) 'Toward a discursive ontology of media', *Critical Studies in Mass Communication*, 9 (3), 229-49.

Brundson, C. (1989) 'Text and audience', in E. Seiter et al. (eds), *Remote Control*, London: Routledge.

Cashmore, E. (2002) *Beckham*, Cambridge: Polity.

Castoriadis, C. (1989) *The Imaginary Institution of Society*, Cambridge: Polity.

Cavicchi, D. (1998) *Tramps Like Us: Music and Meaning among Springsteen Fans*, New York and Oxford: Oxford University Press.

Chaney, D. (1993) *Fictions of Collective Life*, London: Routledge.

Cherry, B. (2002) 'Screaming for release: femininity and horror film fandom in Britain', in S. Chibnall and J. Petley (eds), *British Horror Cinema*, London: Routledge.

Chin, B. and Gray, J. (2001) 'One ring to rule them all: pre-viewers and pre-texts of the Lord of the Rings films', *Intensities, the Journal of Cult Media*, 2, < http://www.cult-media.com/issue2/Achingray.htm > .

Chodorow, N. (1978) *The Reproduction of Mothering*, London and Berkeley: University of California Press.

Chodorow, N. (1989) *Feminism and Psychoanalytic Theory*, Cambridge: Polity.

Christenson, P. and Peterson, J. P. (1988) 'Genre and gender in the structure of music preferences', *Communication Research*, 15 (3), 282–301.

Cicioni, M. (1998) 'Male pair-bonds and female desire in slash writing', in C. Harris (ed.), *Theorizing Fandom: Fans, Subculture and Identity*, Cresskill, NJ: Hampton Press.

Clerc, S. J. (1996) 'DDEB, GATB, MPPB, and Ratboy: *The X-Files'* Media Fandom, 'Online and Off', in D. Lavery et al. (eds), *Deny All Knowledge: Reading the X-Files*, Syracuse, NY: Syracuse University Press.

Cohan, S. (2001) 'Judy on the net: Judy Garland fandom and "the gay thing" revisited', in M. Tinkcom and A. Villarejo (eds), *Key Frames: Popular Film and Cultural Studies*, London and New York: Routledge.

Cohen, S. (1972) *Folk Devils and Moral Panics: The Creation of the Mods and Rockers*, London: McGibbon and Kee.

Collini, S. (1992) *Umberto Eco: Interpretation and Overinterpretation*, Cambridge: Cambridge University Press.

Couldry, N. (2000) *The Place of Media Power: Pilgrims and Witnesses of the Media Age*, Comedia, London: Routledge.
Couldry, N. (2002) 'Big Brother as ritual event', *Television and New Media*, 3 (3), 283–93.
Crafts, S. D., Cavicchi, D. and Keil, C. (1993) *My Music*, Hanover, NH: Wesleyan University Press.
Craib, I. (2001) *Psychoanalysis: A Critical Introduction*, Cambridge: Polity.
Creed, B. (1993) *The Monstrous-Feminine: Film, Feminism, Psychoanalysis*, London: Routledge.
Cumberland, S. (2000) 'Private uses of cyberspace: woman, desire, and fan culture', *MIT Communications Forum*: < http://web.mit.edu/comm-forum/papers/cumberland.html >.
Dayan, D. and Katz, E. (1992) *Media Events: The Live Broadcasting of History*, London and Cambridge, MA: Harvard University Press.
de Certeau, M. (1984) *The Practice of Everyday Life*, Berkeley and Los Angeles: University of California Press.
De Man, P. (1982) 'Introduction', in H. R. Jauss, *Toward an Aesthetic of Reception*, Minneapolis: University of Minnesota Press.
Debord, G. (1995) *The Society of Spectacle*, New York: Zone Books.
Dell, C. (1998) ' "Lookit that hunk of man": subversive pleasures, female fandom and professional wrestling', in C. Harris (ed.), *Theorizing Fandom: Fans, Subculture and Identity*, Cresskill, NJ: Hampton Press.
DiMaggio, P. (1979) 'Review essay: on Pierre Bourdieu', *American Journal of Sociology*, 84 (6), 1460–74.
Doss, E. (1999) *Elvis Culture: Fans, Faith and Image*, Lawrence, KA: University Press of Kansas.
Eagleton, T. (1983) *Literary Theory: An Introduction*, Oxford: Blackwell.
Eco, U. (1962/1989) *The Open Work*, London: Hutchinson Radius.
Eco, U. (1981) *The Role of the Reader: Explorations in Semiotics of Texts*, London: Hutchinson & Co.
Eco, U. (1986) *Travels in Hyperreality*, London: Picador.
Eco, U. (1994) *The Limits of Interpretation*, Bloomington: Indiana University Press.
Eco, U. (2000) *Kant and the Platypus: Essays on Language and Cognition*, New York: Harcourt Brace.
Elliott, A. (1996) *Subject to Ourselves: Social Theory, Psychoanalysis and Postmodernity*, Cambridge: Polity.
Elliott, A. (1999) *The Mourning of John Lennon*, Berkeley: University of California Press.
Elliott, A. (2001) *Concepts of Self*, Cambridge: Polity.

Elliott, A. (2002) *Psychoanalytic Theory: An Introduction*, 2nd edn, Basingstoke: Palgrave.

Erickson, B. (1996) 'Culture, class and connections', *American Journal of Sociology*, 102 (1), 217–51.

Evans, W. (1990) 'The interpretative turn in media research', *Critical Studies in Mass Communications*, 7 (2), 147–68.

Exley, F. (1968) *A Fan's Note: A Fictional Memoir*, New York: Random House.

Fenster, M. (1991) 'The problem of taste within the problematic of culture', in *Communication Theory*, 1 (2), 87–105.

Fish, S. (1980) *Is There a Text in this Class?*, Cambridge, MA: Harvard University Press.

Fish, S. (1981) 'Why no one's afraid of Wolfgang Iser', *Diacritics*, 11 (1), 2–13.

Fiske, J. (1983) 'Dr Who: Ideology and the Reading of a Popular Narrative Text', in: *Australian Journal of Screen Theory*, 13/14.

Fiske, J. (1986) 'Television: polysemy and popularity', *Critical Studies in Mass Communication*, 3 (2), 391–408.

Fiske, J. (1989a) *Reading the Popular*, Boston: Unwin and Hyman; rep., London: Routledge, 1991.

Fiske, J. (1989b) *Understanding Popular Culture*, Boston: Unwin and Hyman; repr. London: Routledge, 1991.

Fiske, J. (1992) 'The cultural economy of fandom', in L. A. Lewis (ed.), *The Adoring Audience*, London: Routledge.

Fiske, J. (1993) *Power Plays, Power Works*, London: Verso.

Fluck, W. (2000) 'The search for distance: negation and negativity in Wolfgang Iser's literary theory', *New Literary History*, 31 (1), 175–210.

Foucault, M. (1979) *The History of Sexuality: An Introduction*, vol. 1, London: Allen Lane.

Frank, L. and Smith, P. (eds) (1993) *Madonnarama*, Pittsburgh: Cleis Press.

Freud, S. (1905/1977) *On Sexuality: Three Essays on the Theory of Sexuality and Other Works*, Harmondsworth: Penguin.

Freud, S. (1914/1984), 'On narcissism: an introduction', in *On Metapsychology: The Theory of Psychoanalysis, 'Beyond the Pleasure Principle', 'The Ego and the Id' and Other Works*, Harmondsworth: Penguin.

Freud, S. (1923/1984) 'Beyond the pleasure principle', in *On Metapsychology: The Theory of Psychoanalysis, 'Beyond the Pleasure Principle', 'The Ego and the Id' and Other Works*, Harmondsworth: Penguin.

Freud, S. (1927/1982) *Civilization and its Discontents*, London: Hogarth Press and the Institute of Psycho-Analysis.

Frith, S. (1996) 'Youth culture/youth cults', in S. Frith and C. Gillett (eds), *The Beat Goes On: The Rock File Reader*, London: Pluto.

Frow, J. (1987) 'Accounting for tastes: some problems in Bourdieu's sociology of culture', in *Cultural Studies*, 1 (1), 59–73.

Gadamer, H.-G. (1965/1996) 'Sprache als Medium der hermeneutischen Erfahrung', in D. Kimmich et al. (eds), *Texte zur Literaturtheorie der Gegenwart*, Stuttgart: Philipp Reclam.

Gans, H. (1966) 'Popular culture in America: social problem in a mass society or asset in a pluralistic society', in H. S. Becker (ed.), *Social Problems: A Modern Approach*, New York: Wiley.

Gantz, W. and Wenner, L. A. (1991) 'Men, women, and sports: audience experiences and effects', *Journal of Broadcasting and Electronic Media*, 35, 233–43.

Ganz-Blättler, U. (1999) 'Shareware or prestigious privilege? Television fans as knowledge brokers', *MIT Communications Forum*:
< http://web.mit.edu/comm-forum/papers/ganz-blattler.html > .

Geertz, C. (1975) *The Interpretation of Cultures: Selected Essays*, London: Hutchinson, Basic Books.

Gelder, K. and Thornton, S. (eds) (1997) *The Subcultures Reader*, London: Routledge.

Geraghty, C. (1991) *Women and Soap Opera*, Cambridge: Polity.

Giddens, A. (1990) *The Consequences of Modernity*, Cambridge: Polity.

Giddens, A. (1991) *Modernity and Self-Identity: Self and Society in the Late Modern Age*, Cambridge: Polity.

Gleason, P. (1983) 'Identifying identity: a semantic history', *Journal of American History*, 69, 910–31.

Goffman, E. (1959/1990) *The Presentation of Self in Everyday Life*, London: Penguin.

Goffman, E. (1968) *Asylums*, Harmondsworth: Pelican Books.

Grant, B. K. (2000) 'Second thoughts on double features: revisiting the cult film', in X. Mendik and G. Harper (eds), *Unruly Pleasures: The Cult Film and Its Critics*, Guildford: FAB Press.

Gray, J. (2003) 'New audiences, new textualities: anti-fans and non-fans', *International Journal of Cultural Studies*, 6 (1), 64–81.

Green, S., Jenkins, C. and Jenkins, H. (1998) 'Normal female interest in men bonking: selections from the *Terra Nostra Underground* and *Strange Bedfellows*', in C. Harris (ed.), *Theorizing Fandom: Fans, Subculture and Identity*, Cresskill, NJ: Hampton Press.

Groeben, N. (1977) *Rezeptionsforschung als empirische Literaturwissenschaft: Paradigma durch Methodendiskussion,* Kronberg: Athenäum.

Grossberg, L. (1985) 'Critical theory and the politics of empirical research', in M. Gurevitch and M. R. Levy (eds), *Mass Communication Review Yearbook,* Beverly Hills, CA: Sage.

Grossberg, L. (1992) 'Is there a fan in the house?: the affective sensibility of fandom', in L. A. Lewis (ed.), *The Adoring Audience,* London: Routledge.

Hall, S. (1980) 'Encoding/decoding', in S. Hall, D. Hobson, A. Lowe and P. Willis (eds), *Culture, Media, Language: Working Papers in Cultural Studies, 1972–1979,* London: Hutchinson.

Hanmer, R. (2003) 'Lesbian subtext talk: experiences on the internet chat', *International Journal of Sociology and Social Policy,* 23 (1/2), 80–106.

Hargreaves, J. (1986) *Sport, Power and Culture,* Cambridge: Polity.

Harrington, C. L. and Bielby, D. (1995) *Soap Fans: Pursuing Pleasure and Making Meaning in Everyday Life,* Philadelphia: Temple University Press.

Harris, C. (1998a) 'Introduction', in C. Harris (ed.), *Theorizing Fandom: Fans, Subculture and Identity,* Cresskill, NJ: Hampton Press.

Harris, C. (1998b) 'A sociology of television fandom', in C. Harris (ed.), *Theorizing Fandom: Fans, Subculture and Identity,* Cresskill, NJ: Hampton Press.

Hartley, J. (1996) *Popular Reality – Journalism, Modernity, Popular Culture,* London: Arnold.

Harvey, D. (1990) *The Condition of Postmodernity: An Inquiry into the Origins of Cultural Change,* Oxford: Blackwell.

Haynes, R. (1995) *The Football Imagination: The Rise of Football Fanzines Culture,* Aldershot: Arena.

Hebdige, D. (1979) *Subculture: The Meaning of Style,* London and New York: Routledge.

Herman, E. and McChesney, R. (1997) *The Global Media,* London: Cassell.

Hesmondhalgh, D. (2002) *The Cultural Industries,* London: Sage.

Hill, A. (2002) '*Big Brother*: the real audience', *Television and New Media,* 3 (3), 323–40.

Hill, A. and Palmer, G. (2002) '*Big Brother*', *Television and New Media,* 3 (3), 251–4.

Hills, M. (1999) 'The dialectic of value: the sociology and psychoanalysis of cult media', Ph.D. thesis, University of Sussex.

Hills, M. (2002) *Fan Cultures,* London: Routledge.

Hills, M. and Jenkins, H. (2001) 'Intensities interview with Henry Jenkins', *Intensities, the Journal of Cult Media*, 2: < http://www.cult-media.com/issue2/CMRjenk.htm > .

Hinerman, S. (1992) ' "I'll be here with you": fans, fantasy and the figure of Elvis', in L. A. Lewis (ed.), *The Adoring Audience*, London: Routledge.

Hoberman, J. and Rosenbaum, J. (1983) *Midnight Movies*, New York: Harper.

Hodkinson, P. (2002) *Goth: Identity, Style and Subculture*, Oxford: Berg.

Holt, R. (1989) *Sport and the British: A Modern History*, Oxford Studies in Social History, Oxford: Oxford University Press.

Holub, R. C. (1992) *Crossing Borders: Reception Theory, Poststructuralism, Deconstruction*, London and Madison: University of Wisconsin Press.

Honneth, A. (1986) 'The fragmented world of symbolic forms: reflections on Pierre Bourdieu's sociology of culture', in *Theory, Culture & Society*, 3 (3), 55–66.

Horton, D. and Wohl, R. R. (1956) 'Mass communication and parasocial interaction: observation on intimacy at a distance', *Psychiatry*, 19 (3), 188–211.

Hoxter, J. (2000) 'Taking possession: cult learning in *The Exorcist*', in X. Mendik and G. Harper (eds), *Unruly Pleasures: The Cult Film and Its Critics*, Guildford : FAB Press.

Hunter, I. Q. (2000) 'Beaver Las Vegas! A Fan-Boy's Defence of Showgirls', in X. Mendik and G. Harper. (eds) *Unruly Pleasures: The Cult Film and Its Critics*, Guildford: FAB Press.

Huyssen, A. (1986) *After the Great Divide: Modernism, Mass Culture, Postmodernism*, Bloomington: Indiana University Press.

Ingarden, R. (1973) *The Cognition of the Literary Work of Art*, Evanston, IL: Northwestern University Press.

Iser, W. (1971) 'Indeterminacy and the reader's response in prose fiction', in J. H. Miller (ed.), *Aspects of Narrative*, New York and London: Columbia University Press.

Iser, W. (1975) 'Die Appellstruktur der Texte: Unbestimmtheit als Wirkungsbedingung literarisher Prosa', in R. Warning (ed.), *Rezeptionästhetik. Theorie und Traxis*, Munich: UTB/ Wilhelm Fink Verlag.

Iser, W. (1978) *The Act of Reading: A Theory of Aesthetic Response*, Baltimore: Johns Hopkins University Press.

Jameson, F. (1991) *Postmodernism, or, The Cultural Logic of Late Capitalism*, London: Verso.

Jancovich, M. (2001) 'Placing sex: sexuality, taste and middlebrow culture in the reception of Playboy magazine', *Intensities, the Journal of Cult Media*, 2, < http://www.cult-media.com/issue2/Ajanc.htm >.

Jancovich, M. (2002) 'Cult fictions: cult movies, subcultural capital and the production of cultural distinctions', *Cultural Studies*, 16 (2), 306–22.

Jary, D., Horne, J. and Buckle, T. (1991) 'Football fanzines and football culture: a case of successful cultural contestation', *The Sociological Review*, 39 (3), 581–98.

Jauss, H. R. (1982) *Toward an Aesthetic of Reception*, Minneapolis: University of Minnesota Press.

Jenkins, H. (1991) '*Star Trek* rerun, reread, rewritten: fan writing as textual poaching', in C. Penley et al. (eds), *Close Encounters: Film, Feminism and Science Fiction*, Minneapolis: University of Minnesota Press.

Jenkins, H. (1992) *Textual Poachers: Television Fans and Participatory Culture*, New York: Routledge.

Jenson, J. (1992) 'Fandom as pathology: the consequences of characterization', in L. A. Lewis (ed.), *The Adoring Audience*, London: Routledge.

Jones, S. G. (2002) 'The sex lives of cult television characters', *Screen*, 43 (1), 79–90.

Jones, S. G. (2003) 'Web wars: resistance, online fandom, and studio censorship', in M. Jancovich and J. Lyons (eds), *Quality Popular Television*, London: British Film Institute.

Kaes, A. (1989) *From 'Hitler' to 'Heimat': The Return of History as Film*, London and Cambridge, MA: Harvard University Press.

Kellner, D. (1984) *Herbert Marcuse and the Crisis of Marxism*, Berkeley: University of California Press.

Kellner, D. (1995) *Media Culture: Cultural Studies, Identity, and Politics between the Modern and the Postmodern*, New York: Routledge.

Kellner, D. (2003) *Media Spectacle*, London: Routledge.

Kermode, M. (2001) 'I was a teenage horror fan: or, How I learned to stop worrying and love Linda Blair', in M. Barker and J. Petley (eds), *Ill Effects: The Media Violence Debate*, London: Routledge.

Kielwasser, A. P. and Wolf, M. A. (1989) 'The appeal of soap opera: an analysis of process and quality in dramatic serial gratifications', *Journal of Popular Culture*, 23 (2), 111–23.

King, A. (1998) *The End of Terraces: The Transformation of English Football in the 1990s*, London: Leicester University Press.

King, B. (1992) 'Stardom and symbolic degeneracy: television and transformation of the stars as public symbols', *Semiotica*, 92 (1/2), 1–47.

Klein, M. (1946/2000) 'Notes on some schizoid mechanisms', in P. Du Gay, J. Evans and P. Redman (eds), *Identity: A Reader*, London: Sage.

Kovel, J. (1980) 'Narcissism and the family', *Telos*, 44, 88–101.

Kristeva, J. (1981) *Desire in Language: A Semiotic Approach to Literature and Art*, Oxford: Blackwell.

Kristeva, J. (1988) *In the Beginning was Love: Psychoanalysis and Faith*, New York: Columbia University Press.

Krzywinska, T. (2000) 'The dynamics of squirting: female ejaculation and lactation in hardcore film', in X. Mendik and G. Harper (eds), *Unruly Pleasures: The Cult Film and its Critics*, Guildford: FAB Press.

Lacan, J. (1949/2000) 'The mirror stage', in P. Du Gay, J. Evans and P. Redman (eds), *Identity: A Reader*, London: Sage.

Lamb, P. F. and Veith, D. L. (1986) 'Romantic myth, transcendence and *Star Trek* zines,' in D. Palumbo (ed.), *Erotic Universe: Sexuality and Fantastic Literature*, New York: Greenwood Press.

Lancaster, K. (2001) *Interacting with Babylon 5*, Austin: University of Texas Press.

Lanfranchi, P. and Taylor, M. (2001) *Moving with the Ball: The Migration of Professional Footballers*, Oxford: Berg.

Laplanche, J. and Pontalis, J.-B. (1973) *The Language of Psychoanalysis*, London: Hogarth Press.

Lasch, C. (1979/1991) *The Culture of Narcissism: American Life in An Age of Diminishing Expectations*, New York and London: W. W. Norton.

Lebeau, V. (1995) *Lost Angels: Psychoanalysis and Cinema*, London: Routledge.

Lehtonen, M. (2000) *The Cultural Analysis of Texts*, London: Sage.

Lembo, R. and Tucker, K. H. (1990) 'Culture, television, and opposition: rethinking cultural studies', *Critical Studies in Mass Communications*, 7 (2), 97–116.

Lentricchia, F. (1980) *After the New Criticism*, Chicago: University of Chicago Press.

Lewis, G. H. (1987) 'Patterns of meaning and choice', in J. Lull (ed.), *Popular Music and Communication*, Beverly Hills, CA: Sage.

Liebes, T. and Katz, E. (1990) *The Export of Meaning*, Oxford: Oxford University Press.

Lindlof, T. R., Coyle, K. and Grodin, D. (1998) 'Is there a text in this audience? Science fiction and interpretive schism', in C.

Harris, (ed.), *Theorizing Fandom: Fans, Subculture and Identity*, Cresskill, NJ: Hampton Press.

Linville, P. W. (1985) 'Self-complexity and affective extremity: don't put all your eggs in one cognitive basket', *Social Cognition*, 9, 94–120.

Livingstone, S. (1998) *Making Sense of Television: The Psychology of Audience Interpretation*, London: Routledge.

Marcus, G. and Fisher, M. (1986) *Anthropology as Cultural Critique*, Chicago: University of Chicago Press.

Marcuse, H. (1956/1987) *Eros and Civilization: A Philosophical Inquiry into Freud*, London: Routledge.

Marcuse, H. (1964/1991) *One-Dimensional Man: Studies in the Ideology of Advanced Industrial Society*, 2nd edn, London: Routledge.

Mason, A. and Meyers, M. (2001) 'Living with Martha Stewart media: chosen domesticity and the experience of fans', *Journal of Communication*, 51 (4), 801–23.

Massey, D. (1994) *Space, Place and Gender*, Cambridge: Polity.

Mathijs, E. (2002) 'Big Brother and critical discourse: the reception of *Big Brother* in Belgium', *Television and New Media*, 3 (3), 311–22.

McAdams, D. P (1997) 'The case for unity in the (post)modern self: a modest proposal', in R. D. Ashmore and L. Jussim (eds), *Self and Identity*, Rutgers Series on Self and Social Identity, Oxford: Oxford University Press.

McKee, A. (2001) 'What is the best *Doctor Who* story? A case study in value judgements outside the academy', *Intensities, the Journal of Cult Media*, 1, < http://www.cult-media.com/issue1/Amckee.htm > .

McKinley, E. G. (1997) *Beverly Hills, 90210: Television, Gender and Identity*, Philadelphia: University of Pennsylvania Press.

McLaughlin, T. (1996) *Street Smart and Critical Theory: Listening to the Vernacular*, Madison: University of Wisconsin Press.

McLuhan, M. (1964) *Understanding Media: The Extension of Man*, London: Routledge.

Mead, G. H. (1934) *Mind, Self, and Society from the Standpoint of a Social Behaviourist*, Chicago: University of Chicago Press.

Medhurst, A. (1991) 'Batman, deviance, and camp', in R. E. Pearson and W. Uricchio (eds), *The Many Lives of Batman: Critical Approaches to a Superhero and his Media*, London: Routledge.

Mendik, X. and Harper, G. (2000a) 'The chaotic text and the sadean audience: narrative transgressions of a contemporary cult film', in X. Mendik and G. Harper (eds), *Unruly Pleasures: The Cult Film and its Critics*, Guildford: FAB Press.

Mendik, X. and Harper, G. (2000b) 'Introduction', in X. Mendik and G. Harper (eds), *Unruly Pleasures: The Cult Film and its Critics*, Guildford: FAB Press.

Merck, M. (1987) 'Introduction: difference and its discontents', *Screen*, 28 (1), 2–10.

Metz, C. (1974) *Film Language: A Semiotics of Cinema*, New York and Oxford: Oxford University Press.

Meyrowitz, J. (1985) *No Sense of Place: The Impact of Electronic Media on Social Behaviour*, New York: Oxford University Press.

Miklitsch, R. (1998) *From Hegel to Madonna: Towards a General Economy of Commodity Fetishism*, Albany, NY: State University of New York Press.

Mikos, L., Feise, P., Herzog, K., Prommer, E. and Veihl, V. (2001) *Im Auge der Kamera: Das Fernsehereignis Big Brother*, Berlin: Vistas.

Miller, A. (1987) *The Drama of Being a Child*, London: Virago.

Miller, D. (1992) 'The young and the restless in Trinidad: a case of the local and the global in mass communication', in R. Silverstone and E. Hirsch (eds), *Consuming Technologies: Media and Information in Domestic Spaces*, London: Routledge.

Miller, T. and McHoul, A. (1998) *Popular Culture and Everyday Life*, London: Sage.

Mitchell, J. (1974) *Psychoanalysis and Feminism*, London: Allen Lane.

Modelski, T. (1983) 'The rhythms of reception: daytime television and women's work', in A. Kaplan (ed.), *Regarding Television*, Los Angeles: University Publications of America and the American Film Institute.

Moody, R. A. (1987) *Elvis After Life*, Atlanta: Peachtree Press.

Morley, D. (1986) *Family Television: Cultural Power and Domestic Leisure*, Comedia, London: Routledge.

Morley, D. (1991) 'Where the global meets the local: notes from the sitting room', in: *Screen*, 32 (1), 1–15.

Morley, D. (1994), 'Active audience theory: pendulums and pitfalls', in M. R. Levy and M. Gurevitch (eds), *Defining Media Studies: Reflections on the Future of the Field*, Oxford: Oxford University Press.

Morley, D. (2000) *Home Territories: Media, Mobility and Modernity*, Comedia, London: Routledge.

Morley, D. and Robins, K. (1995) *Spaces of Identity: Global Media, Electronic Landscapes and Cultural Boundaries*, London: Routledge.

Morley, D. and Silverstone, R. (1990) 'Domestic communications:

technologies and meanings', *Media Culture and Society*, 12 (1), 31–55.

Morse, M. (1983) 'Sport on television: replay and display', in A. Kaplan (ed.), *Regarding Television*, Los Angeles: University Publications of America and the American Film Institute.

Mulvey, L. (1975) 'Visual pleasures and narrative cinema', *Screen*, 16 (3), 6–19.

Nightingale, V. (1994) 'Improvising Elvis, Marilyn, and Mickey Mouse', *Australian Journal of Communication*, 21 (1), 1–20.

Nightingale, V. (1996) *Studying Audiences: The Shock of the Real*, London: Routledge.

Osgerby, B. (2000) 'Stand-by for action: Gerry Anderson, Supermarionation and the "White Heat of Sixties Modernity" ', in X. Mendik and G. Harper (eds), *Unruly Pleasures: The Cult Film and its Critics*, Guildford: FAB Press.

Pearson, R. E. and Uricchio, W. (eds) (1991) *The Many Lives of Batman: Critical Approaches to a Superhero and his Media*, London: Routledge.

Peary, D. (1981) *Cult Movies*, New York: Delta.

Penley, C. (1991) 'Brownian motion: women, tactics and technology', in A. Ross and C. Penley (eds), *Technoculture*, Minneapolis: University of Minnesota Press.

Penley, C. (1992) 'Feminism, psychoanalysis and the study of popular culture', in L. Grossberg et al. (eds), *Cultural Studies*, London: Routledge.

Penley, C. (1997) *NASA/Trek: Popular Science and Sex in America*, London: Verso.

Peterson, R. and Kern, R. M. (1996) 'Changing highbrow taste: from snob to omnivore', *American Sociological Review*, 61, 900–7.

Phillips, A. (1998) *The Beast in the Nursery*, London: Faber and Faber.

Postman, N. (1985) *Amusing Ourselves to Death: Public Discourse in the Age of Show Business*, New York: Viking.

Radway, J. (1987) *Reading the Romance: Women, Patriarchy and Popular Literature*, London: Verso.

Rathzel, N. (1994) 'Harmonious *Heimat* and disturbing *Ausländer*', in K. K. Bhavani and A. Phoenix (eds), *Shifting Identities and Shifting Racism*, London: Sage.

Redhead, S. (1997) *Post-Fandom and the Millennial Blues: The Transformation of Soccer Culture*, London: Routledge.

Redhead, S., Wynne, D. and O'Connor, J. (1997) *The Clubcultures Reader: Readings in Popular Cultural Studies*, Oxford: Blackwell.

Relph, E. (1976) *Place and Placelessness*, London: Pion Limited.

Rheingold, H. (2000) *The Virtual Community: Homestanding on the Electronic Frontier*, Cambridge, MA: MIT Press.

Ritzer, G. (1996) *The McDonaldization of Society*, Newbury Park: Pine Forge Press.

Ritzer, G. (1998) *The McDonaldization Thesis: Explorations and Extensions*, London: Sage.

Rodman, G. B. (1996) *Elvis After Elvis: The Posthumous Career of a Living Legend*, New York and London: Routledge.

Rojek, C. (2001) *Celebrity*, London: Reaktion Books.

Rorty, R. (1989) *Contingency, Irony and Solidarity*, Cambridge: Cambridge University Press.

Roversi, A. (1994) 'The birth of the ultras: the rise of football hooliganism in Italy', in R. Giulianotti and J. Williams (eds), *Game without Frontiers: Football, Identity and Modernity*, Aldershot: Arena.

Russ, J. (1985) 'Pornography by women for women, with love', in *Magic Mommas, Trembling Sisters, Puritans and Perverts: Feminist Essays*, Trumansberg, NY: Crossing.

Sandvoss, C. (2001) 'Football fandom and television in the triangle of universalization, globalization and rationalization', Ph.D. thesis, LSE, University of London.

Sandvoss, C. (2003) *A Game of Two Halves: Football, Television and Globalization*, Comedia, London: Routledge.

Sandvoss, C. (forthcoming) 'Gender and fandom in global soccer', in L. K. Fuller (ed.), *Sports Rhetoric Globally*, Binghamton, NY: Haworth.

Scannell, P. (1996) *Radio, Television and Modern Life: A Phenomenological Approach*, Oxford: Blackwell.

Scannell, P. (2002) '*Big Brother* as television event', *Television and New Media*, 3 (3), 271–82.

Schickel, R. (1986) *Intimate Strangers: The Cult of Celebrity*, New York: Fromm.

Schmidt, S. J. (1980) *Grundriß der empirischen Literaturwissenschaft*, vol. 1: *Der gesellschaftliche Handlungsbereich Literatur*, Wiesbaden: Vieweg.

Schultz, T. (2000) 'BB ist überall', *Medienwissenschaft*, 2, 141–7.

Schulze, L., White, A. B. and Brown, J. D. (1993) '"A sacred monster in her prime": audience construction of Madonna as low-other', C. Schwichtenberg (ed.), *The Madonna Connection: Representational Politics, Subcultural Identities, and Cultural Theory*, Oxford and Boulder, CO: Westview Press.

Schurr, K. T., Wittig, A. F., Ruble, V. E. and Ellen, A. S. (1988) 'Demographic and personality characteristics associated with persistent, occasional, and non-attendance of university male basketball games by college students', *Journal of Sport. Behaviour*, 11, 3–17.

Schwichtenberg, C. (ed.) (1993) *The Madonna Connection: Representational Politics, Subcultural Identities, and Cultural Theory*, Oxford and Boulder, CO: Westview.

Sennett, R. (1977/1992) *The Fall of Public Man*, New York and London: W. W. Norton.

Sexton, A. (ed.) (1993) *Desperately Seeking Madonna*, New York: Delta.

Silverstone, R. (1994) *Television and Everyday Life*, London: Routledge.

Silverstone, R. (1999) *Why Study the Media?*, London: Sage.

Skuse, A. (2002) 'Vagueness, familiarity and social realism: making meaning of radio soap opera in south-east Afghanistan', *Media Culture and Society*, 24 (3), 409–27.

Spigel, L. (1990) 'Communicating with the dead: Elvis as a medium', *Camera Obscura*, 23, 176–205.

Spigel, L. (1992) *Make Room for TV: Television and the Family Ideal in Post-War America*, Chicago: University of Chicago Press.

Sportfive (2002) *European Football: Markets, Events, Clubs, Media, Brands*, Hamburg: Sportfive.

Stacey, J. (1994) *Stargazing: Hollywood Cinema and Female Spectatorship*, London: Routledge.

Tankel, J. D. and Murphy, K. (1998) 'Collecting comic books: a study of the fan and curatorial consumption', in C. Harris (ed.), *Theorizing Fandom: Fans, Subculture and Identity*, Cresskill, NJ: Hampton Press.

Taylor, C. (1998) *The Beautiful Game: A Journey through Latin American Football*, London: Victor Gollancz.

Tester, K. (1994) *Media, Culture, and Morality*, New York: Routledge.

Theodoropoulou, P. (1999) 'Mapping out Fanland', unpublished dissertation, LSE, University of London.

Thomas, L. (2002) *Fans, Feminism and Quality Media*, London: Routledge.

Thompson, J. B. (1995) *The Media and Modernity: A Social Theory of the Media*, Cambridge: Polity.

Thornton, S. (1995) *Club Cultures: Music, Media and Subcultural Capital*, Cambridge: Polity.

Tomlinson, J. (1999) *Globalization and Culture*, Cambridge: Polity.

Triepel, H. (1938/1974) *Die Hegemonie: Ein Buch von führenden Staaten*, 2nd edn, Aalen.

Tulloch, J. (2000) *Watching Television Audiences: Cultural Theories and Methods*, London: Arnold.

Tulloch, J. and Jenkins, H. (1995) *Science Fiction Audiences: Watching Dr Who and Star Trek*, London and New York: Routledge.

Turkle, S. (1997) *Life on the Screen: Identity in the Age of the Internet*, London: Phoenix.

UFA (1998) *UFA Fußballstudie: Marketinginformationen für Vereine, Medien und Werbung*, Hamburg: UFA Sports GmbH.

Vermorel, F. and Vermorel, J. (1985) *Starlust: The Secret Fantasies of Fans*, London: Comet.

Vermorel, F. and Vermorel, J. (1992) 'A glimpse at the fan factory', in L. A. Lewis, (ed.), *The Adoring Audience*, London: Routledge.

Wann, D. L., Bilyeu, H. K., Brennan, K., Osborne, H. and Gambouras, A. F. (1999) 'An exploratory investigation of the relationship between sport fan motivation and race', *Perception and Motor Skills*, 88, 1018–84.

Wann, D. L., Melnick, M. L., Russel, G. W. and Pease, D. G. (2001) *Sport Fans: The Psychology and Social Impact of Spectators*, New York: Routledge.

Wertham, F. (1955) *Seduction of the Innocent*, London: Museum Press.

Wilkins, J. (1641/1707) *Mercury*, 3rd edn, London: Nicholson.

Williams, J. and Taylor, R. (1994) 'Boys keep swinging: masculinity and football culture in England', in T. Newbourn and E. Stanko (eds), *Just Boys Doing Business*, London: Routledge.

Williams, R. (1974) *Television: Technology and Cultural Form*, London: Fontana.

Willis, A. (2003) '*Martial Law* and the changing face of martial arts on US television', in M. Jancovich and J. Lyons (eds), *Quality Popular Television*, London: British Film Institute.

Willis, P. (1977) *Learning to Labour: How Working Class Kids Get Working Class Jobs*, Farnborough: Saxon House.

Winnicott, D. W. (1951/2000) 'Transitional objects and transitional phenomenon', in P. Du Gay, J. Evans and P. Redman (eds), *Identity: A Reader*, London: Sage.

Winnicott, D. W. (2000) *Playing and Reality*, London: Penguin.

Žižek, Slavoj (1989) *The Sublime Object of Ideology*, London: Verso.

Žižek, Slavoj (1991) *Looking Awry: An Introduction to Jacques Lacan through Popular Culture*, Cambridge, MA: MIT Press.

Note: All online material accessed on 28 October 2003.

INDEX